MISPLACED CHILDHOOD

MISPLACED CHILDHOOD

A TRUE STORY OF RESILIENCY AND CHILD ADVOCACY

JOAN ULSHER

Rehm Press

Court Appointed Special Advocates™ and CASA™ are trademarks. Historical reference copyright © 2022 by The National CASA/GAL Association for Children.

The logo is a trademark ™ of Child Advocates San Antonio.

Scripture quotation taken from the Holy Bible, New International Version copyright © 1973, 1978, 1984 by International Bible Society.

Excerpts from The H$_2$O Workbook: A Biblical Path to Hope, Heal & Overcome for the Thirsty Soul copyright © 2018 by Miriam E. Callahan.

Excerpts from The Magnolia Story by Chip and Joanna Gaines copyright © 2016 by Chip and Joanna Gaines. Used by permission of HarperCollins Christian Publishing.

Historical reference copyright © 2022 by the ASPCA. The American Society for the Prevention of Cruelty to Animals.

Historical reference copyright © 2022 by the NYSPCC. The New York Society for the Prevention of Cruelty to Children.

Historical reference copyright © 2022 by EMCF. The Edna McConnell Clark Foundation.

Historical reference copyright © 2022 by The Annie E. Casey Foundation.

Reference to "license to care" from I Speak For This Child copyright © 1995, 2001 by Gay Courter.

"CASA ... Angel by Their Side" words and music copyright © 2021 by Rick Cavender.

Publisher's Cataloging-in-Publication (Provided by Cassidy Cataloguing Services, Inc.).
Names: Ulsher, Joan, 1968- author.
Title: Misplaced childhood : a true story of resiliency and child advocacy / Joan Ulsher.
Description: San Antonio, Texas : Rehm Press, [2023] | Includes bibliographical references.
Identifiers: ISBN: 979-8-9883061-0-8 (Paperback) | 979-8-9883061-1-5 (eBook) | LCCN: 2023908321
Subjects: LCSH: Ulsher, Joan, 1968- | Christian women--Religious life--United States. | National CASA/GAL Association. | Court-appointed experts--United States. | Foster children--United States. | Volunteer workers in child welfare--United States | Abused children--Services for--United States. | Child welfare--United States. | LCGFT: Autobiographies.
Classification: LCC: HV6626.52 .U57 2023 | DDC: 362.76/0973--dc23

First paperback edition
Published by Rehm Press | San Antonio, Texas
publisher@rehmpress.com

Praise for *Misplaced Childhood*

"It is rare to read a book so vulnerable and courageous. Joan shares her life story in this utterly compelling read. Joan describes her devastating childhood and connected events as an adult in a raw, gripping way. I guarantee you will not be able to put *Misplaced Childhood* down. If you ever wanted to truly understand the impact on children that experience such events, this is the book to educate you.

Despite this childhood, Joan has had an incredible military career and a wonderful family. Joan now serves children in the foster system via her CASA advocacy with Child Advocates San Antonio. These children are blessed to have Joan. Her lived experience, which is shared so openly in the book, allows a lens into the innermost feelings of the young people she serves. Joan is passionate about protecting children, currently leading a team advocating for legislative change in a broken system.

Joan did not write this book for her healing or gratification. Joan wrote it to support her local CASA agency and, more importantly, to let others who have suffered know they can be amazing humans!

Joan has my personal thanks as a child from the foster system, for facing her own past with deep courage to write a book that will be influential and healing for others, for years to come. All for the good of others ... "

-Angela White, President & Chief Executive Officer, Child Advocates San Antonio

"' ... kids are the future of our community, and they are in crisis now.' The urgency of this statement from *Misplaced Childhood* is a call to action. The book also speaks to the impact of childhood trauma; how it became a filter for all of Joan's experiences and relationships until she was able to turn that trauma into a roadmap for action. In addition to trauma, Joan also discusses resiliency, the power of love, faith, and purpose in a way that is insightful, educational, and inspirational. After reading this book, I hope many feel called to become CASA volunteers—Joan didn't have one but became one later in life and sees how CASA advocacy can help create a more positive future for a child. Joan unabashedly invites readers to consider child advocacy for their purpose-filled life while highlighting the challenges and successes of children on her caseload as a CASA."

-Vicki Spriggs, Chief Executive Officer, Texas CASA

"*Misplaced Childhood* is both a deep dive into how the author survived years of horrifying abuse at the hands of her parents (and her cries for help were ignored by authorities) and how she turned her pain into advocacy by becoming a Court Appointed Special Advocate (CASA). She understands what is happening from the inside out and inspires others to join the cause."

-Gay Courter, *The New York Times* Bestselling Author, *I Speak For This Child: True Stories of a Child Advocate*

"'I was human but felt unprepared to live like one.' Like Joan Ulsher, many of us want a meaningful life, but never quite figure out how to pull it off. With courageous honesty and refreshing insight, Joan has figured it out! Her journey to relationship, forgiveness, and ultimately redemption in a life of service to others drew me in. Joan always does excellent work. This book is no exception!"

-John Witte, Founder of The Istoria Project

"This entire book hooks you from the beginning with nothing but truth and full transparency. Joan was vulnerable from beginning to end. A must-read for people interested in child welfare and advocacy."

-Ruchi Davis, Children's Court Manager, Bexar County, Texas

"In this beautifully written memoir, Joan shares personal accounts of endured childhood abuse and how she decides to choose the bravest yet most difficult path to use her pain for a purpose—to advocate for foster care children who do not have a voice or a safe person to lean on. She had every reason to be angry at the world, but instead, she is standing hand in hand with children struggling to see their own light. The heavy heart I felt in my chest slowly became lighter as I pieced together the puzzle of her life. I feel more inspired to make a greater difference in the lives of others."

-MJ Leigh, Foster Care Alumni

" ... Joan Ulsher's book is a gift of the heart that highlights the power of love, advocacy, and resilience. A poignant memoir that reminds the reader that resilience nurtures endurance, recovery from setbacks, and the impetus to forge beyond the pain and the agony with tenacity, perseverance, and courage. It is also a call to action to seek opportunities to get involved in advocacy organizations like CASA that help individuals be the best they can be ... "

-The Honorable Peter Sakai, Bexar County Judge

"Joan's vulnerability is captivating from beginning to end. You will feel inspired following her journey from abuse to advocacy for children in foster care. This book is an instrument for changing lives!"

-Michele Jech, Executive Pastor, CityChurch, San Antonio

"Equally as incredible as she is, Joan's story provides a powerful and engaging perspective for all champions of youth in foster care to learn. Her resiliency shines through. *Misplaced Childhood* is an inspirational narrative that helps anyone with lived experience in foster care beat the odds and triumph. Her ability to be vulnerable is appreciated. Her advocacy is admirable. Her story is memorable. Our village is even stronger because she is a part of it. A must-read for all those considering volunteering as CASA or GAL advocates in their communities."

-Airika Crawford, LLMSW, Project Director, Bexar County Fostering Educational Success Program

"From heart-wrenching to heartwarming, this true story of rising above childhood abuse, and finding ways to advocate for children through CASA, will inspire you to find ways to reach out to those in our communities who are the most vulnerable ... the children. This well-written book on a very serious subject will give you insights and ideas that can help you reach out and speak up for the child next door, because oftentimes, that is as far as you have to go to find a child in need."

-Yolanda Bryant, Author, *One Child at a Time: The Mission of a Court Appointed Special Advocate (CASA)*

"Joan displays incredible strength as she faces her own traumatic experiences—shining a bright light on the very issues that we were taught to keep locked in the dark! By facing the darkness, Joan empowers youth impacted by the foster system or juvenile justice system to find their voices to advocate for themselves and others, no longer silent, no longer ashamed of their traumas ... "

-Josey Garcia, Foster Care Alumni, Retired U.S. Air Force Veteran, and Texas State Representative

"Children deserve our very best care and education, especially those unprotected from abuse and neglect. This compelling, original memoir—told with purpose, will challenge you to serve children struggling in the foster care system in America. Joan's lived experiences story—trauma, tragedy, and triumph—can be their story too. Her journey demonstrates that 'our past does not define our future.' There is hope! Joan bravely takes us by the hand and walks us through her process of becoming a CASA advocate. The process is rigorous and not easy, but every child we help will only need to know someone loves her. If you would like to change children's lives for the better as Joan has, *Misplaced Childhood* is a must!"

-Holly Elissa Bruno, Bestselling Author, *Happiness Is Running Through the Streets to Find You: Translating Trauma's Harsh Legacy into Healing*

In Memory of Joey
November 17, 1966 – March 14, 1986

CONTENTS

PREFACE

The CEO & president of Child Advocates San Antonio, Angie, planted the seed for this project. Over lunch one day, we shared stories about our childhood and the major events that shaped how and why we became "Court Appointed Special Advocates," or CASA advocates, for children in foster care. As we talked, I skipped many details about my childhood abuse and foster care experiences, but I sensed Angie still understood what fueled my passion and steered my purpose. Our past experiences and journey shared a similar path.

She suggested that I write a book about my story. Initially, doubt surfaced about my internal "voice" being used to tell the important story about childhood abuse and CASA's role. I was as passionate about being a voice for children as any advocate, but making my life's story public seemed intimidating. Her confidence in me was encouraging, and our conversation implanted itself in the back of my mind. Several months later, the final inspiration revealed itself on a rainy day at a cemetery in my hometown.

The unplanned trip to Buffalo led to the development of this story. What happened there changed my perspective about sharing my voice. On the plane back to Texas, I reflected upon my childhood and professional experiences. Focusing on how my life had changed, evolved, and blossomed while working towards a purpose-driven life clarified my mission. Serving abused and neglected children was an important story to tell.

I started the initial draft in the notes section of my cellphone. Three hours later, as the wheels of the plane were touching down at the San Antonio airport, three sections of my story—from childhood to my journey into child advocacy—were outlined.

When I thought about other books about CASA, child advocacy, and foster care experiences, I felt compelled to write a different kind of narrative. I wanted to provide a glimpse into the CASA/GAL advocacy role through the eyes of a survivor of childhood abuse and neglect as well as through those of a CASA advocate whose remarkable journey was fashioned by the kids whose lives are impacted by this role. The ensuing hybrid memoir developed naturally. I recognized that a project like this meant taking personal and professional risks. Exposing my life to the public while sharing the CASA/GAL process seemed worth the risk. It was a balancing act.

While drafting this story, I faced hardships and felt powerful emotions about my experiences. There were times when I thought this memoir would never become a reality. With perseverance I moved forward, gathering facts about the CASA/GAL role, and describing how and why I became a child advocate. I explored the volunteer advocacy mission from recruitment and training to selecting a case, advocating for children's best interests, and through evolving advocacy efforts into specific education and legislative agendas. I agonized over details about my life experiences and how those details could affect my family. Much of what I reveal in these pages marks a new level of transparency, and some of what I share may surprise those closest to me.

I also share several stories about the children to whom I was assigned along with my process of becoming an advocate and my own experiences. My goal is not to detail the horrors these children lived but to inspire people to want to become child advocates themselves and to make a difference in children's lives.

This is a true story. My memory may be imperfect, but I did my best to honor the story within. Several pseudonyms were used to represent actual persons and children in my account. Some identifying information about my children's stories has been withheld to protect their privacy. This is serious content—scenes depicting child abuse, incest, domestic violence, alcohol consumption, and suicide are examined. If you are not ready to read about these topics, please come back later.

My story and experiences will not necessarily be the same as other court appointed special advocates' stories. We are all on an exceptional journey shaped by the children whose lives we influence. My journey is somewhat unique but not rare.

My passionate advocacy for abused children ultimately meant this project could help recruit and retain more volunteer court appointed special advocates (CASAs). I hope readers recognize that purpose and understand that this is an urgent call for more child advocacy efforts in every community. This project may even offer confidence to those trying to follow their compass. Maybe an adult child with a past like mine needs to read this story to validate their experiences. Overwhelmingly though, informing readers about the critical role a volunteer advocate plays in the foster care arena is what became the driving force for me to see this project through to completion.

Weaving my childhood and advocacy experiences together was meant to inspire, not shock. It was vital for me to share the CASA mission from a unique perspective, first as a child without an advocate and then as an advocate, trying to make a difference in the world one child at a time. Whatever part of this story motivates you will be what is right for you.

There are tens of thousands of children with similar childhood experiences to mine. If my story can inspire any of those children, current volunteer child advocates, people interested in serving children, and you, I will have been successful with this project. Promoting child advocacy on any level is a reward worthy of this risk.

Net profit from this publication will directly benefit the nonprofit organization Child Advocates San Antonio and its mission. Thank you for reading my story.

PROLOGUE

It had been thirty-five years since my brother Joey was buried in Holy Cross Cemetery's Garden of Joyful Mystery and my first visit since his funeral. Buffalo was no longer my stomping ground, but that was no excuse. He deserved more.

Plot number 115 was difficult to find in the pouring rain that April. I did a grid coordinate search for nearly an hour before discovering the overgrown grave. It was a simple granite military headstone inlaid in the grass. The years showed neglect. The marker was sunk deep into the ground, and I immediately peeled back the dense grass and scraped mud from the engraved headstone with my fingers.

The rain stopped, and Joey's name, etched into the grey granite, was now visible. I talked to my brother for the first time in over three decades. I finally said aloud the things we had kept secret. I asked for his forgiveness for not speaking up about the abuse sooner. He had protected me when I could not protect myself, and I acknowledged this. A burden lifted.

There were more ways to honor my brother.

Memories and emotions flooded me. Joey never got a chance to share his story, but I could make that right. This story could make a difference for children like we once were—young and innocent. My siblings and I endured shocking abuse and neglect as children. We did not have Court Appointed Special Advocates back in the day. CASA did not exist. Yet, by the grace of God, here I was, serving children in foster care as a volunteer child advocate in Bexar County, Texas.

As a child, I could not define resiliency. Finding my voice, healing my soul, and becoming stronger after trauma became a lifelong process. Developing resiliency empowered me to fight for the most vulnerable children in our community. Consequently, I became a fierce advocate for children in foster care because of what I overcame as a defenseless child.

Joey did not get that chance.

Resilience

I would define my resilience as:

(1) each time I "bounced back" from tough times in life

(2) my ability to keep functioning despite what life threw at me

Resiliency

I would define my resiliency as:

(1) when I overcame and became accustomed to trauma, it did not pull me down anymore

(2) repeated composure in the face of being exposed to things that ordinarily would cause harm

PART 1
SURVIVING

"'For I know the plans I have for you,' says the LORD.
'They are plans for good and not for disaster, to give you a future and a
hope.'"
NIV Jeremiah 29:11

Chapter 1
Secrets

The year was 1986. The place was Buffalo, New York. I was a senior at Mount Mercy Academy High School, a private all-girls Catholic school. There was no such thing as the internet or cell phones. MTV (Music Television) and iconic movies would define 1986 for ages. This year was etched in my memory for other reasons.

My parents could not afford the school's tuition. Arrangements were made between my mother and the Sisters of Mercy, the Catholic nuns affiliated with my high school, for me to work off my tuition. Their living quarters, or convent, were on the top floor of the red brick school building. Clearing the dinner tables and washing dishes were my dues in exchange for the free private education provided. My parents, working-class people, barely made ends meet. We were poor during much of my childhood, so I was grateful for this opportunity.

My mother worked the night shift, 11:00 p.m. to 7:00 a.m., as a registered nurse at a nearby Catholic hospital. My father was an electrical worker on the afternoon shift, 3:00 p.m. to 11:00 p.m., at Bethlehem Steel, about five miles away on Route 5 in the City of Lackawanna. Around 1980, the plant laid off hundreds of employees, and my father was one of them. The economy was on a slide. Recession, they said on the news. But as a child, I did not understand the ramifications for our family or community.

My dad was a war hero. He had served in the U.S. Navy in WWII and the U.S. Army during the Korean War. He was comfortable with his veteran friends. After he was let go, we all believed my father was leaving for work every day, but instead, he was going to one of several bars—the VFW, American Legion, or the Knights of Columbus. Whichever bar he went to did not matter. The results were always the same. He came home violently drunk at unpredictable times. This became his daily routine, and it lasted for years.

We were a family of six and lived with little privacy in a four-bedroom, one-bath, two-story single-family home built in 1920. Neighbors' houses were separated only by a single driveway or swatch of grass. Single-pane windows did little to conceal the noise within.

Our house was in a constant state of disrepair. The living room walls were covered in dark-colored, fake wood paneling. The paneling was installed by my father to cover the holes in the plaster. The damage came from violent episodes. Red linoleum was laid over badly worn hardwood floors. Orange and avocado green appliances, standard colors from the era, added a splash of color to the dark and drab house interior. My father tried to manage household repairs himself when or if he was briefly sober. It was my first exposure to what we call "do-it-yourself" (DIY) or "sweat equity" projects today.

We referred to streets in our South Buffalo neighborhood as "the blocks." The streets were arranged in neat rows, parallel to one another and perpendicular to the primary business road. Our schools were minutes away, and we always walked—sun, rain, or snow. Busing was not an option.

I had three siblings. Joey and I were number two and three, right in the middle. My older sister, Diane, was heavyset and dark-haired like my dad. My father revered Diane and always put her on a pedestal. She was also popular and outgoing. Diane avoided most of the abuse by not being home often. Resentment over this pushed us apart. She was the oldest and maybe wisest in ways to protect herself. My younger brother, John, was a wiry kid with wavy dirty blond hair. He was an instigator, and he was my mother's favorite. John never thought twice about tattling on Joey or me to take the attention off himself.

Joey and I felt like we were the odd ones out. We felt rejected and shared that feeling. Remarkably, we were often mistaken for fraternal twins even though we were about nineteen months apart. Our features were similar. Tall slim frames topped with short brown straight hair distinguished us from Diane and John. Our fair complexion and freckles made us look incredibly alike. The fact that I was a tomboy deepened our resemblance. There was a connection between us. Joey and I were caught in the middle, which was not a good place to be. We endured the worst of the abuse.

Alcoholism accelerated trouble for us. My parents' drinking habits were different. While my father drank socially outside the house, my mother isolated herself and drank alone. My father would viciously beat my mother after coming home drunk. We often tried to intervene, but by injecting ourselves into the situation, we would become the focus of our dad's rage or even my mother's. It did not matter, however. My mother and father were what I would call "equal opportunity abusers."

No one was safe from them.

We experienced fear and anxiety daily.

We went without heat on some cold Buffalo winter days and nights. I remember stuffing newspaper in the hole in my bedroom window to keep the snow out. The freezing air seeped through gaps in the window and the poorly insulated walls making it difficult to sleep. Bitter winters concerned me the most. Playing or escaping outside was problematic without proper snow gear. But remaining indoors on frigid days made me more vulnerable to abuse. The cold affects me today and reminds me of how trapped I felt as a child.

Hand-me-down uniforms worn in elementary, middle, and high school were commonplace for us kids. Plastic bread bags worn over my socks inside my winter boots kept my feet dry while walking to and from school. The success of having dry feet after trudging through the snow occasionally turned into failure when I arrived at school and realized I did not have shoes in my backpack. Because of the family dysfunction, I learned early to plan for what I needed. It did not always go well. Walking the halls in socks with large holes in the heels was embarrassing. The ridicule from my middle school classmates solidified my shame.

I also recall the indignity of making the grocery rounds on Saturday mornings with my mother. We would pick up free loaves of bread, a government-issued five-pound block of cheese, five-dollar grab bags of food from the General Mills cereal plant, and reduced milk from the dairy. I never went through the cafeteria line at Mount Mercy Academy during my four-year tenure because I was too ashamed to ask whether lunch was included with my waived tuition. This was something I should have never felt shame about. It is a reality crippling many families even today.

There was some relief in the summers. The City of Buffalo Parks Department sponsored a free summer lunch program for several years in the late 1970s. My brothers and I quickly figured out the program. We could descend upon the playground behind Public School 29, only four streets away, for "first dibs." We had all attended kindergarten there and needed no assistance coming or going. Impatience consumed us while we waited for the clock above the playground to indicate 11:20 a.m. when the city truck would finally arrive.

We would score a free cardboard lunch tray almost daily. We savored the pint of chocolate milk, baloney or ham sandwich on white bread hand-wrapped in plastic wrap, apple, and cookie. Balanced meals were rare in our house, so these lunch routines were special. We scarfed the meal down, often leaving remnants of ketchup, breadcrumbs, or chocolate chips smeared on our faces and clothes.

We raced back toward our house and nearly a mile farther to the public pool at Cazenovia Park. The city truck had one more stop before reaching "Caz." Running down my street, I liked to make a game of not stepping on the sidewalk cracks.

"Step on a crack, break your momma's back!" I would shriek while looking back to see if John was keeping pace.

One day, Joey stopped ahead of me when his shoelace came undone. As he bent over in front of me, I crashed into him.

But a skinned knee did not phase me. No one would be concerned over an additional cut, scrape, or bruise. The enormous red scrape on my knee blended in with the other marks. The marks were never questioned. They were not worth crying over anymore.

John laughed as he passed us.

He was breathless.

"Hey, you stepped on a crack!" I yelled as he pulled ahead.

It was a game to outpace each other. Joey and I pushed and shoved each other while scrambling to our feet. That summer was unusually hot and sticky. Sweat wet my hair and soaked my clothes. We ran the whole way, stopping only to cross McKinley Parkway and Abbott Road to avoid being struck by a car. We would reach the park in about twenty minutes. Cazenovia was a large lush green park. The leaves on the trees were green, and the canopy provided momentary shield from the sun as we winded our way along the dirt path to the pool house. Chestnuts scattered the path and made a crunching noise under our feet.

Most of the time, we could jump in line and enjoy another free lunch just as the rear door of the city panel truck was opening. The metal roll-up door rattled as it went up. The sounds of children laughing and playing abruptly turned into cheers. My excitement grew in anticipation of another treat. Our plans were often foiled when we were recognized from the school playground and denied a second serving by the city workers. The food stains on our clothes or faces gave us away. At other times, the workers smiled and said, "Here you go, kid, enjoy." I imagined they knew we needed a break.

Looking back now, I equated our neglect and abuse with my parents' struggles while teetering on the edge of poverty and how they dealt with it—through alcohol. This form of survival afflicts many families across the country today. As a young child, I felt sad and longed for a normal family life. Daydreaming during my idle time offered temporary relief from reality and allowed the pain to drift away.

These feelings were kept buried among other secrets not disclosed to my friends. Later, I would learn that some of their families had struggled too. Times were tough in South Buffalo when we were kids. Families kept secrets. Shame was an emotion that grew from these experiences and followed me for most of my adult life. However, some of my secrets shocked my closest friends decades later when I finally shared the truth. None of my friends knew what happened in our home during those earlier years.

Keeping secrets nurtured the shame and humiliation of my life.

Chapter 2
Sacrifice

Some of my earliest childhood memories are of my siblings and me escaping from a basement window to race to the nearby police precinct to summon help. The violence was unrelenting. Our outcries were repetitive. We got tremendous practice with our escape routes and calling for help. When I was in the third grade, I could visualize the fastest route to the police precinct in my head whenever the violence was the worst.

The most accessible basement window to unlock and swing open was above the washing machine. It did not stick in the frame from layers of peeling paint like the others. A sturdy metal milk crate adjacent to the washer gave us a head start. In a couple of leaps, I could be out of the window and onto the grass next to Mrs. Jackson's house.

My only obstacle to the front yard and the street was a wooden picket fence barely three or four feet high. The rails were easy to climb for a tomboy like me. Grabbing a branch from the small tree in front of the fence helped me gain my balance to jump to the other side. If I ever had trouble, Joey always stayed back to help me. Together, we would dash up the narrow street towards South Park Avenue, turn right, and head north for three blocks. Reaching the Fifteenth Police Precinct on the corner of Whitfield Avenue took five or six minutes.

Running felt good!

The building was intimidating. A set of wooden double doors was too heavy for me to pull open unassisted. Joey and I pulled together. Once inside, a few stairs separated us from an enormous wooden barrier. This time when we went in, we stopped at the police sergeant sitting behind the barrier at a heavy-duty desk, which was designed to separate the public from the public servants. The dark wood tone and dimly lit building were ominous. Maybe it was to intimidate criminals, but the effect on me was petrifying. The desk towered over us. I could not see the top, and the police sergeant could barely see Joey or me.

"Back up!" the sergeant barked the order.

We obeyed, and like robots with arms against our sides, we slowly took one or two steps back from the desk.

"Now I see you two. What do you want?"

Joey spoke first as he gasped for air. "Please, officer, we need your help. My dad is going to kill my mom. He's drunk."

"This better not be a waste of my time."

The gruff reply was familiar. The officer lowered his newspaper and positioned his reading glasses at the end of his nose. He glared at us over the rims.

I did not move an inch and concentrated on catching my breath. My knees were locked together, and I felt a faint feeling overcoming me. What was going to happen to us?

"How old are you?"

"I'm eight, sir," I replied while timidly looking away.

"And how old are you, boy?"

"I'm almost ten." Joey also nervously looked down at the floor.

"*Humph.* I think I remember you now. Tell me your address again, and I will send a squad car when a patrolman is available." The officer raised his newspaper before finishing, and we could no longer see his face.

We were not reassured. The tone of the conversation was dismissive. My shoulders slumped, and I dragged my feet while turning back to the stairs and the heavy door. We always hurried back to the fray, hoping our dad had passed out while we were gone.

Help from authorities was inconsistent. If the police or a Child Protective Services (CPS) investigator did arrive, we knew it immediately. The pounding at the front storm door resonated through the entire first floor of our house. They never rang the doorbell like ordinary people.

Finally we would hear it. *Bang, bang, bang*! The quick pounding got everyone's attention.

My mom always made Joey and me accompany her to the foyer. She would place one hand on my shoulder and the other on Joey's arm after answering the door. The pressure from her nails would dig deep into my shoulder, leaving bruises and cutting my flesh. My bruises were not usually visible, but Joey always had an array of cuts and bruises on display on his biceps. The newer purple and red marks blended with fading brown and yellow bruises. This was most obvious in the summer when he wore sleeveless shirts. The bruise and abrasion patterns varied and repeated all year long.

"Nothing is going on. It must be some misunderstanding," Mom would lie to the authorities.

Joey and I always quickly recanted and followed her lead. "Yes, sir, everything is fine," we would mumble, nodding to affirm the sham.

I would remain rigid and concentrate on not wincing despite my mother's firm grasp on my shoulder. The pain would pulsate into my neck and down my right arm. Pursing my lips concealed my pain and maintained the façade. We were scared. Joey's eyes did not hide his fear. The vacant stare and wide-open appearance of his eyes I knew always mirrored mine. This was unconscious and would go unnoticed by the police officers or investigators. They left every time.

When the coast was clear, my mother would release her grip on us and slap Joey. He stopped pulling away when he saw the hits coming long ago. The blow always landed hard. Hearing the *slap* from her hand on his face made me shudder as if I felt the sting myself. My brother and I shared the pain.

"You are a liar. You did this. I wish you were never born," she would yell at him.

The day or evening abuse continued. We had turned away help from the authorities out of fear. The near-miss from abuse being detected in our home never persuaded my parents to change their ways.

It is hard to believe how many times this scenario played out month after month as I reflect today. For five to seven years, we sought police protection regularly. Sometimes John or Diane joined us. Each episode yielded the same negative results. In 1980, the Fifteenth Police Precinct on the corner of South Park and Whitfield Avenues closed and moved into the building formerly known as Public School 29. The route mostly stayed the same. Passing the identical eight houses, we would reach South Park and turn left to the new destination. We had to travel four streets to the south, one more than before, but we were getting older and faster. The results were the same. Our voices were silenced when we returned home. Intimidation became our internal prison walls.

We repeatedly recanted out of fear.

Sometimes, none of us made it out of the basement windows. My father had started to set traps to deter our escape. The accessible windows we could reach were now partially blocked. He had hung rebar, pipes, and scrap lumber horizontally on the basement wall below the small square windows.

I remember the dreadful feeling that washed over me when we knocked something over in the desperate scramble to escape. Time appeared to stop momentarily as a metal bar hit the cement floor and made a loud *clank-clank* sound. Noise exposed us! A good soldier like my dad would have no problem hunting us down now. We had only seconds to make it out. My heart beat out of my chest and initiated a panic response. He knew where we were. It would not be long before we were caught.

"Run," I whispered, barely hearing the words myself.

Joey jumped up out of the chest-high window.

"Joan, grab my hand," he cried while reaching back through the darkness.

I gulped hard. It was so difficult to swallow.

John hid under the stairs while Diane confidently walked back upstairs, avoiding detection. We were at the mercy of each other now. One of us escaped, but someone would have to be caught for the rest of us to get away through another route. It seemed inevitable.

Frozen in fear, I cried, "Joey, I can't reach."

The rebar and pine lumber scraps continued falling from underneath the window ledge. Three dim incandescent bulbs lit the basement, and I barely saw the hazard, let alone my hands in front of me. Frustration about needing to be more careful stressed me.

"Darn, it's my fault. Go. I'm sorry."

Panic overcame me as I accidentally created more noise by knocking down more pipes. Careless, I could not avoid a mishap. My bare feet were cold and wet from the damp concrete basement floor. Blood began pooling beneath me when I stepped on a nail protruding from one of the fallen scraps of lumber. Adrenaline pumped and suppressed the pain.

Joey ran for help.

My luck ran out. Turning around into my father was my fate. As I was dragged upstairs by my short hair, I caught a glimpse of John through the open stair treads. My father saw him too. Our fate was sealed this evening, or was it?

Joey did return in time. The authorities did not. The distraction of Joey opening the front door allowed us to flee from my father's grasp. Joey was the new target.

Refuge for me was an upstairs walk-in attic. It was cold and dark, but my father would not find me again tonight. Sleep was not possible as my heart was rapidly pounding in my chest. The wooden floor was uncomfortable, and I tried not to move to keep the floorboards from creaking. I was also hypervigilant of any noise in the hallway. John, Joey, and Diane were on their own, exposed or hiding. This worried me. I could only wish my father passed out soon. Hours would pass before I felt safe to go to my bedroom.

Eventually, my dad nailed all the windows shut when we outsmarted him too many times. We were so desperate to be spared a beating that we even resorted to turning on one another. We sacrificed each other to save ourselves and find a better hiding spot. This was us in survival mode. It was indeed the survival of the fittest. We blamed one another for causing the abuse—even though we knew that was not true.

The abuse was routine in our house. Therefore, I assumed it was typical for other children—like our friends. Could this be something not ever spoken about openly? I could not believe we were terrible and deserved such vicious punishment. Why was this happening? Why did my parents treat us so cruelly?

Physical abuse and domestic violence were not the only trauma we faced. Neglect and emotional abuse were prevalent as well. At times, I resembled a war-ravaged soldier incapable of rational, emotional thought. Words of affirmation or love were foreign to us and internalizing the hate-fueled rhetoric was commonplace. Others, like schoolteachers, noticed my waning attention span and vacant stare. My elementary school teacher would snap her fingers at me in class. Snap, snap, snap!

"Joan, Joan, pay attention."

A *Huh*! was barely audible while I raised my head off my desk.

"Read the next passage," she demanded.

I had no idea where we were in the assignment. My mind wandered. Her ruler slapped my forearm. There was no flinch from me. Desensitized by my parent's abuse, the slap from the Catholic nun had no effect.

She said I was daydreaming in class. But from my perspective, I did not recall thoughts or dreams. The trauma created a vacuum of creativity within my mind. How was I supposed to act? Or think? Nothing mattered. Not even us.

Other times, I was talkative and disruptive. I craved positive attention but knew little about what was required to receive it. There was no nurturing and no love at my home. Thriving was nearly impossible.

As a small child, I played outside with my siblings and neighbors until the streetlights came on. No one checked on us. My dad was likely out drinking, and my mother was sleeping off her night shift or slowly getting drunk alone inside the house. We often wandered off and got into mischief at a nearby cemetery, vacant buildings, and well-established businesses.

It was the need for more supervision that was problematic. I followed my older sister to local retail stores and learned how to shoplift clothes by shadowing her. My shame and guilt drove me away from her. There was no way I wanted to be a thief even if I tried to justify needing clothes. The possibility of getting caught scared me straight. I tried hard to be good to stave off the vicious beatings. Hanging with my brothers became more routine. My sister and I grew further apart.

The outlook with the boys was not much better. My brother Joey nearly blew off his thumb playing with illegal fireworks he got from a friend. The M-80 pyrotechnic exploded as it left his hand in front of our house. I dove onto the grass several feet away and covered my ears. His right thumb was mangled. The tip of his index finger above the nail bed was bleeding profusely. He was not taken to see a doctor. A beating was levied for the transgression instead.

The skin on his hand never healed. Both hands developed severe dryness and cracking. The wounds were made worse when he anxiously picked at the dry skin. His fingers and hands often bled from the deep cracks. He was bullied at school because of this condition, yet my parents never had him examined by a doctor. The appearance of his hands frightened even me.

The pain must have been unbearable. He suffered from this for as long as I recall seeing him alive.

Being naïve and undisciplined, I found trouble as well. Once, a large bag of ice melt used for thawing ice and snow was left open in the garage. Reaching inside the bag and grabbing a handful of the crystals, I noted how they resembled rock candy. Rock candy was crystallized sugar and brightly colored with food dye. It was popular at the time. I ate the white and blue substance without recognizing its poisonous nature. It tasted sweet, probably from its antifreeze chemicals, and I did not recognize the danger. I also encouraged Patrick, a neighbor the same age as me, to eat it. It was not very smart. Patrick told his mom, and she called my mother. The evening would include another beating. Dinner was withheld, and I was sent to my room. I felt horrible about my friend. The sick feeling I had in my stomach lasted several days, but losing my friend was far worse than the temporary nausea.

Our escapades put us in danger several times. We were young children and needed supervision. But the neglect carried into our basic needs. Food, clothing, heat, safety, and medical care were lacking when my parents were incapable of caring for themselves. An ample supply of beer and cigarettes at the house was a priority over our needs.

—

This life was not what I saw on TV. I enjoyed watching *The Brady Bunch*, *The Partridge Family*, *Little House on the Prairie*, and *Eight is Enough*. I idolized the fictional television parents and dreamed I would live with the characters in these programs one day.

Slam! It was the front door. I was snapped back into reality. He was drunk again.

Everyone ran for cover. If only I could get a break tonight. If only no one would touch me tonight!

My dad staggered through the house shouting, "Carol, Carol!"

He found my mother halfway between the bathroom and her bedroom at the back of the house. My mother was beaten with his fists while preparing for her overnight nursing shift. Dad grabbed her by her hair and threw her against the linen closet near the stairs, causing the nearby dog food and water dishes to spew their contents across the floor.

Joey came out of hiding. He defended my mother from my father. "Dad, please stop," he wailed.

Diane and I scurried to shut the windows. The crank arms were difficult and slow to close. Faster! I wound them tight, panting from breathlessness.

My father was holding my mother down with one hand. She was on her knees. Her makeup was smeared around her eyes as she cried hysterically. My dad tightened his grip on her hair.

She cried out again, "Fran, you are hurting me!"

He used his right hand to swing at Joey.

"Shut up; you are worthless. Don't you hear me?" My dad slurred his words and staggered. He nearly fell over as Joey dodged his wayward swing.

I watched from behind the action in the kitchen, paralyzed in fear. How my father managed to drive home in this condition night after night momentarily bothered me.

My mom screamed in agony, "Please, Fran, I have to go to work ... I'm sorry, I'm sorry," she cried.

My father was shaking her while trying to grab Joey. Joey dodged him again. Diane joined in and tried to pull my mother away from my father.

We all pleaded in unison, "Dad, please stop!"

This type of unprovoked attack happened often. I was worried we had not shut the windows fast enough. We were always afraid of the neighbors hearing what was happening. We were embarrassed. This night was no different.

"Where's my dinner, bitch?" he growled.

"I will get it, Dad. Here, I will get it for you," I said, thrusting myself into the mix.

Careful to keep my distance in the kitchen, I glanced over my left shoulder to see if a path was clear to run if he moved toward me. The front door was not unreachable by any stretch. Quick calculations of the distance between my dad and me to the door were reassuring. The odds were in my favor.

Diane calmly pleaded with my dad. "Dad, please, she has to go to work. Joan's getting your dinner."

My dad stood up and released his grip on my mother's hair. I watched him move sluggishly, terrorized by his name-calling. The world slowed momentarily. "Bitch!" he yelled as spit flew from his mouth, kicking my mother a last time and causing the dog bowls to fly further across the floor. My mother slid quietly down the door jamb of their bedroom.

Diane helped my mother. Joey started cleaning up the water and the spilled dog food. My mom's hair curlers and some small chunks of hair were scattered amongst the dog food kibble and soaked by the spilled water outside the bathroom.

I never did get my father any dinner that night. He was incoherent and stumbled to the living room. At this point, my father had been sleeping on the couch regularly. Their marriage seemed to be over, but this is how we existed. Unfortunately, this made me vulnerable to my father's interest.

Good, Dad passed out. I watched him crash onto the couch.

It is not me again tonight.

Meanwhile, my mom quickly turned against Joey with misdirected anger. "You bastard," she screamed at him. "I hate you."

Joey had not done anything wrong. He was physically closer to my mother as she slowly recovered from the vicious attack. He hurriedly mopped up the mess on the floor with rags. It was common for her to take her anger out on him. She never dared to hit my father back, so Joey became her punching bag.

Confused and afraid, I ran upstairs while my mother was reeling at Joey.

My mother needed to get to work, but she physically assaulted Joey instead. She never went to work. Like many other nights, she called in "sick."

Alone and afraid, I cried myself to sleep, steeped in guilt and shame about Joey's cries and torture. My tabby cat, Kipling, curled on top of me, was often my only comfort source. Her purring and the heat from her body through the bed linens were soothing. My father accidentally killed Kipling several years later. She had climbed inside his station wagon's motor on a frigid winter day. He found her after the car had trouble starting.

Joey was the sacrificial lamb. It seemed to become his self-ascribed role. His sacrifice often protected me from my dad like he tried to protect my mother that night. My mother openly despised him, whether she was drunk or not. The worst physical abuse from Mom and Dad was always directed at Joey.

Joey usually gave himself up to my dad and took the most severe beatings from both grown-ups so we could get away. He tried to protect me even when I could not save him.

On one occasion, Joey pulled me away from my father as he was stripping his belt from his pants. His timing was impeccable. Able to jump off the couch, I darted into the dining room a few feet away. I was afraid of my father but deeply worried about what would become of Joey, so I remained nearby.

Joey taunted my dad to take attention away from me. "You can't hurt me!" he cried. "You are a no-good drunk. I hate you!"

Joey misjudged the safe zone. My dad was quicker than usual and grabbed him, yanking him from his feet. He had a firm grasp on Joey now. He stood tall over him and quickly dragged him into the dining room. I was afraid he was coming for me too. Instead, he ordered Joey to choose a belt for his beating while reaching for another belt hung across the dining chair.

Joey kept taunting him.

I begged, "Joey, stop. Please, you are making it worse." My voice was whiny but detectable from my nearby hiding place. Fear immobilized me. What had Joey done?

"Choose!" yelled my dad.

The choice was always between a worn-out wide white leather belt with holes throughout it or the thinner brown and black reversible leather belt only about an inch wide. The leather on both was stretched and cracked in several places. I knew them both well and often suffered the distinct bruise patterns they left behind. We all did, even if we did not have a choice.

My choice would have been the wide belt, but Joey chose the thinner leather belt tonight. It flowed quickly through the air and left deep cuts in our flesh from its sharp and narrow width. It sounded like the crack of a whip. The thin belt was the most severe choice.

Joey was yanked back to the couch and forcibly stripped.

The *snap* of the belt against Joey's bare bottom shattered my spirit.

Joey shrieked in pain. "I am sorry. I am sorry," he wailed.

My father held him down over his knee with his right hand and struck him from the left. The belt whirled in the air.

Frozen in fear, I hid under the dining room table.

"I'll give you something to cry about," my dad said as he continued to beat Joey.

Snap, snap, snap. I did not count how many times Joey was beaten, and an eternity passed. Joey was whimpering quietly and lying lifeless on my father's knee. My dad's arm flowed through the air, grasping the thin leather belt tightly.

How much longer? I agonized silently.

"Dad, stop. Please stop," I begged from under the dining table.

My father paused briefly and looked directly at me. He had one eye that presented a cold steel expression. It was fake. "Lost it in the war," we were told. The truth was that he lost it in a drunken rage after the war. One of my uncles punched him directly in the eye socket and popped his eye out. My only image of him was with his prosthetic eye. There were always so many lies told within our family. The other eye was bloodshot. His gaze was frightening. Drunk was an understatement.

"Oh no," I muttered under my breath as I slowly backed myself farther into the dining room out of his view.

"You're next!" he exclaimed.

Snap, snap, snap.

Joey stopped crying. He gave up. Like we usually did.

Sometimes we wrestled the belts away from my intoxicated father if we were lucky. He was too strong for us, though, and the smack of his hand would fall instead like a sledgehammer against our tiny bodies. It was a calculated risk to try this maneuver. We were too young to gauge how genuinely drunk or in control he was. We were powerless.

My hatred towards my parents for drinking and abusing us, neglecting us, and lying to the authorities and the neighbors did not make me proud. The abuse did not draw me closer to my siblings. Maybe it should have. I was numb. We probably all were. We lived like strangers, not brothers and sisters. Each of us was damaged in separate ways, and we could barely fend for ourselves, let alone one another. There were times we tried to be united, but when one of us got caught, the rest resorted to self-preservation, except for Joey.

He was selfless.

His sacrifice saved me more than once.

No one in my family ever heard the words "I love you" when we were growing up. I reasoned that I felt tolerated when my parents were sober. They turned into monsters when they drank, which seemed like nearly every day. We needed a protector. We needed an advocate. Yet there was no one to speak for us. If there were ever pleasant times, those memories are misplaced. The darkest times are the memories that have haunted me.

We were rarely safe at home. If my dad was at work or at a bar getting drunk, my mother was home getting drunk. They were on different shifts, so their alcohol-fueled stints could start early in the day and span long after sunset.

Windows and doors were shut to hide the noise from the neighbors.

The neighbors must have known. How could they not? The proximity of all the houses had to reveal hidden secrets. We had targets on our backs when the door closed. And in the light of day, the marks, scratches, and bruises glistened in the sun. They were as colorful as our clothing. Someone needed to notice.

Would help ever arrive in time?

Chapter 3
Interventions

I made my first report of sexual abuse when I was approximately twelve years old. Finally, the police and CPS had to respond to our outcries. There was no taking it back this time. I felt destroyed.

It first happened when my father came home drunk again.

"Joan, where are you?" he called out. His footsteps came from the stairs. The stairs groaned under his weight. The sound became louder. "Joan, honey, where are you?" His drunken tone was suspicious and sinister.

He found me upstairs in the bedroom I shared with my sister on our piss-stained queen-size mattress that lay on the floor. We shared it with the bed bugs, lice, and fleas that infested our house. There was nowhere to hide in my room.

Where was Diane tonight?

Too late! I was fully awake now. My father's silhouette appeared in the door frame and blocked the dim hall light I left on nightly. It seems odd that I was afraid of the dark. Worse demons lurked in my house, even in the light of day. Darkness was not the enemy. I was immediately yanked off the mattress like a fish snagged from a creek bed. Dragged downstairs by my arm, I knew this would end badly for me. Kicking and thrashing wildly was useless and only added to my injuries. My efforts to free myself were met by my dad's counterattack. He slammed me against the wall and stair railing to gain complete control and power over me. I was too small and weak.

"Stop, leave me alone," I wailed. No one was within earshot.

Where were my siblings? No one was home! It was late. My mother was already at work, but where were Diane, Joey, and John? Were they hiding?

I feared for my life, but I succumbed to his power. My will was fading. My father turned into a madman.

He forced me onto the couch in the living room. My arm was red and hurt from him dragging me through the house. My face burned when it was forced into the scratchy tweed-like fabric. It was rough and smelled of cigarette smoke and body odor.

"Stop kicking. I am going to teach you this, so you don't learn it on the streets," he slurred.

"Dad, no—" I screamed and kicked more.

My father turned me over and pinned both my wrists against my side. Fighting back guaranteed nothing except more pain. At over six feet tall, my father was strong and towered over me like a monster. I was overpowered. The smell of alcohol on his breath was too close.

"No, no, no—stop!" I continued to scream louder than ever before.

No one came to rescue me.

He laid on top of me, and I was paralyzed by the sound of his belt being unbuckled and his zipper unzipping.

I left my body. This sexual assault escalated to what I now understand were long-standing "grooming" behaviors from him. My father controlled me with force, punishment, coercion, and manipulation. The molestation persisted for many years. The word molestation repulses me and is difficult to say aloud today.

When I made the report, despite the fact that I was in shock, I was still able to be specific about the details of this event. Revealing the additional years of abuse under our roof was not possible. From what I remember, no one asked if any other abuse had happened.

Other secrets were preserved. My mother manipulated us into believing the police and parents of our neighborhood friends were bad and could not be trusted. This influence kept us from revealing the true extent of the horrors behind our front door.

The trigger for the brutality in our house seemed to stem from my parents' alcoholism, their hatred towards one another, and their struggles with money.

Model parents? No.

We were genuinely decent kids. Of course, we stepped out of line on occasion, probably no more than any other kid testing limits. Our mischievous ways usually resulted in receiving grace from a business owner or neighbor. Maybe they felt sorry for us? We were lucky our parents never found out about some of our escapades. Nevertheless, nothing justified the brutality or emotional and physical toll we endured. No child deserved this kind of treatment.

My father was arrested the night he sexually assaulted me the first time.

My mother had come home during her nursing night shift. It seemed like she appeared shortly after the incident. It was long after midnight, and my siblings were still not home. After it happened, crying hysterically, I locked myself inside the single bathroom of our two-story house. At the time, I believed she had been the one to call the police, but in hindsight, it is more likely a concerned neighbor alerted her to return home from work and called the police themselves.

When the police came, my father was already long gone, but they would soon find him at a local bar. I had not told my mother what happened, but somehow, she knew. I will never know how.

"Are you going to handcuff me?" I asked the police officer.

"No, that is for criminals. You did nothing wrong, little girl."

The officer guided my mother and me to the backseat of the police cruiser. We were taken to the new police precinct location for an official statement. When the police cruiser pulled up to the curb, I was immediately discouraged. I had been here before. It never mattered.

My mother bailed my father out of jail the next day.

Later, she would tell the authorities and my court-ordered therapist,

"Joan needs help. I do not know what to do with her."

Turning towards me, she snarled the words, "Queen Elizabeth!"

I was named after Saint Joan of Arc and Queen Elizabeth II. She only used my middle name when she wanted to berate me. The derogatory way she expressed my middle name disappointed me. My mother did not welcome my complaints about the abuse and frequent outcries over the years. She was embarrassed by me.

"It's all about Joan. You want to get your way," she barked.

I felt unwanted.

She implied something was wrong with me and not my father; I knew it immediately and was confused. Why would she protect the man who beat her for years, beat us, and molested me? Why did she not protect her child?

My dad came home after the arrest. Again, I was not safe. We were not safe. Someone would have to pay for his brief incarceration. It would be me again. I was marked. Disrupting their perfect life behind the battered storm door on Mariemont Avenue may have been a mistake.

Court-ordered therapy was paralyzing for me. It involved my mother and father with the therapist and me in the same room. This made no sense to me. Was consent not granted for me to have privacy? Was I suspected of lying?

There was a brief meeting with a judge at a courthouse in downtown Buffalo. My memory is unclear, but the image of an older man wearing a black robe leaning over the side of his desk to speak with me is imprinted in my head. He spoke calmly and asked me to tell him what had happened. He made me feel safe. Certain I had told him about the abuse, I felt things would improve. The judge was supposed to make things better. Did he not believe me? He ordered the therapy.

It was astonishing that the therapist, Lisa, expected me to tell her what had happened and detail the unspeakable abuse in front of my father and mother! Unbelievable! I was expected to continue to speak easily of the single "event" leading up to my father's arrest. Where was I going to get the courage and strength? There was no one to advocate for me. There was no one to speak for me.

It was humiliating enough when I had had to describe the single sexual assault to several male police detectives weeks earlier at the police station. They questioned me for hours about specific details. I did not understand what I had been through at the time. I only knew it was wrong; that was clear in my mind. I described what happened as best as I could while never looking at my mother for comfort. We never spoke about my report. There was no trust between us.

There was also no physical evidence. The police did not attempt to collect any, and I was never taken to the hospital.

It would not have mattered anyway as I showered immediately after the incident. My father had pounded on the bathroom door. "Joan, I am sorry. Please do not say anything," he cried. He knew he was wrong again.

My arms were wrapped around my scrawny legs as I sat in the tub. The lukewarm water washed him and his odor away. Sobbing alone, I had difficulty finding peace. My tears washed away with the water.

"I did this for your own good," he said, trying to justify his actions. A few moments later, I heard the front door slam.

———

It was not possible for me to cooperate during therapy under the conditions Lisa set. Could this be why my father was never convicted? I desperately needed someone to speak for me as a child. There was no one to be my voice. There were no CASAs or other child advocates available yet. My mother would send me back to school after these family therapy sessions with a doctor's note that read:

"Please excuse Joan from class today. She had an appointment with her psychiatrist."

Humiliation turned my face and neck red with hives each time I handed over the note at the administrative offices of Saint Ambrose Middle School.

One of my friend's mothers worked in the office and often received my excusal note. I was ashamed and embarrassed. What if my friends found out?

My inability to participate in this therapy may have led to the prosecution not pursuing the case against my dad. I had shut down. The trauma was incapacitating. How could they prosecute him if I could not speak for myself? But how could I speak up when I feared what would happen at home after we left the therapist's office?

I remained in my home with my perpetrator during the legal process. My dad gave me a puppy as a gift, maybe a consolation prize—another manipulation. I loved the puppy, not because it was a gift, but because the puppy, whom I named Captain, loved me back. This was the comfort I needed since losing Kipling.

I did not know how to find my voice. *Somebody, please help me.* Secrets were sealed again. Before I knew it, the case was over. The abuse, however, was not.

<hr>

A year later, I thumbed through the phone book and found Lisa's phone number. I dialed it from a payphone on South Park Avenue, minutes from my house.

"Lisa?" I asked when a woman answered the phone.

"Yes. This is she."

"Are you still a therapist?" I inquired.

"Yes, who is this?" She sounded worried.

I told her my name. "A judge said I had to see you after my father hurt me."

I did not wait for acknowledgment and spoke rapid-fire.

"I was your client a long time ago. I want to come back."

The sound of her shuffling through files in her desk or file cabinet resonated through the payphone receiver. *Swoosh, clang.* Metal drawers opened and closed.

After a long pause, I heard her sigh wearily, extinguishing my hope. She must have found my file.

This call was too late. I shook my head and clutched the receiver with white knuckles. I was angry with myself for waiting so long.

"I remember you," she urged, but her tone was not believable.

There was no one else to turn to. Assuming I was simply another old case file to her, a manila folder, a forgotten story, my heart sank. I pleaded my case one final time.

"Lisa, can I see you again? Without my parents this time. I need to know what I did wrong. Why did no one believe me?"

The payphone *beeped*, indicating it needed more coins, so I did not hear if she said "yes."

She did not.

Asking for help again, I pleaded for empathy. She listened and explained how she could not help me now. Clutching the receiver closer to my ear, I was sure I heard her wrong. Being told "no" was incomprehensible to me. I had not prepared for this outcome.

She recommended someone named Tina, a counseling intern at a local college, and offered her phone number as someone who could see me "pro bono." I did not understand the term, but she explained—at no cost. She did remember my situation. I scribbled Tina's name and number on my arm with the pen dangling on a spiral cord from the phone booth. The phone disconnected. The coins had run out.

At home, I transferred the information to a note and hid it in a drawer. Secretly, I washed the ink from my arm to avoid any inquiries from my parents. The saved information would come in handy much later.

Rejection washed over me.

⚊

High school freshman orientation had begun. We were gathered in the auditorium at Mount Mercy Academy. Teachers lined up against the walls and appeared to size us up as the principal, Sister William Marie, spoke from the stage. We were instructed about policies, locker assignments, uniform requirements, and the code of conduct.

I nervously shifted and could not stand or sit still. There were more than a hundred new students in the room. Were their eyes on me? Maybe I was being paranoid? I always felt judged. It was my shame. My restlessness did draw more attention to me. The freshman principal, Sister Mary Clare, was hovering behind me. She touched my shoulder. It was more of a poke or jab rather than a gentle tap. "Pay attention," she stated in a stern voice.

"Yes, Sister," I said, shifting nervously again.

Sensing her eyes on the back of my head, I turned around and looked directly at her.

"Do you smoke?" she asked.

It caught me off guard. "No, of course not," I replied earnestly.

She looked at me with disbelief. Her lips and eyes showed her doubt. The head tilt was my final confirmation.

Yup! She did not believe me. Humiliation consumed me, and I tuned out the rest of the speakers from the stage in front of me. The smell of smoke permeated my clothes—everything I owned. My mother was a chain smoker, and now my new freshman principal had me pegged as a smoker and a liar. What a first day! It was a disaster.

Unbeknownst to me, one of my neighbors had alerted the school administrators to the abuse at my house. Several years later, my next-door neighbor Mrs. Cleary, revealed how she had felt helpless all the years listening to the turmoil in our house. This was during a visit with her shortly after graduating high school.

"Joanie, I did not know what to do. It was so horrible for you. I am sorry we did not do more sooner," she sobbed as she spoke to me.

She recounted what she heard through her bedroom window. She was the one who called the high school and asked them to look out for me. The school did know! They had been watching me. I was not paranoid.

Her bedroom window was straight across from our kitchen. Our driveway separated the houses. The Clearys were barely fifteen feet away. None of us ever went to their door for help in all those years. That was a mistake I had to let go of. I was grateful for her.

"I called the sisters at Mount Mercy Academy. I was so worried about you," Mrs. Cleary explained.

This disclosure surprised me, and I felt proud of her. I hugged her. Secretly, I loved how she was the only person ever to call me "Joanie." It always made me feel special.

"I'm going to be fine," I said, trying to reassure her. I heard the doubt in my voice, and I was not even sure of the validity of my statement. Convincing myself was more difficult than convincing her.

She gave me several homemade cookies, which reminded me of how nice she had always been when I was a child.

As a freshman, I believed the teachers could see the damage in me on the first day of orientation. My suspicions were correct. My neighbor had tried to intervene. If only I dared to speak up as a child. Crying out for help seemed an impossible task most days. How could I ever trust an adult? My mother instilled the belief in me that adults were not trustworthy and that what happened in our family needed to stay in the family.

This was my normal.

In my sophomore year, Mrs. Kane, my English teacher, won my trust. I overcame the fear my mother instilled in me. Mrs. Kane became my confidant. Talking with her came easily. I do not recall how this relationship came about. I imagine I was just desperate for help at that time. She was pleasant, engaging, and a genuinely caring person. She made herself available to counsel or mentor me in between classes. Receiving attention made me feel special. Some days I struggled to relate. Other times were peppered with superficial conversation from me. Could I be ready to release the burden inside me? My voice was stirring inside. Mrs. Kane eventually did help me feel comfortable with revealing some of my secrets.

I must have hinted about the abuse. She was patient with me, and at my teacher's insistence, I called Tina, the therapist Lisa had recommended two years prior. Mrs. Kane arranged for me to leave school in the afternoon every week and travel by city bus, transferring routes until I reached the college student health center about ten miles away. Mrs. Kane and Tina were the first adults I trusted with my fears.

Tina agreed to see me weekly for counseling throughout high school. As a minor, consent would have been required from my parents. In this case, there was none. It was a lucky break for me. My friends did not even notice when I was missing from class for several hours during the school day each week. The absences never affected my attendance or grades either. A pass was automatic and not questioned.

This was some of the first kindness I felt in my young life. It warmed me inside. The accommodations my neighbor, teacher, and a volunteer counselor—essentially outsiders—were making for me filled the void of not feeling loved by my parents. The school professionals protected my privacy. Privacy from my parents was priceless during this period.

The abuse was uninterrupted at home. I became afraid to share details again. It had been an epic risk and total failure when I had provided painful details before since nothing seemed to come of it. My timidness and secrecy made it hard for Mrs. Kane or Tina to help me. Fear and brainwashing by my parents influenced my behaviors. Chaos and fear were familiar feelings for me.

You could consider me a troubled youth at that time. Academically I did well and participated in many extracurricular activities to keep me out of the house, but I had trouble relating to others, especially adults trying to help me. This was how trauma affected me. My dark side was something I rarely exposed—it was a depressing and anger-filled cavity where I could not visualize a life of comfort or joy. I did not want anyone to know what I was honestly thinking. I hated my life and carefully lived life in secret. My friends were oblivious because of my shallow and enigmatic exterior.

In early spring, a pair of CPS investigators appeared at the house. The doorbell sounded instead of the usual pounding. This took me by total surprise. Neither Joey nor I had alerted the authorities this time.

There we stood, shoulder to shoulder, again in the foyer. Joey and I were stoic, not flinching from the wounds inflicted by my mom's nails and grip. How was this not recognized by the investigators? The man and woman were strangers and unfamiliar from previous encounters at our house. The man spoke directly to my mother. "There's been a report made to social services about children in this home."

My mother did not reply and squeezed my shoulder harder.

"The report concerns Joan," the man added while appearing to confirm with a glance down at his clipboard.

The woman smiled at me and bent down closer to my level. "Is that you, sweetie? Are you Joan?"

I had been outed! My memory blanked, but I remember Joey pleading, "Tell her, Joan. Tell her, Joan."

We had talked previously of going to the authorities together but needed help to muster the power to do it again. We had not initiated this encounter. This would become only the second time either of us spoke up and did not recant in front of my mom.

I confirmed the investigator's concerns with a nod and a muffled, "Yes. It is true. Please help us."

Was I hearing my voice? What was I getting us into now?

The strangers directed several questions at my mother, and a heated conversation ensued. My mother was furious.

Joey and I pleaded to be taken away.

"Go ahead, take them if that's what they want," she said, scowling.

Joey and I were finally removed from our home and entered foster care the same day. Looking back towards the house, I saw my mother slam the door when my brother and I were directed to the black sedan.

So much of our childhood had been destroyed, and we were now teenagers. I believe I was fifteen. Joey was almost seventeen. Could the trauma be reversed, or was it too late for us? Resiliency was a foreign word with no meaning for me at this age.

Joey and I did not embrace or speak during the ride to social services. Neither of us knew how to express ourselves in a healthy way. This day, regrettably, would turn out to be the last time I saw my brother alive.

It was too late for Joey.

Chapter 4
Loss

Foster care came too late and ended too soon. How long I spent in foster care is not measurable. Most of my memories are suppressed. Facts about my care under Child Protective Services have long since been erased. Trauma had a negative effect on me. There were at least two foster placements and numerous stays at a shelter for girls starting when I was about fifteen.

The first foster family, the Barkleys, lived south of Buffalo in what locals called the South Towns. They had a farmhouse. When I arrived, a bunch of kids younger than me were playing in the yard. My new foster brothers and sisters squealed with delight when the CPS caseworker pulled up the long driveway.

Barbara, my new foster mother, was initially pleasant to me. I kept my distance. Not being used to affection, I pulled away when she attempted to hug me at the door. Her warm nature quickly disappeared when the CPS caseworker left.

"Here are the house rules—" Barbara rambled off meal routines, bedtime, chores, and other nonsense while sticking her finger at my chest. Her tone was accusatory and overbearing. It seemed she was trying to aggravate me on purpose. My shoulders tensed up. Aggression did rub me the wrong way, and the finger-pointing was rude. She reminded me of my maternal grandmother and looked like a short untidy older Ronald McDonald character. The bright red color of her hair was evidence of a do-it-yourself dye job. But the bushy perm—tight curls likely strangling the blood flow in her head, I imagined—really set off her clownlike appearance. Her sagging skin and neck jowls showed her age. What was she doing with a bunch of kids at her age? I wondered.

"If you try to visit your father or run away, we will report you to the authorities, and you will go to 'juvie' hall," she threatened.

"Why would I go visit my father?" I asked.

"Do not talk back to me. Just do as we say, and there will not be any trouble. You hear me, Missy?"

"Yes," I replied as I hung my head low.

My caseworker left a black trash bag with a few belongings she had collected from my house after my removal. I dragged the bag towards the bedroom Barbara pointed to. The bag symbolized my limp and lifeless body.

The initial treatment bothered me. It would be a challenge to take this clown seriously. I was a good student, a hard worker, and not a troublemaker. Defeated thoughts overcame me again. My foster parents' comments and controls felt threatening and intimidating. The scrutiny and blame from the Barkleys were too much.

I wondered what had happened to my brother. Where was Joey? We were separated forever. How could I ever find my way back to him? Who was going to protect me now? I felt so alone. Closing my eyes, I tried to picture Joey. I wanted to remember him. Was he also thinking about me?

The only thing I ever asked of my foster parents was a ride to the bus stop in the nearby Village of Hamburg from week to week. The CPS caseworker agreed I could continue going to work and gave me bus schedules. This was instrumental in helping me navigate three bus routes from the country into the city. Volunteering at the Buffalo Zoo was a means to reach my goals. It was like work to me. Becoming a zoologist, veterinarian, or even a herpetologist, was my dream early on. These dreams motivated me to excel at school and work. I hoped success would be the way out of my dysfunctional life.

The Barkleys resented when I asked for more rides, week after week. They reminded me they were not a taxi service.

"How do we know you will not see your father?" Barbara would regularly accuse me.

It was humiliating to hear this accusation. *I never wanted to see my father or my mother again.* I internalized more hatred for Barbara than even my father at that moment.

"This arrangement is not working," I cried. "I hate it here. I did nothing wrong. Can't I go to work? Please, can I have a ride?"

She judged me and what happened to me. No one in their right mind would think a child wants to get molested again. It was ridiculous to accuse me of trying to go home! Their comments made my skin crawl. Disappointed, I secretly hated these people too. Time seemed to move so slowly. This scenario played out often.

Mr. Barkley was unlike his bossy wife, but he never hushed her. He dutifully would drop me off at the bus stop when the sun came up and pick me up before dinner, always doing what she directed. He said little on those short drives.

One day early in my stay, I came home from the zoo to find Barbara in my bedroom. She had been going through my belongings.

"Where'd you get this?" she demanded.

She held up a wad of money, about three hundred dollars of my savings. It took me several years to earn it. A paper route, lawn mowing, shoveling snow, babysitting, and even dog walking allowed me to make cold, hard cash.

My brothers and I hustled to make some cash from an early age. We got hooked on making money by combing the neighborhood for discarded beer cans or pop bottles when we walked to and from elementary or middle school. Five and ten-cent refunds per find could yield a pocketful of change to spend on penny candy at the corner grocery store. As we got a little older and braver to stray upwards of two to three miles from our house, we could collect enough to splurge on a chocolate and peanut parfait at the French

Custard Ice Cream Shop on the corner of Okell Street and South Park.

"Did you steal this?"

"No, I earned that. What are you doing going through my belongings?"

"You live in my house. Nothing belongs to you."

"It's mine!" I exclaimed to no avail.

"I am reporting this to your caseworker. You are not allowed to have all this cash."

"How am I supposed to pay for the bus?" I asserted.

"I can give you two dollars each week if you do your chores."

"That's my money. Give it back."

"You stole it! You are not getting it back," Barbara unilaterally decided.

Pleading my case was pointless. There were so many times I'd had to go without as a child. Fending for myself was necessary for me. Figuring out how to make some money was a survival skill I needed to circumvent this life. It made me proud to endure and succeed. Poverty was not going to be my future. Diligent work was my chosen discipline for a ticket out of this life. The money was never returned. Barbara went through my room weekly. It was a shakedown; I was branded a criminal.

—

It felt like a lifetime had passed before a new placement was available. The CPS caseworker said the Barkleys had asked for me to leave. They rejected me because I was too much trouble for them. I was the trouble! No, I could not believe this reality either. The caseworker drove me to another unfamiliar neighborhood. The area was North Buffalo. It closely resembled the blocks and houses I was familiar with in South Buffalo. At least I was closer to my work at the zoo.

At the second foster home, I was greeted on the front porch of the duplex by my boss Myra from the Buffalo Zoo, and her mom, Virginia, a docent in my department. What a coincidence. How did this happen? Cue the development of a red rash on my neck! Hives appeared on my exposed skin, revealing my nervousness and embarrassment. *There was nothing lower than this point.* As I mulled over the situation, I wondered how to save face.

They lived in the same duplex as the new foster family and had been advised of the new placement by their neighbors. I am sure they wanted to make me feel at ease with their familiar faces welcoming me at first, but it was awkward and humiliating.

My shame was heavy.

My secrets were not for random disclosure. How much did Myra know? What did she think of me? How could this possibly be? Various thoughts crossed my mind. My hard-earned cash reserve was also gone. Barbara kept it. An allowance from the new foster parents would be necessary unless I could figure out another way to make money.

Myra and I rode the bus to the zoo together. She often paid my fare. We never spoke about my personal life. I felt safe with Myra. The zoo was also a safe zone. I cannot recall a single other image, encounter, or conversation from this foster home. How was everything else at this foster home suppressed? It is like a blackout in my mind. Trauma controlled me this way.

I was a prisoner of my past.

On my sixteenth birthday, Jim Fowler from *Mutual of Omaha's Wild Kingdom* television show fame was giving a presentation at the zoo. My volunteer position included impromptu public speaking about the zoo animals in our collection. As part of the presentation with Jim Fowler, I brought a great horned owl named Bruce onto the stage. My boss was impressed with my performance and poise. This was the day I was offered a paid position at the Buffalo Zoo.

"Well, Brat, you did good," Myra said, smiling at me.

Myra's nickname for me was "Brat." I never minded it. She made me feel special and appreciated. Those were good feelings. I was comfortable with her.

She was always incredibly supportive. I loved her attention and that of my other boss, Marty. They trusted me with dozens of wildlife diets for the animals in our department, chiefly, their care and feeding. This motivated me to work hard and earn new responsibilities. I learned so much about being a zoologist from them, and they often playfully teased me. It was the only way either could get me to smile or laugh.

"The volunteer program is ending. What do you think about staying on as a part-time employee?" Myra asked me.

"Are you kidding? Yes, of course, I would love it."

"It's not great money, but we can pay you minimum wage. It's a little over three dollars an hour."

"This is perfect. Thank you. I want to do this job forever."

At sixteen, I could not even comprehend how to apply for or obtain a paying job, or for that matter, how much it would cost to live on my own eventually. This opportunity was one I was grateful for. It affirmed and recognized my work ethic. My employment with the zoo lasted for many years while I attended high school and some college. They always accommodated my schedule and welcomed me back after extended periods away at college.

It is troubling that I do not recall any other experience at the second foster home. Not even a face or name come to mind. There are many recollections about working at the zoo with Myra and Marty and memories of friends and high school. Recollections of my foster experiences are subconsciously blocked, even today. Was more trauma blocking my memories? Myra was kind and supportive. She never pried. But what happened in the apartment above her? What happened with my foster family?

There is also no imprinted memory of someone consistently helping me through this foster care experience. Who was my CPS caseworker? How can nearly all images be erased? Memories only exist for a couple of transfers, with a few comments here and there.

Ultimately, I was returned home by CPS, but the time and dates did not stick with me. Additional abuse ensued, and the trauma continued to consume me. Trauma has lifelong consequences on the brain. Gaps were created in my memory and will last my entire life. This was the way my body tried to survive. It was random. Some images surface from time to time, but many are functionally gone. Erased.

Running away from home became my only option to avoid the dysfunction after my foster care experience. Survival was paramount. Going to the police had always been ineffective. Mrs. Kane, at Mount Mercy Academy, introduced me to the McAuley House. The two-story residential house was two blocks from my high school. It served as an emergency shelter for girls. The Sisters of Mercy from the convent affiliated with my high school ran it.

Each time I overstayed the maximum nights allowed with the sisters, I had to return home. It was always a short respite. Believing there was nowhere else to go was a bit discouraging, but McAuley House would welcome me again and again. Back at home, my absence was not noticed. There were no questions. I fell back into the lineup. My parents were usually drunk every day or night, so it was no surprise that they consciously never recognized my absence.

Loneliness hurt.

What about my brother, Joey? I never wanted to go home, and discharge from foster care was not my choice. My opinion or input was not gathered. Did I not have rights? Clearly, I said something, right? My brother never came home. Did he have different rights? Did he have a say in this decision?

I asked my mother about Joey but never about my case.

"Joey is a permanent ward of the state," she replied in a manner that was more boastful than embarrassing. "We don't need to talk about Joey."

"But what happened to him, Mom?"

"I requested a 'PINS' petition, a person in need of supervision," she explained.

Ward of the state meant he was never coming home. My heart sank. Suspicious of what happened, I knew my parents could not be trusted. Joey had not done anything wrong. Had my parents conned CPS and convinced them we were disobedient and not victims? Who made these decisions? Who spoke for us? What had I done wrong? What had we done wrong? I felt betrayed by the system. My voice, our voices, were barely heard.

I missed my brother.

Joey aged out of foster care in late 1984 and enlisted in the U.S. Army. When I turned seventeen a year later, I joined the U.S. Army as well but needed my parents' cooperation to sign the enlistment papers. My senior year was about halfway through, and changes were in order. Seeing my parents sit together on the couch while my recruiter provided the paperwork for their signatures was one of my few recollections of ordinary family acts from my youth.

Signing up for the delayed entry program in the U.S. Army Reserves was my decision alone. An army uniform now hung in my closet. I was proud to wear it one weekend a month. This was the first step toward taking control of my life. Following in my brother's footsteps was also an influential factor.

Joey sounded happy and energetic in most letters he wrote about basic training and his advanced individual training in artillery. His career and lifestyle were fascinating, and understanding he was "safe" really impressed me. Joey shared his dream of a new life in the military and his future. It was a positive picture but did not fully mask his pain.

He continued to write for over a year, and it was nice to have a connection. His coping and release, he told me, was from listening to a band he heard of while stationed in Germany. The band was Marillion from the United Kingdom, and he wrote about their *Misplaced Childhood* album in the last letter I ever received from him. Joey was right about the lyrics. The words had meaning for me right away. The music solidified the connection. *Misplaced Childhood* remains an inspirational album to me.

Joey found freedom far from our family and the hardships we knew in South Buffalo. His life choices empowered me to follow suit, escape my childhood, and strive to break the cycle of abuse.

It was a cloudy, cool day in March, and I walked to my parents' home from high school like usual. Spring had come early, and all the snow had melted from the sidewalks. It was Friday, and I was about to learn how safety could be deceptive. As I approached the brick steps at 54 Mariemont Avenue, Father Stanton from the local Catholic Church parish, St. Ambrose, stood on our stoop alongside a man in an army uniform.

I paused when I immediately recognized the man. The army officer was my company commander—a superior in my chain of command. My brief stint in the military at this point had warned me to be wary of the commander. A junior-ranking soldier did not need extra attention, and it was safest to do your work while staying under the radar. This was a sign of trouble. What had I done? Captain Smith was far from the 365th Combat Support Hospital in Niagara Falls. Father Stanton greeted me when I approached the bottom step, but the officer did not know who I was. I had only been assigned to his unit for about four months. Panic was building inside me. It did not take long to realize he was not here for me.

No one appeared to be home. Captain, now an adult dog, was barking endlessly on the other side of the door. My attention turned to the cream-colored wood-paneled station wagon drawing near the house. My father drove a Chrysler Le Baron Town and Country wagon. He was living beyond our means. My vacant gaze followed the wagon as it rolled up in slow motion. My dad pulled into the driveway. My mother was with him in the front passenger seat. This was different. They never went anywhere together.

My parents lived like strangers under the same roof, exactly like I did with my siblings. My mind searched to understand this moment. I was having difficulty processing the situation. What were they up to? Why were these men here? One answer was provided by my mother when she spotted Father Stanton. She closed the car door and spoke. "We just signed divorce papers."

Without a moment to spare, my mother turned to me. "This is your fault," she said.

Naturally, I was blamed for my father's arrest and now the "surprise" divorce.

My mother's quip fell flat on me.

Was happiness going to come for me at last? No, what was going on? Something was not right. The divorce was long overdue, but I had no time to celebrate.

Father Stanton was unflappable. He dismissed my mother's remark as if it had never happened. "Carol, Fran, can we come inside?"

My parents stared and said nothing.

"I'm sorry, this is Captain Smith. He has an important message for you," Father Stanton urged.

My parents walked up the stairs, passing the men. The silence was unusual. They seemed to know more than I could imagine. They sat together on the couch. *That damn dreaded couch*. I hated everything about it. It was the focal point of the living room and reeked of my father. It was also the trigger to so many brutal memories. I stood nearby, careful not to get too close.

Captain Smith announced he was serving as a local casualty notification duty officer. Dread immediately washed over me. Casualty? The word hung like a raincloud over my head. A storm was brewing. What was happening? He handed a Western Union telegraph to my parents. My brother was serving in the army in Germany at the time.

My mother read the message aloud. "On behalf of the Department of the Army, we regret to inform you that Private Vincent Joseph—died of an apparent suicide—" my mom continued reading, but the words eluded me.

I could not believe what I was hearing. Time froze. Joey was gone forever.

Captain Smith provided details about Joey's death. I visualized my brother's last moments as Captain Smith relayed how he was discovered in his barracks room on base. My parents were in denial and suggested other explanations. The words "life insurance, personal effects, and military honors" were only bits and pieces of what I heard before fading deep into my subconscious. I had left my body again. Dissociation, the "leaving of one's body," is an unconscious method of survival for many trauma victims. It is a form of survival during a "fight or flight" moment. This was commonplace for me.

The U.S. Army would posthumously promote Joey to private first class as a consolation. Captain Smith was sure of this. He talked about a mistake Joey had made one time. He was reduced in rank for this mistake. Restoring him to his highest rank was the least the army could do.

The captain departed after expressing his sympathies for my parents' "loss." However, their loss happened years earlier when Joey was placed in foster care and eventually in a state-run boy's home. They did not deserve any sympathy now. I felt a pit in my stomach. The empty feeling was surreal. I said nothing. Father Stanton talked about the funeral arrangements with my parents, and I walked away without a glance or acknowledgment.

My hopes for Joey being safe and me becoming safe one day faded. Dreams were rapidly extinguished. My older brother committed suicide sixteen months after aging out of foster care. He was alone.

I felt alone.

Breathing was suddenly the focus of my attention. I gasped for air. It was a panic attack. Terrible guilt about Joey's suicide weighed heavy on my heart. He protected me, yet I was not there for him when he needed me. I found some brief comfort holding my dog, Captain, in my lap on the floor of my bedroom.

Wondering what the future had in store for me unexpectedly became a real worry.

Chapter 5
Adjustment?

After graduating high school in 1986, I left for basic training at Fort Jackson, South Carolina followed by an advanced individual training program with the Army Medical Department at Fort Sam Houston in San Antonio.

It had only been four months since we buried Joey. I focused my energy and emotions on my training. Somehow, I compartmentalized my past and tried to blend in and act normal, whatever that was. This was done by deliberately walling off thoughts, feelings, and emotions and not allowing them to surface. The U.S. Army was my chance to break free.

When my army training concluded, I returned to New York. On my first day back, I was overcome with shock and anger. My mother had put my dog, Captain, to sleep during my absence. She killed him for no reason other than resenting that he was a gift from my father.

It was incomprehensible. She killed my dog. It reminded me of the blame she placed on me for the divorce and for my father's absence from the home now. The little amount of life insurance she had received from the army after Joey's death was split with my father. It was drying up. She told me I needed to leave.

The spring college semester started in a week. Leaving again was easy, but I needed somewhere to come back to. I was torn between fear of my family and anxiety about my new freedom. Because I was moving between cities, I transferred army reserve units from Niagara Falls to Syracuse, the nearest military base to my intended college community. Attending the State University of New York College at Oswego, about three hours from Buffalo, was my new priority. At first, I made several trips back to my childhood home during breaks from school when the dorms were closed. Working at the zoo and a local veterinarian's office allowed me to continue to afford my college aspirations.

My mother's drinking was escalating in Buffalo. She was a wreck. She drank two dozen or more cans of beer nightly when she was not working or early in the morning when she came off her night shift. A friend from her work, a nurse named Mike, often brought her marijuana and other drugs so they could get high together in our house. She blared her stereo and rocked herself in an oversized antique rocking chair in the dining room. A can of beer was always in her one hand, and a cigarette in the other. She played her record albums all day and night. The music of Bob Seger, Leo Sayer, Pink Floyd, Neil Diamond, Bob Dylan, Janis Joplin, Elton John, and many more could be heard immediately outside the house, muffled slightly by the closed doors and windows.

The violence was over now. Joey's name was never mentioned again, and I believe she carried guilt about his suicide. When home from college, I spontaneously scurried around to close the windows to keep the neighbors from hearing her drunken singing. I extinguished her cigarettes to prevent a fire as she lay slumped over, passed out, in her rocking chair.

My emotions alternated between sadness, anger, guilt, and sympathy. I did not know what to feel while observing her decompensate further. Settling on feeling sorry for her permitted me to feel less hatred. I was evolving, and I struggled to respect her despite this growth. She had great taste in music, and respecting her interests was at least a start to my healing.

Regrettably, I lost contact with my friends. I was so alone. We did not have the convenience of social media, and I distanced myself from anyone who could offer support. I no longer felt welcome in Buffalo. I said my last goodbyes to Myra and Marty when I made the difficult decision to end my employment at the zoo. Leaving Buffalo for good was necessary though I would miss their friendship and my position.

Like any other traumatized child stuffing painful memories of childhood abuse and grief inside, the cracks slowly began to appear. Struggles in college gradually emerged. Coping was difficult. Academic warnings, referrals to the dean, and more counseling were necessary. I sank into a dark depression. A mentor, Major Walker, Reserve Officer Training Corps, or ROTC, Professor of Military Science, stepped up to guide my army and educational careers as both were in jeopardy, given my shaky emotional health.

My methods to avoid my past were failing. I had turned down a three-year Army ROTC scholarship, quit my job as a resident assistant in the dorms, and even withdrew from multiple classes semester after semester. I needed time off from college on two occasions to regain stability and purpose. Working full-time as an apprentice veterinarian technician near the college gave me a break from academic stress. My medical laboratory technician training from the army and past employment at the zoo qualified me for the position. Graduation had to be pushed back a year, so I could earn enough income to support my college pursuits fully.

Renting a small cottage directly across from Lake Ontario, about a mile from the university in Oswego, was a fresh start. My landlord, Mr. Noun, gave me a break on the first three months of rent. I lived rent-free and put some "sweat equity" into the small two-story cottage to fix it up. It needed cleaning, painting, and some other cosmetic work. Taking on these tasks was a realization of how my father imprinted some basic "fix-it" or homebuilding skills on me. It was a positive influence I had not recognized earlier. Later in my life, I became addicted to rehabbing homes and furniture.

I was not used to managing stress appropriately. The college health and counseling clinic allowed me to continue using their services during my academic withdrawals. Due to my worsening depression, the director of the campus health clinic, Dr. Thompson, and my therapist, Nancy Hale, recommended psychiatric inpatient treatment at a youth hospital for me in Saratoga, N.Y.

Luckily, it was arranged without my parents' knowledge. How it was paid for was undetermined. My time in Saratoga was challenging. I worried too much about my army commitment instead of my mental health. After all, I was juggling my army reservist duties and was not thinking about my academics. My hospital discharge occurred after little change to my overall well-being.

Disclosing this treatment was necessary to obtain a security clearance before becoming a commissioned officer in the U.S. Army. As I feared, the army resisted commissioning me, and I had to undergo several psychiatric evaluations at Fort Drum, N.Y., before being allowed to become a second lieutenant through the ROTC program.

Fortunately, I was given a second chance at a career in the army, which granted a medical waiver for what was described as an "adjustment disorder." They described it as nothing serious considering what I had endured early in life. I mean, after all, what was to be expected? Major Walker was instrumental in seeing me through this process. I was grateful for his guidance.

In the hospital and therapy, I learned coping mechanisms and other healthy ways to deal with stress, flashbacks, and grief. I should have taken the treatment more seriously. The limited skills I took away from that time were helpful in my transition back into college and in becoming somewhat stable.

Running also helped provide a release. Running track, playing soccer, ten-speed cycling, and horseback riding had been outlets for me during my youth. Those activities grounded me and kept me focused on the future while periodically keeping me outside the home. Running daily became a necessity again. Finding new paths from my cottage along the lakefront and onto the college campus made me euphoric each time I accomplished a new goal—a faster time, a longer distance, or a challenging trail.

As the cool air whipped my face, I breathed it in and celebrated its freshness, far away from my mother's cigarette smoke. Visions of Joey and me running to the police station, running to the park for a summer lunch, and running, always running, started to make me whole again. This outlet was working, but people around me expressed worry. My friends at college and especially in the ROTC program recognized that I was pushing myself beyond normal limits. Major Walker cautioned me to slow down and take it easy. He was worried about another mental breakdown and told me so.

Energy seemed to come from nowhere. It was like a natural mania. I was addicted to the runner's high. My mind raced like my running. Looking back, I recognize how unusual my behavior was. I accomplished distances of sixty-two, one hundred, and more than one hundred miles—or a metric century, a century, and a double-metric century respectively—within twenty-four to thirty-hour periods of continuous running in my final years of college. These were distances I was familiar with from riding my bicycle but running them was extreme. My endless energy needed an outlet. No doubt, I was running from stress and my memories. It was working.

Music was also a necessary conduit for healing during my running. I was drawn to much of the same music my mother used to play. This was another positive influence from my past, now from my mother. Wearing headphones while I ran offered me emotional therapy. It brought balance to the exhaustive running.

My rebound and integration back at school were noticeable. Major Walker was the first to name my turnaround "resiliency." I changed my declared major from zoology to psychology to make up lost academic ground. My academic improvements and performance in my military program helped me earn the Distinguished Military Graduate designation from the ROTC program.

Intermittent therapy helped. Soon resiliency was even becoming obvious to me as I overcame several obstacles. I worried about how I would continue to deal with my grief and keep my emotions in check when I left Oswego. My support system was in place there and helped keep me stable.

Leaving would create a vacuum in my support system again.

———

Graduation was upon me, and I entered active duty in the army. Convinced I needed to lock away my anguish and childhood memories to ward off another meltdown, I created emotional walls again. What a foolish plan. Repeating the same fatal mistakes from my past, I buried my trauma. Falling into old coping methods like this seemed comfortable and safe, but it was not a wise choice.

I left New York and my family behind. I had no intention of ever living there again. My military career would provide a new family and take me far from home as I knew it. My biological family was toxic, and I needed to stay far away to avoid being sucked into the same cycle of alcoholism and violence. Sealing off memories the way I was used to was akin to bandaging an open wound with a dirty dressing. If only I could have predicted the consequences later in my life, I could have avoided additional suffering.

———

It took nearly a lifetime to heal from the trauma I endured as a child. My misplaced childhood was marked by police inaction and inconsistencies in child protection services. I was failed on many levels, but probably none worse than the court-ordered family therapy. Facing my father in a so-called therapeutic environment destroyed any self-esteem or courage I had within me.

Child advocacy centers like CASA and others did not exist in my early years. They evolved later and spread across the country out of the need to protect other children like me. Societal norms when I was a child were different from those today. Cities, states, and the nation evolved with an interest in safeguarding children better. Fortunately, outcries of abuse are taken more seriously today.

Many childhood memories are hidden in my subconscious, perhaps misplaced. However, enough vivid recollections of my childhood have guided my transformation from a defenseless and fragile child to the fierce and persistent volunteer child advocate I am today. This was resilience.

My parents' alcoholism led to severe emotional, physical, and sexual abuse and neglect. Unlikely people would help me find my way. Secrets long since locked away would eventually become exposed as I learned to accept my past, forgive my abusers, and seek to turn my experiences into tools that would help me communicate and relate to traumatized children as their CASA advocate.

There was a plan formulating right before me. The path to healing was ahead of me. I was an adult. Surely life would be more manageable now. I did not expect the road ahead to be paved with more challenges.

As a young person, I had no idea my life's trajectory would change forever.

PART 2
ADULTING

"Unmet needs are difficult for most of us to acknowledge
because it's not about what *happened* to us—
it's about what *didn't happen*."
Miriam E. Callahan—*The H$_2$O Workbook*

Chapter 6
Feeling Human

Early in my life, I recognized that there were always people looking out for me. There was no question that a handful of critical people impacted and influenced the successes in my life. These people showed me what humans are capable of. I learned of humanity—the qualities that make us human, such as loving and having compassion, being creative, and having emotions. These were assets needed for my survival.

Acknowledging that my dreams of fictional TV parents were unrealistic fantasies, I sought out positive role models to learn from instead. My survival can be attributed to these movers, believers, healers, and dreamers who stepped into my life's path and remained steadfast. They guided me whether it was apparent or not. These adult role models were secretly influencing me. My life was reshaped because they stepped up to protect me or provide mentorship. Their interposition in my life shaped how I wanted to relate to others. Several of these people are a steady presence in my life today, and I have openly thanked them. Others may not even know the impact they had on me. These are conversations I look forward to having.

Helping teenagers or young adults struggling to find their way through life early on is something I had always wanted to do. While stationed at Alaska's Fort Richardson after college graduation, I volunteered weekend evenings at Covenant House, a teen runaway shelter in downtown

Anchorage. This was my first official army assignment, and I was excited to get involved in the community.

Unfortunately, I never felt a lasting connection with the youth there. They were transient and cycled in and out from one weekend to the next, making establishing a rapport difficult. There was never an opportunity long enough to make a connection.

Seeing different faces each weekend reminded me of how I came and went from McAuley House in South Buffalo. I tried to make the most of the intermittent contact with youth in Alaska by drawing from how the Sisters of Mercy made me feel comfortable. My experience reminded me to be patient, not force any connection, and let it occur organically. I persisted for some time, hoping a single contact might make a difference for one of the lost children. Regrettably, I do not think it ever happened.

I was promoted to First Lieutenant during my first year at Fort Richardson. A promotion party was in order. I invited all the single lieutenants and a few single captains with whom I was familiar. Getting into a new relationship was not on my mind. But one particular captain attracted my interest.

This captain, Andy, was about eight years older than me. He was an acquaintance from work. His sense of humor and maturity were unusual among my other lieutenant friends who were loud, rambunctious, and drank too much. Andy was a measured man. He caught my attention while playing with my dogs, who responded affectionately. Animals can sense good people. I filed this positive sentiment away for later.

Several weeks after the party, we met again at the Officer's Club on the military post. My friends were as loud and obnoxious as before, but Andy noticed me and sent a drink over. The music was deafening, and I had difficulty asking the waitress where the drink came from. While scanning the room, I recognized Andy at the bar. He was the only person facing my table. Raising my glass, I waved him over to join me and my friends.

He did join us, but what was I thinking? The music from the band was earsplitting. One could not think, let alone talk, under these conditions. This would be awkward. Undeterred, Andy grabbed the drink cup napkins from the table and began to write. It was not uncomfortable at all. I liked his confidence.

You should get more mature friends, he scribbled in ink.

Like who? You? I teased a reply on the four-inch square napkin.

He nodded. He was confident; I liked his approach.

What's wrong with my friends? I wrote.

His facial cues, a side smile that made his eye twinkle, and a playful eye roll indicated they were not worthy.

We passed the quasi-napkin notes back and forth, trying to "one-up" each other with humor, sarcasm, or wit. He was more skillful at flirting than I was.

Going to ER in a few minutes. Wanna come? I wrote. ER was the abbreviation for Eagle River. It was north of Fort Richardson. My friends knew of a band playing not far from where I lived. Many of them lived in the same area.

Why? Do you need some adult supervision? He quipped.

Another proverbial eye roll and warm smile, this time from me. *Yes. I do, but I don't know any adults!* I fired back.

He smiled, and a boyish grin spread across his handsome face. This was beginning to feel more like a date.

I had not known I was connecting with my future husband that night. It was unexpected. We hit it off well. During this military assignment, Andy gave me a bit of a distraction from my past. My dating experience was extremely limited in high school and college. Those encounters were informal, and I never committed to anyone. They never seemed like authentic relationships. My heart was an empty pit before Andy. Expressing myself in a healthy way was routinely a challenge.

Andy taught me to laugh and love. His playful ways first warmed me to the idea of love. He persisted. We were a little shy about commitment but enjoyed each other's company early on. We went to the theater, comedy shows, dinner, and the movies. He had two young children and had experienced a bitter divorce in his not-so-recent past. I was the rebound. Meeting his family and children made me feel more attached to him and them.

His extended family lived in Anchorage, adjacent to Fort Richardson. They were so normal. They modeled how families were supposed to relate. This was the family I had longed for during my childhood. It was only a short time before Andy and his family invited me on fishing and camping trips. They accepted me as one of their own. Their weekly activities included me. This was what family was meant to be. I felt loved.

This relationship was a giant leap of trust for me. Trust issues stemmed from my abusive past. I tried to keep my inadequacies from Andy. There were many awkward moments when I fumbled my way into returning his affection. He always made the first move. Reciprocating the moves he made through handholding, gazing into my eyes, and even a kiss drew me closer to him.

I was becoming pretty attached to this perfect man. He offered safety and security, though he was afraid of becoming trapped by an unwanted pregnancy. I assured him I was not interested in bearing children. The "why" was never discussed. My fear of continuing the dysfunctional family gene pool made me cautious. My intense fear of hurting a child the way I was hurt reinforced my decision never to have children. Luckily, proper safeguards never put us in a difficult situation.

As my relationship with Andy grew into a steady romance, I pulled away from my volunteer efforts at Covenant House. My military responsibilities consumed my other weekends, and my career started to take me to multiple locations worldwide. I began to accept my new life in the army as a career.

Thoughts of Joey and the missed opportunities for us to reconnect in the army were frequent troubles that crippled my will. Wearing an army uniform reminded me of my brother and losing him five years earlier.

The army was more challenging than I had expected. There were plenty of trials. Developing mental toughness was a necessary step to achieving success. My first active-duty assignment was in a light infantry division. This was not a haven for female soldiers. Within minutes of arriving at Fort Richardson, I was confronted by the noncommissioned officer in charge after duty hours. He was an older gentleman. The weathered skin on his face mirrored the number of chevrons in the rank he wore on his uniform sleeves. He was a senior master sergeant, one of the highest enlisted ranks in the army. His swagger indicated many years of service and commitment to the "man's" army.

"Ma'am, what unit are you signing into?"

The chewing tobacco bulging from his cheek pouch made it difficult to understand him. He looked long and steady at me. This soldier was the designated welcome wagon after hours.

I was too tired for any nonsense. The ten-day trip from my training program at Fort Sam Houston in San Antonio to Anchorage, Alaska, was rugged. The interstate from Texas to California could be considered the scenic route, if you consider thousands of miles of highway scenic. Shouldering the western coastline, I drove without worrying about time or place until I reached northern Washington State. On the ferry from Bellingham to Haines, Alaska, I had a short rest.

Winter conditions in Alaska and parts of Canada are unpredictable. This December, there was plenty of snow. Although I had my brand new 4-wheel drive SUV I had purchased after college graduation, after disembarking the ferry in Haines, Alaska, I made a novice decision to drive the Alaska-Canadian, or Alcan highway, alone. My dog, a two-year-old Akita named Dakota accompanied me. I had missed the loyalty and affection of a dog after Captain's sudden death and adopted Dakota as a companion to ward off loneliness in college.

Fortunately, I had met four fellow military soldiers and their families on the ferry, all heading to Anchorage. One of the mid-grade enlisted soldiers insisted I convoy with the group for safety. We negotiated a snowstorm through the southern portion of Alaska, entered Canada, and after a couple more treacherous and icy days, entered Alaska again.

***

I focused my attention again on the crusty noncommissioned officer at Fort Richardson. His tobacco habits disgusted me.

"I'm signing into the medical company in the 306th Forward Support Battalion, Master Sergeant."

"Well, this is the 6th Infantry Division, ma'am. You have the three worst things going for you. First, you are a *fe*-male," he said in a southern drawl, elongating the word "female" for emphasis. Without pausing, he spit his tobacco and, in so doing, set the exclamation point on his statement: "You're medical." This was followed by another tobacco spit into his soda can. "And you are a second lieutenant. You might as well pick up your bags, turn around, and get out of town," he finished with a sneer. His derogatory introduction was a shock.

"Well, *Sergeant*," I purposely addressed him at the lower grade of sergeant, which is not a common way to handle a senior enlisted soldier, but I felt no guilt. Master sergeants are the eighth highest enlisted rank in the army and are entitled to more respect, but this "gentleman" was not earning it from me. He was not amused.

His intimidation had fallen flat. Regardless of how many years he had served, as a commissioned officer, I outranked him. No one would ever push me around again. I did my time as an enlisted soldier. Now a "butter bar," a gold-toned second lieutenant bar, adorned my uniform shoulder. It was earned through demanding work, grit, and determination. I was an officer. He was no gentleman.

These were not the pleasantries I expected at my first duty station.

"Equal opportunity" was not necessarily equal for all in the 6th Infantry Division. Infantries were comprised of ground warfighters. Women were not always equally respected in this environment. The battalion's command climate reflected the master sergeant's sentiments. There were only three female officers in the battalion. Harassment of the junior female officers was common. Men outnumbered me by at least sixteen to one. I experienced discrimination and sexual harassment from a lieutenant and two higher-ranking captains early in this tour of duty. Why did life have to be so harsh? When would I catch a break?

Meeting Andy changed everything. He was playful, kind, and generous. We were suitable for one another. His patience allowed me to risk becoming close to him and loving him. Andy's attention acted like kryptonite on my stress. He made me feel at ease, comfortable, and loved. My anxiety faded around him.

A promotion and key positions as an executive officer and treatment platoon leader in the medical company were behind me. Unexpectedly, I was catapulted into a lieutenant colonel's job in the division support brigade. This was a step up, and finally, outside of the oppressive environment I first faced in the medical company. As the newest chief of the division medical operations center, I served in the most senior medical service corps position in the entire infantry division in Alaska. A vacancy created the opportunity, and several senior leaders trusted me to fill the void despite my junior rank. Andy also changed positions, and now we worked directly down the hall from one another. We were discreet with our relationship at work.

We both took our careers seriously. Although I needed more experience for my new position, perseverance and a strong work ethic helped me overcome any perceived deficit. The job was ordinarily held by a senior officer three ranks higher than my first lieutenant grade. The trust instilled in me from the chain of command overshadowed any previous unfair

challenges I faced as a female officer in the medical company. I had come
a long way from my original enlistment as a private in the U.S. Army
Reserves. Joey would have been proud.

—

The first real test of my bond with Andy came from separation. My new
"chief" role allowed me to serve as the task force commander of a small
interdisciplinary medical team set to deploy to Africa. The responsibility
for the humanitarian and training mission fell on my shoulders. My
deployment was to the island nations of Comoros and Madagascar off
the southeastern tip of the African continent for several months. The
separation from Andy proved to be what made me long for a more
permanent relationship with him.

Exploring the world while serving my country was exciting but filled
with challenges. The mission in Africa was exhausting. My team faced
unbearable heat, squalid accommodations, mosquitos, and the ever-present
risk of vector-borne disease, questionable food or water sources, and
vigilance in case injury or a terrorist strike required evacuation from the
islands. These were daily realities. I was the only female and the officer in
charge, and several men on my team were jealous and insubordinate. They
challenged and questioned my authority. Harassment ensued once again. I
ignored their hostilities to ensure the mission continued.

My team wanted the conveniences afforded in the United States,
including a nine-to-five workday and lazy weekends of relaxation and
exploration during this deployment. Islanders, native to Comoros and
Madagascar, did not have the fortunes we had as Americans. I scolded my
team's selfishness and arrogance. Villagers from all over the islands traveled
for many weeks to our location. Receiving first-nation medical care was a
significant event for them. We had ample medication and medical supplies
to distribute, and the medical professionals on my team could meet their
needs. Sacrifices were necessary to treat as many patients as possible, and
in the end, we did. Over twenty-seven hundred impoverished Comorian

and Malagasy locals received first-rate medical care from the American military resources I organized and managed. This was a "once in a lifetime" opportunity for them.

The long and difficult mission made me yearn for the feelings of comfort I had developed with Andy back in Alaska. Missing him was an understatement. I had never felt this way about anyone before. The connection was deeper than I had imagined, and I desperately wanted to be in his arms and laugh with him again. Even hearing his voice briefly could fill the void. A couple of village entrepreneurs in Comoros were willing to figure out a way to make the phone call and negotiated the final cost as I pointed to Alaska on a faded and tattered world map. An eight-minute phone call to Alaska would cost me more than one hundred U.S. dollars in cash.

The two Comorian men sat on rickety wooden crates on the dirt floor of my hostel lobby. The lobby was like no other in the States. The open-air space was littered with salvaged items, a random truck tire, scrap wood, several crates, a rusted bicycle with no rubber wheels on the rims, and a collection of tools—primarily sharp machetes and shovels. The awning made from a patchwork of palm fronds provided a place for us to conduct business safeguarded from the scorching sun.

Surprisingly, they created a working phone from a wooden box of makeshift wires. The black-handled receiver connected to the contraption was the only item resembling a modern telephone. A third man sprang up a tree, barefoot, with great ease and agility while gripping a lengthy coil of wire in his teeth. One end was connected to the contraption, and the other was linked to a box precariously attached to the roof of the adjacent building. There was no rotary dial on the crude device. The final twisting together of several wires established the connection with an operator elsewhere on the island, I assumed.

The men spoke into the receiver using their native Shingazija language, a Comorian dialect similar to Swahili with a distinctive Arabic influence. Their words produced a beautiful blend of sounds with a musical quality of rhythm, pace, and timing. Andy's phone number, written on a pad I handed the men, was communicated to the operator. After twenty anxious and curious minutes, the men gave me the receiver.

Ring, Ring, Ring. Success! The locals celebrated their joy with me and quickly motioned me to a crate. Reconnecting with Andy for eight glorious minutes was exactly what I needed. It recharged my internal battery. My heart was whole again, carrying me through the rest of the deployment.

The villagers who helped make the connection shared their earnings. It was much-needed income for them, and their community connection left an impression on me. Before my final departure, I left my military boots, miscellaneous clothing, and other personal items for their families. Purchasing handmade crafts and paying them more than they asked was another way to express my gratitude. The poverty I experienced as a child was nothing compared to what these people endured. It was humbling. How could I ever think I was teetering on poverty compared to what I observed in these countries? I was richer than I ever understood despite the difficult and lacking conditions I sometimes faced as a child. The average annual income for most islanders on Grand Comoros during that period was the equivalent of two hundred U.S. dollars. One hundred and twenty dollars for a phone call was insignificant to me now. I was no longer a poor kid from South Buffalo. I had made it.

———

Shortly after returning to Alaska from Africa, I was served orders for a promotion to Captain and additional training. It was time to move to another duty station. This was army life. The training took me temporarily back to Fort Sam Houston again. Andy and I stayed together in a long-distance romance. Several months at Fort Sam Houston in San Antonio allowed me opportunities to see Andy. His children were now living with his ex in nearby Houston, three to four hours away, and he made the most out of visiting them and me on several trips.

Meanwhile, I pressed the army for an assignment to Fort Lewis outside Tacoma, Washington, to be geographically closer to Andy while he was on an extended assignment in Alaska. It was granted. We were able to maintain our growing relationship with the proximity.

I faced different hardships in my new assignments. Fortunately, I had Andy in my life, but what I went through I kept secret. Andy was the most influential person in my life then and now, and today, he is decisively one of the most generous people I know. I owed him more, yet I did not want to burden him with my struggles.

The hardships and challenges reminded me that I was not a robot.

I was human but felt unprepared to live like one.

Chapter 7
Silence

Incidents in the military would continue to tie me to my past. *There was no escaping it*. The trauma had a stranglehold on my mind. Ten years had passed since my brother's death. College, additional army training and experience, and two promotions were behind me. I had managed to create a relationship with Andy without disclosing my secrets. I was silent and carried on my struggle in private. Why could I not keep my childhood experiences behind me?

As a company commander at Madigan Army Medical Center in Fort Lewis, Washington, I was responsible for several hundred soldiers, officers, and their families in my unit. After one fateful occasion, I traveled to a Midwestern town to tell grieving parents that their son, Private Douglas, a soldier under my command, had committed suicide. The circumstances of my soldier's death reminded me of Joey's suicide.

Private Douglas was a trainee under my command. I wore the same style of government-issue drab olive green Class A uniform worn by my previous reserve company commander, Captain Smith, when he announced Joey's death. I was about to give a similar somber decree to Private Douglas's parents. The same words from the Western Union message I had heard before unconsciously flowed from my mouth.

Memories transported me back in time. I truly mourned Private Douglas's tragic death. But Joey's loss, a decade removed, came front and center in my thoughts. Old wounds were reopened. The responsibility seemed mine. Two nineteen-year-old men left the world too early, and I had failed both or so I told myself.

Andy traveled to the Midwest in a heartfelt show of support. I needed him. We became engaged a few days later. Sadly, my trauma deleted the happy memory of our engagement. I remember nothing of that day or the surrounding days. Andy and I began our life in marriage six months later and set out for new military assignments near Tokyo, Japan, as husband and wife.

To me, it felt like I was sleepwalking through life. Trauma flatlined my memories and my view of the present. As the years passed, my happy memories became inconsistent. Struggles emerged again. The suicide of my brother, Private Douglas, and others during my career in the army would place a tremendous burden on my heart. This led to crippling and debilitating depression. Andy felt the strain too, but not knowing the underlying causes, he could only continue to be present and supportive.

Many of these experiences accumulated during a single overseas army assignment in Japan shortly after our marriage. During this assignment, one of my additional duties was as a casualty affairs officer at the medical facility where I worked. I did not ask for this duty. It was expected of me. The duty included handling and processing the newly deceased—all of them—whenever I was in the country during this period. This was different from the role of a casualty notification officer, where making a notification was the objective. There were countless deaths during these three years. However, the suicides of fellow service members or their family members were the hardest to deal with emotionally.

The medics at the military clinic were the first responders, and I followed them to the scene as a casualty affairs administrator. They were typically younger and fragile. I felt responsible for leading them through these tragic situations and modeling a calm demeanor. They were also unprepared for what we all experienced as a team.

One particular image of a soldier who jumped to his death from his housing apartment complex was seared into my mind. It was horrific. The parking lot below the open window to the housing complex filled up with onlookers. I motioned for the medical personnel to form a perimeter. Their supervisor, a sergeant first class, was already on top of it. Military police and crime scene investigators arrived. They were efficient.

The summer sun scorched the earth. The temperature was approaching one hundred degrees at midday. The soldier's body was getting too warm. Concerns flooded my mind. We need to move faster. The heat would affect the autopsy. There were too many people gawking at the scene. *Act now!*

When the investigation team released the scene, the medics carefully removed the soldier's body, placed it in a white plastic body bag, zipped it up, and loaded him into the waiting ambulance. I bagged and tagged the additional body tissue and bone fragments scattered near the body. This was my first direct experience with a deceased person. It would not be the last. Other events like this haunted my memories for decades. This was pain that continued to put pressure on my broken life.

Additionally, I prepared death certificates, placed toe and body tags on the bodies, wrote transportation notices, and presented the next of kin with numerous documents for signature. These duties and roles were my responsibility as an army patient administration officer. This was my duty. Whenever an American died at my military installation overseas, I was called to perform these duties. Staffing shortages meant I had no assistant or army noncommissioned officer in my department to assign these duties.

There was never any debriefing for these experiences. I felt unprepared in my military training for talking to the next of kin. Several of the clinic physicians shied away from the immediate family. They wrongly dumped the burden of notifying the waiting family in the next room on me.

"There was nothing that could be done," I would state. "I'm so sorry for your loss."

The raw emotions and reactions I witnessed pained me. The encounters became internalized with my childhood trauma. It was not possible to walk away from their pain. I had to approach them again. There were at least six official documents to present before I could have a body transported to Okinawa for autopsy. It was overwhelming and emotionally draining.

These events affected me in profound ways. Another thing I could not get out of my head was the smell of burnt flesh. A family of six brought a four-year-old male victim through the emergency room door. The smell of burnt flesh is almost indescribable. Once you recognize it, you know exactly what it is. It is the scent of a combination of rotten meat, sulfur, and chemicals. It permeated the emergency room corridor. Every family member had also been burned to some extent while trying to rescue the four-year-old, whom they told us, was trapped in their burning house. There was nothing that could be done for the child. It was horrible.

The family was distressed. There was no time for shock or horror. Emotional and physical responses were turned off again—another form of dissociation. Survival mode became automatic. I went to work on my paperwork and prepared for another uncomfortable conversation with another grieving family.

These experiences were a new level of stress, internal trauma, grief, and regret. I carried the scenes of these deaths and others alongside the trauma I experienced as a child inside my core. No faith, or god, gave me the strength to manage these memories alone. There was also no conscious control over what I remembered and what memories were misplaced. Regardless, I did not believe I was ready to talk about the pain.

Three years passed under these conditions until I received a full scholarship to the University of Pittsburgh for a master's degree program. The scholarship was awarded by the army for my stellar career performance to date. We relocated from Japan to a quiet suburb in Moon Township, outside Pittsburgh, Pennsylvania.

With my feet back on U.S. soil, I believed a little therapy would be helpful and found a professional nearby. My mind had been searching for ways to compartmentalize the images and memories of the tragedies in Japan. These experiences were packed alongside my childhood memories. It had been ten years since I had had any form of counseling. The silence needed to be broken.

My experiences in Japan led to the diagnosis of post-traumatic stress disorder shortly after beginning therapy. My childhood trauma undoubtedly had something to do with my vulnerability to this mental health crisis. Despite my struggles, I still managed to excel in my graduate studies.

Death would come calling again.

It would hit me close to home unexpectedly again.

Chapter 8
Broken

Looking back at my relationship with my mother brings sadness to my heart. She tried her best. I do not believe she knew how to be strong. Where did things go wrong for her, I often wondered. I imagined it started with her mother. My maternal grandmother was a wicked woman. She chain-smoked cigarettes and drank a lot as did my mother.

We did not have many family connections. My "Gram," as we called her, was a temporary babysitter but otherwise not connected to us. Our family was isolated and cut off from aunts, uncles, and cousins. Fallouts between family members were common. My mom was likely embarrassed and ashamed about our abuse, including from her. So there were very few family connections.

Perhaps my mom was trapped in a cycle of abuse from an early age. There were smiles on my face in the few pictures from my childhood. We must have been happy at one time. My mom must have been happy at one time too. How did things go so wrong? Why did they get so bad?

My selective memories disturbed me. The painful parts of my past clouded any decent or happy memories. Maybe my mom did not know how to break free from my father when we needed her the most. Domestic violence can be a vicious cycle. We experienced it regularly.

My mom was dependent on my father. He was the primary breadwinner from early on. When he was laid off, it put added pressure on my mom.

Even after thirty years, her salary as an evening shift nurse at a Catholic hospital was less than what I earned my first year as an active-duty army second lieutenant. I was successful early on—owning a home and a new car were triumphant signs that I had overcome the near poverty my parents had faced. They had raised four kids in a terrible economy, and money was always tight for them.

My mom did not even have a driver's license until I was about nine or ten years old. She was a passive person. She never caught a break in life. My life had been hard when I was a child, but as an adult looking back, I realized that time was when my life was only just beginning. I would get opportunities, and those could and would facilitate my growth beyond my past demons.

My mother suffered long and hard. She never got the life she truly deserved. Despite what happened to us, I did believe she deserved happiness.

From an early age, I saw my mother as broken. As a young adult, I worked hard to separate my sense of identity from my past. On occasion, I stayed in touch with my mother over the telephone. Establishing a genuine love for her never occurred. I found myself incapable of that kind of love. Feeling sorry for her seeped into my soul. She was my mother, so I tried to stay in touch.

My heart would sink when she answered the phone, and I could tell she had been drinking. We never spoke of the past. She tried to improve her life. It was a difficult journey for her too. She sold our childhood home and bought a cozy condominium south of Buffalo in the South Towns. Ironically, it was not far from my first foster home. She used the remaining money from my brother's life insurance to relocate and start afresh.

We made small talk over the phone several times a month over several years. My Akita dogs, Andy, his kids, and my military life, wherever that was—San Antonio, Alaska, Africa, Washington, or Japan—were the only topics I felt safe to share. She seemed interested and proud of me. I should have shown her love and thanked her for the moments when she supported me.

⁂

When I was a small child, my mother signed me up for Saturday art classes at the local library. Later, when I was a pre-teen, she got me involved in Girl Scouts and 4-H. My mom sold hundreds of Girl Scout cookies for me at Our Lady of Victory and Mercy hospitals, and I attended Camp Seven Hills two summers on a full scholarship from the cookie sales. Those overnight camping adventures gave me a respite I desperately needed. But I lost my opportunity to thank her for these efforts.

I was selfish, and I was also broken.

Life was unbearable when she drank. I held this against her. As an adult, I recognized that I could have been more appreciative. How do I show her affection? There were no easy answers for me. When I was a child, she connected me with people, distracting me from the horrors of my life. A friend of hers at the hospital gave me horseback riding lessons. This friend, Joanne, saw talent in me and took me to horse shows. It was my mom's connection and arrangement for me.

The relationship soured when my mom showed up drunk at a horse show during the Erie County Fair. She stayed overnight in her car, blaring the radio and singing in a stupor. Joanne and I were in her RV. It was hard to sleep through this. Joanne and I never spoke again after the embarrassing incident. It was heartbreaking to lose this positive and influential connection.

My mom also supported my participation in a local bicycle club, and she was the one who learned of and signed me up for the volunteer position at the Buffalo Zoo before I ended up in foster care. I could not see these were the ways she may have tried to express love for me. She did try, and I squandered it away, never making a real connection with her.

Those activities and other extracurricular activities I participated in at school allowed me to survive. I know now that these were my mom's attempts to help, support, and maybe even love me in the only way she knew how. Regrets flooded my heart and mind. I walked away from my family. They were toxic in my mind, and I did not feel strong enough to stay connected as a family.

———

While on assignment in Japan, I was rocked by unwelcome news from home. My army career, while fast-paced and exciting, was extremely stressful. There were many challenges with handling deaths at my army installation, and I was not expecting tragedy back home. I spoke infrequently with my mom. Diane and John were distant figures from my past. My mother often complained about them during our phone calls, which justified my decision to stay away from them.

The Red Cross notification that my mother was hospitalized with an aneurysm came while I was working at the medical clinic in Japan one day. My sister's phone number was on the message, and I immediately called her. Diane assured me it was caught early, and my mom would have surgery to have it "clipped." She pleaded with me to come home anyway.

An administrative clerk in my army unit arranged for me to take emergency leave and provided me with a plane ticket back to Buffalo. A second call came while I was preparing to leave. My mother had "taken a turn for the worse." I was told, "Come home now."

The next day I was on the plane from Tokyo to Buffalo, New York. It was too late. My mother suffered a stroke during the surgery and died.

My Aunt Nancy, my mom's youngest sister, picked me up at the airport. We stayed together at my mother's condominium with my cousin Jennifer. I was grateful my Aunt Nancy and Jennifer were there. I never really knew them when I lived in Buffalo. It was nice to hear how my mom and her younger sister made amends and communicated regularly. Developing a relationship with them filled an emptiness that had haunted me for my lifetime. I lost my mother, but my family was expanding. We became close after this tragedy. I loved my aunt and cousin. They never judged me how I judged myself about detaching from my family.

When I saw my sister, she was a shell of her former assertive, confident, and outgoing self. This was from years of drinking and drug use. She had a failed marriage, poor credit and debt, and difficulty holding a job or steady housing. She had a son, but whether he was in her life was a mystery at the time. He was a mystery to me as well. My mother's estate attorney, Paul, knew of Diane and her troubles. He contacted me at my mom's condo. He asked me to come to the office.

Andy flew in from Japan a couple of days after me, and we went together to meet Paul. Andy's support was indispensable. My mother had named Diane the executrix of her estate, but Paul wanted to know if I would take over for her. He did not have confidence in Diane, and although he did not say what he observed in her, I suspected he recognized she was not up to the task. I agreed to do whatever it took to take care of my mother's estate. Andy agreed that this was the right move.

My mom did not have much, but at least she was highly organized. My aunt and cousin helped me navigate the arrangements. The difficulties were not over with Diane and John. We were not getting along. They resented me and my success in the military and life. There was no time for trouble right now. I tried to evade them as much as possible and returned to Japan once all my mom's arrangements were taken care of. Avoiding their calls was my game plan.

A profound sadness emerged in me during the month-long stay at my mom's condominium. I was not equipped to deal with loss again. Guilt about not ever thanking my mother for what she did do for me devastated me. She was, after all, my mother. Breaking free of my family's dysfunction was how I survived, but at what cost? It never felt right in my heart. One day I would need to rectify this.

Childhood abuse, suicides, harassment in the military, my mother's death, and the diagnosis of post-traumatic stress disorder added up to too many unresolved issues in my life. I needed to call it quits. Five years after my mother's passing, I retired outside San Antonio, Texas, with my husband, stepson, and two dogs. I was familiar with the nearby military bases, Fort Sam Houston and Camp Bullis, from my twenty-year career in the army reserves and active duty.

San Antonio was a comfortable and safe environment for me. It was vastly different from life in Buffalo, New York. However, my childhood trauma was difficult to bypass and stubbornly followed me like a fly drawn to horse shit. Occasionally, Diane or John would call my house. They would find my phone number online and leave messages on the house phone. I never returned their calls.

I was broken.

People around me were supportive and encouraging, but sometimes it was not enough. My struggles continued.

My life needed to evolve if I was going to survive and eventually thrive.

Chapter 9
Mentoring

I met AJ at a neighbor's barbeque in south-central Texas several years after retiring. He was a couple of months shy of his eighteenth birthday and entering his senior year in high school that fall. AJ was a school friend of my neighbor's son. He was in foster care, and I heard his foster parents were anxiously waiting for him to graduate and move on. This plight immediately drew me to his story. I wanted to meet this young man.

My foster care experience had been buried in my subconscious since late college, and I had not thought about my days at Covenant House Alaska in a long time. Those situations never came up, and I am sure I never mentioned them to my husband. We had been married twelve years at this point. I had a talent for successfully hiding my past experiences from those closest to me.

Even though the pain, depression, and post-traumatic stress lingered most of my adult life, I decided I did not want the trauma to define me anymore. Controlling the pain by not letting secrets get discovered was my go-to defense. Few people "knew" me.

Yet I could not imagine this young man thrust into adulthood so soon without a parachute. I felt compelled to help AJ in any way I could before he aged out of foster care.

We were introduced the same day.

"Hey, AJ?" I asked when I approached him in the neighbor's kitchen. I stuck my hand out to shake his hand. "Nice to meet you. I live across the street."

"Nice to meet you too, ma'am," he stated as he grasped my hand with a solid and confident handshake.

AJ was wearing a Green Bay Packers jersey, oblivious to the football rivalry I had with my neighbors. This was Dallas Cowboys territory!

"I'm going to make a Cowboys fan out of you," I jested. "But first, I have to get you away from these cheeseheads."

I jokingly sneered at my neighbor Bobby and his mom Amanda. It was genuine fun. They were from Wisconsin, and we often harassed one another about our chosen professional football teams' victories and losses.

"I hear you will age out of foster care next summer," I stated.

AJ nodded. "Yes, ma'am," he said.

I explained that I had been in foster care when I was his age. My husband, standing nearby, glanced over at me with a cocked smile and raised eyebrow that expressed his disbelief. Andy did not know this history.

I waved Andy off and returned my focus to AJ.

AJ was incredibly open. He was respectful, well-spoken, and polite. He answered all my questions with "yes, ma'am" or "no, ma'am." I did not probe him for personal details.

We discussed school, his interests, and his plans for next summer. He liked country and Christian music. He participated in sports. The teens, AJ and my neighbor Bobby, played water polo and were on the swim team together at their high school. He was well-rounded and driven. He also seemed so well-adjusted, considering his lengthy foster care history. My interjecting Cowboys fan rhetoric as often as possible kept the conversation flowing.

He had a huge smile in response to my joking. I immediately liked the young man who stood before me.

"Is there anything I can do for you? I remember how difficult it was in foster care," I said.

"I could use a job. Do you know anywhere hiring?" AJ asked.

"How are you with construction?" I replied.

"Well, I do not have any skills, but honestly, ma'am, I want to learn. I am a good worker."

"You never used any power tools, built a fence, cut lumber, anything like that?" I continued.

"No, ma'am. Wait, do you need your fence built? Yes, yes, I want to do it. I need the money."

"I am ready to tear down the six-foot privacy fence at my rental and rebuild it next week. I could use your help. Sure, I'll hire you. How does ten dollars an hour sound?" I offered.

"Seriously? I am in. Count me in." He was excited and hopped up and down. "Thank you. You won't regret this, ma'am."

Initial problem solved. I was excited to get to know AJ better and needed the help. We would start to connect on an employer and employee level the following week. He was eager to learn how to use power tools and try construction. I had construction skills and often enjoyed DIY projects. My dad implanted this drive. I was happy to have an apprentice.

AJ was a diligent worker. We talked from dawn to dusk, working steadily on the fence project. We discussed how sports, family, and career objectives influenced our lives. His motivation was endless. As I shared my DIY knowledge, I recognized AJ as an adaptive learner. I knew I wanted to continue to help him whenever he needed advice or support. He was such a great young man. It seemed unfair to hear how little support was available within the foster care system.

The complexities of the Texas Department of Family and Protective Services system were foreign to me. AJ and I never spoke about the details of his case. I was a novice in this field. It never crossed my mind that dozens of local organizations were available to support AJ, including Child Advocates San Antonio. They were all unfamiliar to me. Even so, I wanted to work with AJ and other youths like him. For now, I embraced AJ like a member of our family.

AJ would age out of foster care, and I wanted to help him succeed. My experience after foster care left me with a void in my life. Maybe being his friend would strengthen his confidence and restore some of mine. Feeling hurt, lonely, or scared and being alone are realities for children exiting foster care at age eighteen. These experiences and feelings affected me while I was in foster care and when I returned home.

I forged a friendship with this young man. He spent many school nights at my neighbor's house. The teens overslept multiple times during their senior year and often came across the street to ask me for a ride to school or swim practice. These encounters allowed me to continue to get to know this young man.

The calling to mentor AJ felt natural. He welcomed my advice and was willing to participate. Our relationship grew. He affectionately calls me "Auntie" to this day. I respected how warm and open he was. High school graduation day came, and AJ transitioned from foster care to independent living and adulthood. My husband and I continued to provide support— furnishings for a new apartment, financial and education guidance, occasional transportation, and assistance registering for community college.

I had no formal training as a mentor, so I followed my instincts and drew from my professional experience as a career army soldier and officer where I had been a leader to young men and women. Now I could extend a hand to this young man. My military experiences gave me the confidence to share my understanding, insight, advice, and guidance with AJ or others.

Nonetheless, I had a past that needed a reckoning. My purpose was forming.

Meanwhile, my goal was to allow AJ to grow at his own pace and learn to recognize his capabilities, strengths, and opportunities. My offering value and respect for his decisions and building him up when he accomplished a cherished goal meant a lot to him. The goals he set were of his choosing. Sometimes he needed a list of options to explore, but due diligence was one of his greatest strengths.

AJ took calculated risks when the situation called for it. It can be called calculated because he had conducted research and formalized his decision-making every step of the way. I trusted AJ's plans, offering an objective perspective as needed.

Once AJ decided to join the army, he went all in. The decision blindsided me, and I never even knew he was considering the army, but I supported him 100 percent. He challenged himself at every opportunity. He has risen to Staff Sergeant, responsible for lower-ranking soldiers. He is airborne qualified and has been deployed to combat zones numerous times. That is a sure testament to his mental toughness and resiliency. He has been entrusted with independent travel all over Germany to participate in additional training in his ammunition specialty by his superiors. We often shared stories about our world travels with the military. We both acknowledged that the army gave us opportunities. The army was critical to overcoming and escaping our backgrounds.

AJ's service in the army made me proud. There were numerous times his stories quietly reminded me of Joey and Private Douglas. It was difficult not to compare their journeys in my mind. In a way, AJ's service and our relationship were helping me close the window to those difficult memories. Because of this, I was committed to supporting AJ and his dreams.

I could not change the past for Joey or Private Douglas now. But through AJ, I could focus on his story and remind him he was loved and supported. My being there for him, "mentoring" him, ignited his voice and strengthened his resilience.

Having a presence in someone's life is powerful and has lasting positive effects. I benefitted from this personally. AJ knows what he wants and is clearing a path to reach his goal. I have never regretted being there for him. The parallels between our life experiences and dreams inspired me to think about helping other teens again. Having a personal connection with someone who is reliable is indispensable for youth self-esteem, growth, and success. I learned this from personal experience and passed it on to AJ.

Over the years, I grew to love AJ like a son and could not bear to see him fail. He never did. His academic objectives and job titles may have changed several times, but he was persevering. He was succeeding.

AJ has beaten the odds in a nation where many kids who age out of foster care instantly become homeless. An army career is his plan for the future. He is saving to purchase a house. He is married and has a five-year-old son whom he dotes on and another child on the way. As he aspires to live life to the fullest, I remind him how proud I am of him.

We never bothered with details of our past experiences in the foster system. Instead, we bonded over the commonalities we shared in our motivations, aspirations, ambition, and interests. The Dallas Cowboys and the U.S. Army were topics we discussed often; in fact, converting him into a die-hard Dallas Cowboys fan might be my biggest success! Football is a passion that enabled our relationship to keep expanding.

There was a time I received two VIP passes for the Cowboys' pre-season minicamp at the Alamodome in San Antonio. I invited AJ as a graduation gift. He was delighted to go. One of his foster brothers was at the dome that Saturday too. He had a general admission pass, and AJ spotted him far above the field in the stands.

"Ma'am, can I go see my brother, Daniel? I want to share my VIP pass with him. Is that okay?"

"Of course. It is yours. It is super generous of you to think of him," I responded.

AJ was that kind of kid. He was always thinking of others. Daniel bounded down the stairs, and the boys exchanged their passes so security could see that Daniel was now granted access to the players on the field. I was so proud of how AJ looked after his younger foster brother. AJ met Coach Phillips and several Cowboys starters when the boys switched back. His face was beaming. He was also asked to attend the late evening sports segment with the Cowboys later that evening by KSAT News. His happiness at that moment was unforgettable. He had the brightest eyes and a contagious smile.

Mentoring AJ helped further prepare me for my journey as a child advocate. I felt human. This is what humanity was. Others challenged me throughout my life, and now I was imprinting and challenging AJ to become his best self. But equally, he was helping me. Because I developed compassion for AJ, the sense of urgency about healing my soul and letting go of my internal controls and the past hurts entered my consciousness again.

Being raised in the Catholic Church had never appealed to me, and I held no true religious convictions for most of my adult life. Faith was something I resisted for years.

Yet I recognized later that God has always placed critical people in my life. There was no other explanation except divine intervention for what was yet to come.

Overcoming my past never seemed possible. Something had to change.

God was going to shake up my life.

Only I did not recognize His plan.

PART 3
FLIP THIS LIFE

"I always thought that the 'thriving' would come when everything was perfect, and what I learned is that it is actually down in the mess that things get good."
Joanna Gaines—*The Magnolia Story*

Chapter 10
DIY

Everyone who knows me today knows I like to fix things, experiment with design, or even remodel spaces. Restoring furniture or renovating houses has been a hobby I have honed throughout my life. My interest in "fix-it" work began in my childhood when I occasionally saw my father performing many much-needed projects at our house. Nearly a lifetime later, I never expected my dad's skills would have been such an enduring influence on me.

Transformation is essential to grow beyond our past. This account is about what God has done in my life and how He has taught me to give back. "Flipping my life" is an analogy for saving me from my past, my mess, and my trauma—it is the path forward. It is a purpose-driven life. It is the path toward resiliency. It may not be right for everyone, but when I found it, it was what I needed.

The skills I have discovered and polished in construction and DIY projects are God's doing. It is a blessing. How does this relate to my child advocacy? This plan was revealed when God first "flipped" or restored my life a decade ago.

This is how I visualized the change in my life. If you enjoy a dose of reality television about renovations or "fix-it" projects, this analogy may ring true for you.

Picture how those DIY reality TV shows begin. This is the show. Imagine a DIY life that had seen good and bad days but lay battered and torn from neglect and abuse. I was subjected to physical, sexual, and emotional abuse long ago and continued to carry the wounds on the inside.

On the outside, I had outgrown the visible wounds. My internal and external structures were neglected, and my spirit felt even worse. I had an empty and cold heart and was not short on anger and bitterness. This was what I imagined an abandoned house looked like. Sensing my exterior paint was peeling and visible to others, I shied away from allowing people to know me authentically. Could the cracks in my walls be seen? This was my shame. My soul was rotting from the inside out. My life was decaying from within.

Emotionally I was like a hoarder. My wants and needs consumed me, and I often neglected those around me, harming relationships without awareness, which seemed more manageable than the right or constructive choices.

Was it too late for this tired and worn-out old house? How much damage had I done by burying the past inside? My parents had treated me as insignificant, and I had believed it. Would my life be a fix or a failure? Did I have an after-repair value? Taking inventory of my strengths and weaknesses gave me pause. There was so much work to be done.

Other people in my life believed in me and told me I had potential—a drive to help teens, talent with DIY construction, and a purpose they seemed to see growing inside me. That would be a good start, but not good enough if I stayed the course alone. My full potential needed to be revealed, and I needed expert assistance.

Categorically, I felt condemned to suffer. Living in my mess got comfortable. Much of it was self-created by not fully exposing my abuse as a child and not seeking healing sooner. Letting go of what I had experienced as a child or what I had experienced in the army was not easy.

Depression and self-destruction overshadowed every aspect of my life and relationships. Nothing in my life was in good working order.

Self-actualization of my full potential required a plan. In God's eyes,

I was a diamond in the rough. God was working in my life, and I was ignoring the signs. My life felt like it was falling apart only because I would not relinquish my self-control. I carefully orchestrated everything in my life, keeping me from organically thriving.

The trauma and grief from my youth were stuffed deep inside me. Somehow, I reasoned that controlling my adult life was a way to rectify what I could not control as a child. I controlled memories and conversations about my past, never really confessing the truth to those closest to me.

My lost and "misplaced childhood" needed healing. The walls were closing in around me. Guilt about the suicides of my brother and Private Douglas consumed me. The same guilt, coupled with the images of the bodies overseas, made me hypervigilant about all external stimuli. I developed anxiety, and it felt like I was asphyxiating myself with poisoned gas.

For all these reasons, my life was an out-of-control DIY project. Despite my brokenness and mess, my life was not foreclosed on. God never gave up. The child in me needed to be healed, and my flesh needed to be restored. My voice needed to be heard.

For thirty-five years, God planted several meaningful people in my life. These people persevered despite my coldness. God had a plan for me—His lost child.

These people were planted for my protection: a concerned neighbor, a high school teacher, a military professor, other military leaders, a nurse, and ultimately a physician. I was superficial, though, and never really allowed many people to know the real me. The people around me were determined however and told me they prayed for me. They shared their stories. There were stories of this God that could restore me, make me whole again, and help me reach my potential. How did others recognize my struggles? How and why was I so blind?

My phony façade did not perfectly shield me from intrusion by others. I was reminded how this God could rehab my life again and again. He alone could flip my life. Yet I would not receive the message. I would not easily relinquish control over my past—the hidden truth. I was not open to change because I did not know how to change. Internal struggles ravaged me. I needed help.

Could God save me?

Chapter 11
Faith

Decades removed from my childhood trauma, I continued to suffer from painful depression. I lacked faith.

Little did I know there were consequences to being distant, aloof, and cold. It hurt other people, resulting in rejection by my stepchildren and their families. I never saw it coming and do not understand what went wrong or exactly when.

A new breaking point developed. My stepson and his wife lived nearby. The falling out started with a text message from his wife. She wanted no more interaction between our households. Confused by the message, I tried to reestablish the lines of communication. That backfired. We were at odds over unrelated and inaccurate assumptions about our relationship. I never fully understood where things fell apart.

The next hammer to drop was when my stepson, Andrew, communicated a sudden ultimatum to my husband. Andrew's wife told him he either needed to cut off his relationship with us altogether, or he could lose his children for good. Andrew's wife's dislike of me was being used to punish my husband. Andy remained by my side, and as a result, he lost contact with his son and grandchildren. It seemed to be such a petty and harsh move. Personal attacks once levied against me now had collateral damage. The guilt I felt about Andy being drawn into my conflict devastated me. Without warning, the broken child that had been stuffed within me for decades resurfaced.

Depression. An increase in drinking. Isolation. Anger. Bitterness. I sat alone in the darkness blaring music—trying to drown out the negative self-talk. I momentarily resembled my mother. This was not a good state to be in.

That was my rock bottom.

The control I once struggled with maintaining was out of my hands. Someone else was calling the shots. Demands to stay away suddenly cramped my style. I was incensed at how I was losing access to my stepson and my grandchildren. I was no longer able to make things better. All communication was cut off. The decision was not mine. I was crushed.

My life did not seem worth salvaging. My mental stability was shattered. Depression was no longer riding shotgun through my life; it had assumed command.

A dark cloud filled my mind. For my husband to have a relationship with his son and grandchildren, I needed to be out of the way. I wondered about ending my life to restore peace in the family. This irrational thought repeated itself over and over in my head.

Images of Joey, Private Douglas, and the victims from my army duties flashed through my mind and played like a movie reel that would not shut off. Once again, I was hypersensitive to the mental images that had given rise to my first experience of post-traumatic stress disorder. It did not matter if my eyes were shut or wide open. The movie reel continued to flicker. Impulses were forming rapidly. Self-loathing and guilt fed the irrational and distorted thoughts. This was personal madness.

Once that negative seed was planted in my mind, my thoughts raced out of control. The exact memories of what unfolded on a Monday evening over a decade ago are not intact. My mood was unstable; after three sleepless nights, I followed through with an impulse to commit suicide.

As I waited for my body to die, my dogs stayed close. They were always loyal and loving. Tonight, they were guarded. I always found comfort and love in animals. Kipling, a tabby cat, and Captain, a spaniel mix, comforted me as a child. Several Akita dogs followed over the years. Tonight, my "fur kids" sensed something was wrong. Staring into their eyes created a moment of clarity within my self-induced psychosis. God had a message for me.

Suicide was not the answer. It was never the answer in my past, either. My impulses were foolish. Recalling how Joey's death affected me so profoundly made me reconsider my actions. Abandoning my dogs, let alone my husband, was the worst thing I could ever morally do.

"Oh, God," I cried out in the darkness. "What have I done?"

God was with me.

I looked upwards and gazed at the stars. They dotted the sky on this clear evening. Their brightness was a sign. The light shut out the darkness of my thoughts. *He, Jesus, is the light!*

My dogs lay patiently by me.

Immediately I remembered the stories of a God that could redeem me. Stories from special people throughout my life. The message was delivered many times and never received until now. I surrendered to the Lord in prayer. This was faith. Confidence, trust, and belief were placed in the God I had rejected for years.

At that moment, I finally gave up managing my disastrous DIY life project. Running my life my way would no longer be a priority. Just as Joanna Gaines says in her book, *The Magnolia Story,* deep in my mess, the going did get good! I relinquished control for the first time through prayer. Freedom came through faith. Freedom included the creativity to explore how to remodel and redesign my life through faith.

Professional help was warranted. My husband initiated the emergency call to 911 while I started the call to God for a new project manager. The perfect carpenter could fix and heal me. Jesus became my carpenter. I became a new believer on a Monday night in my backyard. God saved and redeemed my life. I became His DIY project.

The potential others saw in me was indeed a perfect start. Could I continue this journey with others? What was God telling me to do? My purpose would be revealed as my voice was discovered.

My life started to "flip." But how did the flipping process work?

———

Faith started the journey after the fateful decision that nearly ended my life, but there was more work. Physically, I was fortunate to walk away from a near tragedy. After I cried out to God, my spiritual body started to heal. When I left the hospital, I found the Bible someone had gifted to me many years ago. It was the first time I ever opened it.

I immersed myself in reading the Bible and looked for the address of a church that had been recommended several years prior. Suddenly, all the good advice I had once dismissed appeared as concrete and congruent plans in my head. The disorganized thinking and irrational thoughts were drowned out for good.

What had people been trying to show me all these years? Found it! CityChurch, I remembered the name. Friends in San Antonio spoke highly of this church. I needed a community of believers. "The church that rocked" appeared in the online reviews. It was minutes from my home.

The following Sunday, I was greeted by warm and friendly people. The worship music was uplifting. The song lyrics were beautiful, and the accompanying acoustic and electric guitars, drums, and a keyboard roared within the auditorium. It did not only fill my ears. I felt the decibels on my chest. This church did "rock."

Music always soothed me, and I had used it as a coping mechanism before, but this Sunday, I discovered that music could fill my soul. The worship team played Christian music from groups like Jesus Culture, Hillsong, Bethel Music, and Elevation Worship. That drew me in, but the message preached from the stage sealed the deal. The Word of God fed me. I had been starving all along!

I started attending CityChurch Bandera Road in San Antonio every Sunday and Tuesday. This furnished me with the tools for spiritual recovery. They welcomed me.

⚊

What I called "demolition day" came next. God placed a dumpster in front of me and told me to fill it with my mess. It would not be a painless process. The years of trauma I endured weighed heavily on my heart and mind. There would be no cosmetic fixes. It would take longer than a four-week renovation to fix my brokenness, heal my wounds, and unleash the power of forgiveness. I had to open the wounds inflicted by my parents' abuse and my brother's death so long ago.

With God, I was reminded that everything is possible.

He wanted all the junk, my mess, the brokenness, the damaged parts, the ugly truth, the secrets, and the excess baggage placed in the dumpster. Everything I was hoarding in my heart and mind needed to be disposed of. Demolition was demanding work.

At first, I only wanted to listen and not share my story at church. My mess made me feel afraid and ashamed. I had worn shame on my sleeve all those years, long after leaving my childhood home. God took down my damaged walls to reveal a shaky and unstable foundation. He gutted the horror in my heart and removed the rotten parts.

I hated my parents and other siblings, except Joey, but I needed to find forgiveness to release the pain. Trusting others became more effortless. Even my shame faded as I humbled myself and became more transparent in sharing my story. The anger and bitterness that almost destroyed me were extinguished. It was also mandatory to learn to forgive those who had hurt me and let it go.

It was easy to become absorbed in activities at CityChurch. While my spiritual life was undergoing renovation, I looked for ways to serve others. My spiritual knowledge developed and paved the way to volunteering on the plaza to meet visitors and share God's story. I helped visitors navigate spiritual choices for classes offered on our campus the same way I was shown months earlier. By participating in food collection for our community Food Bank, I expanded the ways I could serve as a Christ-follower. My role grew, and I was asked to serve as a pastor's assistant, first to John and later to Mike. I also jumped at the chance when I was invited to go to Chihuahua, Mexico, to serve as a project manager at the Casa Hogar orphanage, now known as Pies Hermosos Asociación Civil. These volunteer activities paved the way for my service much later at Child Advocates San Antonio. I was on the path. God was navigating.

Each of these steps and every contingency had been decided ahead of time. It was a blueprint for my life. God fully budgeted and funded my rehabilitation. The nails used in my reconstruction had been placed in Jesus's hands and feet thousands of years before I was born.

Perfect timing permitted this rehab. I recognized that God never wanted me to suffer as a child, but now I know how to use those experiences and relate to others in pain. All I had to do was let go of the control of my past. Children are now my focus. And that is the purpose God has opened my heart to.

Because God never forecloses on us, one of the most dreadful houses on the block—me—got a new lease on life, an eternal life. Light now shines through the windows to my soul. The light, Jesus Christ, was always there, even in my darkest times. That dark Monday long ago in my backyard was proof of my new faith.

I now understand what I had been rejecting for years. God is the ultimate project manager, and His Son, Jesus, the carpenter, was sent to die for my sins, fix me, and save me. And that the Holy Spirit was there to keep the fire burning in my furnace that is my heart. It took faith—the confidence to believe that God had been working in my life, even when I locked the doors and boarded up the windows to my soul. There was a unique design plan in the works.

This journey took years of dedicated and disciplined study of God's Word. After three long years, my prayers were answered, and my stepson, Andrew, and my grandkids came back into my life. Andy had stood by me during their absence. We endured together. Healing the relationships and healing my trauma produced a good feeling. I was grateful to start a new life with Andrew and the kids. We were a family again.

God's design was perfect. I was and am following His blueprint. He was meant to flip my life—not me. Rebuilt, re-plumbed, and rewired, and with a new, more substantial foundation, I have been steadily healed and restored.

I am addicted to His rehab. He has made me the confident and competent advocate I am today. This was His plan all along.

God also showed me how my DIY skills could be repurposed for children. This is a story I will reveal later. It is a large part of my volunteer advocacy and philanthropy today.

Long detached from my misplaced childhood, I became a child again—a child of God. It is childhood like none ever. Glorious! Today, I embrace my inner child and care for her by caring for others.

Before my journey and resiliency could be fully realized, the estrangement from my childhood family needed to be addressed.

There was one step left to take.

Chapter 12
Forgiveness

Forgiveness for my father came by happenstance through incidental contact with my sister. My last communication with Diane had been thirteen years earlier when my mother passed away. I recalled a lot of conflict with Diane and John over my mother's estate and vowed to separate myself from them forever. When her affairs were finalized, I left Buffalo and closed that chapter again. I did not need their contact.

I was a child of God now. Forgiveness was always at my back door in my new life I renovated through faith. But I felt doubt. Understanding forgiveness is one thing; practicing it is another. Did I have what it takes to exercise forgiveness?

I received a call from Diane on a Tuesday afternoon. I reluctantly picked up the call after seeing the caller ID. Screening my calls and pleading with my husband to do the same was my usual avoidance method. Diane had left many drunken rants on the answering machine over the years. They were never friendly or purposeful calls, and I ignored them. She resented me, and I assumed this was because I did not want to lament our broken lives through alcohol and drugs the way she had.

"Hey, it's me," she said. I recognized her voice immediately.

"Yes, I am here. What is going on?" I asked hesitantly.

"Dad is extremely ill. He needs to go into a long-term facility. I need help."

"Diane, I have not seen him for decades. I am not sure I am the one who can take care of that."

There was a long pause, and I could hear Diane struggling to compose her words. My heart began to sink. She was impaired. She could not pull off the rest of the conversation without slurring her words and sounding overly emotional. Her struggle with addiction was incomprehensible to me. Incredibly though, I relied on my new faith. She could not manage my dad's needs. It was my duty to act. These people were family. I had always considered her too toxic for me and kept my life separate from hers.

Times were different now. My life was different. Help was warranted. My perspective changed course. I let out an audible sigh.

"Diane, I can be on a plane in a couple of days. I will take care of it."

The rest of the conversation was rushed to coordinate accessing my father's mobile home and finding the long-term care facility. I gasped inadvertently when I hung up the phone. She had always sucked the life out of me, and I had difficulty hiding my obvious disdain for her.

As promised, I departed for Buffalo to help my father within two days. Diane did not meet me at the airport as she said she would. She promised to lend me my father's car. Fortunately, I had reserved a rental car on the off-chance she would not follow through. My intuition was correct. Several calls to her cell phone went straight to voicemail. It was full. Finally, I got a text that said, *I am working.*

I drove from the airport to the restaurant where she waited tables. This was one detail I had managed to remember from our conversation two days earlier. She was not there. The manager reluctantly gave me her home address after much persuasion.

Diane's apartment was easy to find a few minutes down Main Street in Amherst, north of the Buffalo city limits. She did not expect me. Something was wrong. Had she forgotten I was flying in to help our father? She swayed from side to side. It was three o'clock in the afternoon. She was drunk. A half dozen empty whiskey bottles were on the floor behind her, visible through the screen door.

"Did you forget I was coming?"

There was no reply. Her eyes closed as she struggled to form words. "Can I have Dad's key?"

She reached into her pocket to retrieve a set of keys and staggered back, catching herself on the door handle behind her.

"Here, I got it," I said, opening the door to reach for the keyring in her other hand. "Which key is it?"

Her finger indicated the single key on a second ring attached to a slew of keys I assumed were her apartment, work, and car keys. I removed my father's mobile home key and returned the rest to her. We did not speak again during my week-long mission.

The night before visiting my father, I prepared myself by meeting with old high school friends. The new age of social media allowed me to re-establish those long-lost connections. We picked up as if we had graduated only days prior. We talked openly about my visit and how difficult it would be for me to see my father. We reminisced about our high school years. Sadly, my memory was elsewhere. Seeing my father weighed heavily on my heart. I spoke of the abuse and foster care experience for the first time with them. They were so supportive; I cried on the way back to my hotel. They loved me and would have done anything for me in high school. I did not know how to find my voice when I was in pain as a teenager. I thanked the Lord for giving me good friends. It was a genuine relief to expose the truth. The personal exposure brought me peace that night.

The next day I knocked on my dad's room.

I heard him say, "Come in," and I opened the door.

Something stirred inside me. My father was now a frail man with a slight stature. His six-foot frame was no longer intimidating as he stood hunched over with the assistance of a walker barely twelve feet from me.

He called out my name in an unsure and muffled voice. He was surprised by my presence. "I thought I would never see you again in my life. I am so sorry. Please forgive me."

Remarkably, I heard myself say, "I forgive you," before stepping through the door.

Those three words lifted a life-long burden from my heart. It was a miracle I made it through these crucial few minutes and expressed forgiveness with zero reservation. We both were searching for forgiveness. Jesus, the healer, gave me the strength to express forgiveness from deep inside me.

I forgave my worst abuser.

Power cleansed me from within, and I breathed in deeply and exhaled the relief.

The following week kept me busy settling him into his new home and managing his personal affairs. It had been thirty-two years since my father's arrest. While organizing his belongings and cleaning his trailer, I found well-preserved legal papers. My father never had to register as a sexual offender. My suspicion was always correct. Why did he keep these documents? Did he keep them to prove he won? I let the issue go and did not address this with him.

He was settled in a supportive assisted living facility now. I was in a good place, and he was in a good place. It was gratifying to observe that my father was no longer the monster I had remembered from long ago. He said he made peace with God for Joey, and I believed him. We enjoyed our week-long visit. Every day I listened as he shared war stories over lunch at the facility's dining room. We were talking like we knew one another as friends, not as the strangers we were as family. I felt peace.

Shortly after returning to Texas, my sister called again. I did not pick up the phone. She left a voice mail.

"Hey, it's me. There's a change of plans." The tone of her voice was familiar. Her next words, "I hope you are not mad," were barely audible.

But I know what I heard. "Dad begged me to take him out of the nursing home. He was unhappy. He is staying on my couch until I can move him back into his mobile home." The words were slurred and spoken in a familiar scattered rhythm.

Listening to the message twice while closing my eyes, I doubted this plan was a positive solution. I had disposed of all my father's belongings and left Diane instructions on how to sell the mobile home while I was in Buffalo. My father had several medical conditions in his old age and required special care. A vision of my father with no nursing support, medication compliance, or oxygen at my sister's apartment foreshadowed what I feared next. She could not properly care for him.

He died within the week. Diane's call came in, and I stood by the answering machine listening to her leave the message. Anger kept me from picking up the receiver. It would take years for me to move past this moment, and it would be the last time I ever heard my sister's voice again.

We are all a work in progress. The reunion with my father allowed me to exercise forgiveness. It was vital for my healing. There would be more work to do. The forgiveness cycle needed another spin.

——

Eight years after the death of my father, I was called back to Buffalo again to see my estranged sister, who was now on life-support and gravely ill from her lifelong alcohol addiction.

Diane's son, Matthew, had not lived with her since he was a teenager. He was a stranger to me. His Aunt Val, his paternal aunt, made the first contact, first by email, followed by a phone call. It was Val who told me of Diane's rapid decline. It was disturbing for me to hear the news. She spoke favorably of Diane's son who rejected his mother's vices and set his goals on a future in the navy. Wanting to meet the young man she spoke so highly of, I promised to support him and come to Buffalo immediately.

"Thank you for contacting me about Diane's circumstances," I responded. "I cannot wait to meet Matthew."

Matthew arrived in Buffalo before me. Based on the West Coast, he could board an emergency flight from California, much like I did when my mother passed. We met one another at the hospital. Matthew was tall with black hair. He bore a striking resemblance to my father. Diane and Matthew each had my father's dark features and slick black hair. Matthew knew Buffalo General Hospital and swiftly led the way. We went together to the hospital room in the cardiac intensive care unit. The support for each other was mutual and came so naturally.

The week was filled with daily visits to see Diane. In the end, I forgave Diane privately at her hospital bedside. She was not responsive, but I believe she heard me and felt peace before passing. She died several days later, on my birthday. Diane was the same age as my mother when she passed away. I am grappling with regrets about our relationship. Healing is a journey that does not happen overnight. New hurts require going through the forgiveness journey again.

Incredibly, I reached final closure with my father by scattering his ashes at Joey's gravesite on Father's Day. I felt grateful to my sister for holding onto my dad's ashes all those years. It seemed like a proper ending for a man who vowed he had changed. My cousin Jennifer, who stood by me after my mother's death, was by my side in the cemetery. Her support was, once again, indispensable.

My family and my journey were a bit messy along the way. God is a better project manager than I am. He continues to plant more people and friends in my life. Unlike earlier in my life, however, I now know to nurture those relationships. I try to spread a message of hope, healing, restoration, and advocacy—perfect love for us all. I was grateful for the expanding family relations, knowing that when a door closed, another opened. Losing my mother meant gaining an aunt and a cousin. When my father passed, I became closer to his younger sister and her children's extended families— my cousins. Now, losing my sister meant gaining a nephew.

I had developed my voice. I had mastered resiliency. When it was time to spread my wings and fulfill my desire to serve other children outside of mentoring AJ, I looked to my husband.

The time for action was now.

PART 4
LICENSE TO CARE

"It's not in the stars to hold our destiny
but in ourselves."
William Shakespeare

Chapter 13
Finding Purpose

A God-driven purpose was forming inside me. It was time to take the next step. There were others in need—the children in my community, who needed the same salvaging and restoration I underwent myself. These children had futures and success stories within them. I wanted to help them find their path.

My struggles were in the past. I adapted and overcame my trauma with resiliency. My eyes were now open, and I was introduced to a new way of life. I wanted to show others how the grace from a loving God in me could be used to help children who felt alone and rejected. If I had missed the call to child advocacy earlier in my life, I knew others were also missing out on impacting a child's life. It was not too late to make a difference.

My husband, Andy, was the first to apply to be a court appointed special advocate or CASA. He had seen the banners around town for Child Advocates San Antonio and heard the calls for volunteers on the local radio stations.

It did not surprise me that he was undertaking this challenge because he is a natural with children. Andy relates incredibly well to our three grandchildren, especially our youngest, who is disabled and non-communicative. Andy and my stepson, Andrew, have become household experts in tube feeding and caring for his unique and comprehensive special needs. Loving children like we loved our grandchildren made me hurt for children experiencing abuse and neglect and lacking love and resources in the community.

Intrigued and wishing I had heard about this specific volunteer advocacy program sooner, I decided to explore the program further. I mentored AJ for a decade with no formal training. As I learned about the volunteer advocacy program from Andy, my future aspirations became brighter.

This was my purpose! I was sure. Finally, I understood that what I endured no longer needed to be a painful and debilitating excuse for what was wrong with my life before Christ intervened.

My husband withheld the details about his initial application. He did not believe I could perform this kind of work. He also thought I would never pass the interview process if I disclosed my past mental health struggles, depression, and post-traumatic stress, due to childhood traumas and tragic military experiences. I was no longer that broken person though. Healing had come. Child advocacy became the obvious focus of my purpose-driven life. I knew it was my path.

Since retiring from the army in 2005, I have floated from one volunteer job to another trying to find my purpose. A brief stint as a case manager for the Red Cross assisting families of fallen military members hit too close to home. Changing course, I participated in home builds for the Homes for Our Troops and Habitat for Humanity organizations to put my "fix-it" skills to work. Five years of service followed at CityChurch, when I volunteered for their campus and community efforts. As I grew and sought purpose, my heart was always open to where God would lead me next.

I rejected my husband's naysaying and contacted Child Advocates San Antonio, our local community CASA program. My initial inquiry was positive. The recruitment staff were willing to tell me more about the requirements.

The process began immediately. I submitted an application and agreed to the mandatory criminal background check through fingerprinting and validation of my state driver's license. Proof of auto insurance was required, and the program confirmed I had appropriate coverage and no moving violations. These items were necessary so I could transport children if needed. This is something not every state allows for volunteer advocates. There was also a background check through the CPS database. This ensured I had never perpetrated abuse upon a child. I submitted three personal references, and those people were contacted. They made undisclosed recommendations about my becoming a volunteer CASA advocate and representing our city's most vulnerable and fragile population of children.

I disclosed loosely guarded secrets about my past mental health struggles and submitted to the interview process. Speaking openly to the staff within the recruitment department about what my husband worried might prevent my being selected was difficult but I got through it.

My vulnerability reached a new level. During recent spiritual recovery classes and even in front of the consolidated church congregation, I had told part of my personal story. This was a whole new level of transparency. Applying to become a child advocate made me feel more exposed because I revealed truths and secrets I had never spoken of before.

I decided to let honesty dominate my conversation about what I had endured and why I was on a purpose-driven mission to serve youth who had faced what I had experienced. Disclosing my past trauma caused difficult memories to surface. Being measured in my approach with the staff members became a delicate process to keep me from feeling embarrassed.

Sally, an advocate team leader, conducted my final interview. She was a tough but compassionate interviewer. She asked difficult personal questions and had meticulous follow-ups. I searched my memory bank for coping mechanisms for stress and anxiety during the interview. The advice or training learned in therapy or through spiritual growth classes gave me confidence. I wanted to be honest and transparent enough to gain Sally's confidence and trust while demonstrating my competency.

Sally carefully wrote notes each time I responded to her questions.

It allowed time for memories to surface briefly. My mind wandered episodically. Looking around the room, I was transported to my past. First, I was in the large room at the police station. The fluorescent lights above me flickered as they had then. Next, I was in the court-ordered therapist's narrow and overcrowded office. The chair I sat in was equally uncomfortable, and I was beside her desk, no different than now with Sally. Finally, inside the judge's dark chambers, my vision narrowed to see more. My mind flashed through the various scenes and abruptly went blank. Sally was speaking again.

The stark office setting and government-style desks and chairs in the interview room reminded me of those environments as those were the first times I had been asked personal questions. We were getting to the most personal content during the interview now. Tears emerged, but I remained steadfast in my answers.

The questions were methodical, and Sally kept her responses reserved. She knew what she was doing. I assumed she had heard similar responses before. Her skill and professionalism during the interview encouraged me to continue. I had to stop thinking about the environment. It was distracting me. This was a safe zone. I did not have to remind myself a second time. Sally's professionalism and patience provided the fuel for my determination to continue.

There were few clues as to whether my past would prevent me from being deemed fit to represent children. It had been many years since there were any cracks in my stability, and this was an assurance I wanted the advocate team leader to understand unconditionally.

I was truly redeemed, and I was confident of that. I trusted in the Lord's plans and felt reassured. Fears and doubts disappeared. Letting everything out and letting go were my solutions. I disclosed difficult moments from my life, but I did so because I was committed to the process and the work. Serving children in the child welfare system would become the most critical purpose in my life.

My life and Joey's sacrifice needed to bring value to children who had been marginalized within the foster care system. These children needed someone to see them as future success stories. Their experience in foster care and trauma should not be used to define them. They needed to be heard the way I was not heard as a child.

There was a wait for results on the background checks and personal references, but I was optimistic. Trusting the process seemed easier now that it was almost over. With Sally's stamp of approval, I advanced to the training program. The hardest step was over.

The training was next!

Chapter 14
Training

The following week, I received a course overview, including a detailed itinerary for the required two-week training program all potential volunteer advocates complete. The thirty hours of training is a National CASA/GAL Association standard for all programs. The Child Advocates San Antonio mission statement was printed in bold on the first page of the materials:

"To recruit, train and supervise court appointed advocates who provide constancy for abused and neglected children and youth while advocating for services and placement in safe and permanent homes."[1]

The mission was simple and exact. Constancy and advocacy were terms I would often hear throughout this process. This training would prepare me to represent children's best interests when they were removed from their parents due to abuse or neglect. The pretraining documents introduced roles, responsibilities, and strict policies and procedures, but the real orientation was about to begin.

Walking through this process opened doors to my past daily. Every phase of training was a reminder of how the system had failed me. Questions emerged in my mind about how our outcries to the police were dismissed. We recanted too many times to remember, but they could never see

---

1. Child Advocates San Antonio, "Mission Statement," in Course Overview, (November 2018).

through the sham. I was not bitter. There was no time to resent the fact that no one spoke up for me as a child. My past provided the fuel and passion for helping children. It was motivating. Channeling the mistakes in my childhood and foster care experiences reinforced my commitment to my newly discovered mission.

Court appointed special advocates are volunteers. There are no prerequisites before training. The local CASA organization would teach me everything I needed to know. My life experiences would also add value to how I related to the children.

Training started a week after my interview. It was more than I expected, and every presentation captured my attention. Policies, statistics, the parties involved, crucial minimum expectations of advocates, cultural competencies, confidentiality, and more were presented. It was an information explosion! There was much to learn to become a fully functioning volunteer child advocate.

What stuck with me the most are contained within the major topics below. I have highlighted my experiences from the initial training. It is far from a complete representation of everything I have learned. Here I have focused on how this process impacted me and strengthened my quest to become a competent advocate for children in foster care.

Early Child Advocacy

A history lesson introduced us to the beginnings of the child advocacy movement in the United States. This was the first time I had heard of this story. It was fascinating because it had roots in animal advocacy, and animals were my first source of comfort. I paid close attention.

The primary player was the ASPCA or American Society for the

Prevention of Cruelty to Animals. It was founded in 1866.[2] Eventually, the New York Society for the Prevention of Cruelty to Children would evolve, albeit unconventionally, in 1875.[3] Animals had attention and protection for almost ten years before children. This was shocking to learn. Nevertheless, there is an interesting twist to this history. This is the story of the individuals who started the child advocacy movement.

A church worker, Etta Agnel Wheeler of New York, approached the ASPCA society members and told them about a young child named Mary Ellen who was being abused by her foster mother daily. Ms. Wheeler believed the ASPCA was her last hope. Every other organization she approached could not or would not offer help. She must have figured that since they helped animals, they could also help children. Ms. Wheeler's assumption and risk were correct. Henry Bergh, the ASPCA founder, acted quickly and ensured that Mary Ellen was removed from her abusive home. Eventually, the foster mother was convicted of the abuse in 1874.[4] Ms. Wheeler made an impact by speaking as the voice for Mary Ellen. History remembers her as the first child advocate.

At Ms. Wheeler's insistence, Mr. Bergh, with the support of ASPCA legal counsel, approached a philanthropist for help in forming the New York Society for the Prevention of Cruelty to Children that same year. This was a monumental advancement for children's rights. Animal rights activists became the first organization to advance these rights. The new organization for assisting children became the first child protection agency in the world. This was groundbreaking for the child advocacy movement, which would take off years later. A concerned citizen—Etta Wheeler, the ASPCA, and the NYSPCC were improbable heroes to Mary Ellen and

2. American Society for the Prevention of Cruelty to Animals, "History of the ASPCA," Accessed December 2, 2021, https://www.aspca.org/about-us/history-of-the-aspca.

3. New York Society for the Prevention of Cruelty to Children, "History," Accessed December 2, 2021, https://nyspcc.org/about-nyspcc/history/.

4. CASA, "Chapter 2: Child Protective Services, the Courts, and the Parties Involved," *New Advocate Training,* (November 2018), 2, NYSPCC, "History."

children everywhere for years to come.[5]

CASA programs and other child welfare organizations would probably not be around today if it had not been for these unlikely animal and child heroes. This story had a profound impact on me. Animals were my only source of comfort as a child. I learned to respect that child advocacy was born from the passion of those who helped animals but knew children always needed to come first. An important takeaway lesson from this story was also clear—one person can make a difference for a child.

―――

The CASA Model

The history of the volunteer court appointed special advocates model was equally inspiring. In Seattle, a superior court judge named David W. Soukup is celebrated as the founder of this concept. Judge Soukup had recognized a critical deficit when adjudicating children's cases in which the state was involved with their care: judges needed more information. He conceptualized recruiting volunteers from the community and training them to be fact finders to provide necessary information to the court. This information, he imagined, could assist all judges in making life-changing decisions for children in the care of CPS. He secured funding for a pilot program to train the first-ever volunteer child advocates, which launched in Seattle in 1977,[6] about a hundred years after the NYSPCC was incorporated.

The first program was successful, and more programs sprang up across the country. A National Court Appointed Special Advocate/Guardian

---

5. NYSPCC, "History."

6. Child Advocates San Antonio, "Chapter: 1," in New Advocate Training, (November 2018), 6; National CASA/GAL, "It Was a Judge's Idea," Accessed December 2, 2021, https://nationalcasagal.org/about-us/history/.

ad Litem Association (National CASA/GAL Association)[7] was then coined to support state and local programs. Many local programs across the country are called by different names. If you are interested in learning more, please explore what programs exist in your community. At the end of this book, I have included information on how you can connect with a local or state program through the National CASA/GAL Association.

The training was thorough. When I learned about the history and development of the CASA model, I became reflective and wondered what resources had been present in my hometown when I needed help the most—in the early 1980s. Much of my childhood trauma occurred before these programs started nationwide. I became curious about how and when, or even if, there had been a child advocacy program in my hometown when I first entered the foster care system as a teenager in 1983. An investigation into my hometown seemed logical.

It was hard to appreciate that most programs were barely getting off the ground back in the day, but I was undeterred. I researched online and found a CASA program in Erie County, New York. The local program was part of a more extensive network called Mental Health Advocates of Western New York.[8] I sent an email to ask what year they had been founded, and the director replied to say 1991.

Confirmation. They had not been available when I needed help. Fortunately, they have now been admirably serving my former community for over thirty years. My research resulted in mixed feelings. I felt disappointment but also a sense of security. The answers did not erase the pain, but they made more sense. I was resolved to continue this journey so children's voices would be heard and valued in my new community. The

7. National CASA/GAL, "History," Accessed December 2, 2021, https://nationalcasagal.org/about-us/history/.

8. Mental Health Advocates of Western New York, "Court Appointed Special Advocates," Accessed June 3, 2021, https://mhawny.org/program/court-appointed-special-advocate/.

past was behind me—it could not be changed.

—

History of Child Advocates San Antonio

Since my introduction and interest in CASA advocacy began in San Antonio, I was also anxious to learn more about my local program's beginnings. The training provided this introduction. Later, I found additional details about the organization in their archives. I also met with the program's early founders, Ellinor Forland and Betty Zinn of the National Council of Jewish Women, who are credited with the program's formation nearly forty years ago.

According to Forland, in 1983, she and Zinn, past section presidents of the National Council of Jewish Women (NCJW) in San Antonio, were asked to research the next community service project for the council. In considering alternatives, they were told of the CASA model from Seattle. The National Council of Juvenile and Family Court Judges (NCJFC) had already approached the National Council of Jewish Women at the suggestion of the executive director of the Edna McConnell Clark Foundation.

In that era, the Edna McConnell Clark Foundation focused on funding educational and social services for children. It had established a relationship with the NCJW a few years earlier regarding a juvenile justice project and requested that they consider establishing five pilot CASA projects around the country.[9] The goal was to demonstrate whether the concept designed by Juvenile Judge David Soukup in Seattle could be replicated.

Forland and Zinn used examples from the pilots, specifically one in Dallas, as a "cookbook" for establishing a program in San Antonio. After

9. The Edna McConnell Clark Foundation, "About Us," Accessed December 24, 2021, https://www.emcf.org/about-us/.

garnering the support of a local family county court judge and the regional director of CPS, a collaborative relationship was formed. The two women set to work as soon as they got the CPS and judicial go-ahead. By the end of January 1984, thirteen volunteers were trained, twelve of whom were council members. The first children's case to be assigned was in early 1984. Perseverance and determination spurred interest in the program, and new volunteers were sworn in each year.

Child Advocates San Antonio became the third CASA program in Texas. After six programs were formed in Texas—Dallas, Wichita Falls, San Antonio, Austin, Houston, and El Paso—the beginnings of a large, successful professional state organization were formed and based out of Austin. It was coined Texas CASA.[10]

While drafting this story, I was fortunate to meet with these local founders, Ellinor and Betty. We spoke at length about their early experiences. Their efforts improved our community and how child advocacy is provided. I feel deep gratitude for their work.

As a foster care alumni, I began to appreciate how child advocacy was initiated nationwide. It was too late for my siblings and me, but that is why my passion became enriched in the mission today.

Similar CASA programs have expanded since the start-ups in the 1980s nationally and across Texas. Currently, there are 939 programs based on the original CASA model across the country in forty-nine states and the District of Columbia,[11] and seventy-three of them are in Texas.[12]

---

10. Ellinor Forland, "Brief History of CASA in San Antonio," Letter, National Council of Jewish Women, (San Antonio: CASA, 2006), Included with permission of the contributor and CASA.

11. National CASA/GAL, "Our Reach," Accessed December 2, 2021, https://nationalcasagal.org/about-us/national-organization/; National CASA/GAL, *National CASA/GAL Association for Children 2021 Annual Report*, Accessed March 21, 2023, https://nationalcasagal.org/about-us/reports/national-casa-gal-association-for-children-2021-annual-report/.

12. Texas CASA, "Who We Are," Accessed December 2, 2021, https://texascasa.org/who-we-are/.

Abuse and Neglect

Abuse and neglect are difficult topics for most people to discuss. The details can keep a person up at night. My "lived experiences" in childhood deprived me of many restful and safe nights. The specific details of my childhood abuse interspersed throughout this memoir were challenging to write about. There is no sugar-coating it; experiences like mine are still a problem across our nation. Providing detail was essential to express how grave this situation is.

Thousands of children suffer unimaginable abuse each year. People who have not had those experiences sometimes have difficulty relating to abuse and neglect. As a result, training for CASAs needed to be conveyed with sensitivity and authority. We all needed to be fully aware of the magnitude of the problem in our community. Looking around the room, I knew I could not be the only one who shared these lived experiences.

Children deserve safety, and it is often not found in their homes. Independent studies report that more than six million children in America are at high risk for abuse by a family member.[13] A report of child abuse or neglect is made about every ten seconds in the United States. This was my reality. Family members are not the only perpetrators, but they are the most likely. We learned of many high-profile cases of child abuse and neglect. It was awful to hear but essential to our understanding. This was as real as it gets.

Our training covered the four primary forms of child abuse: physical, emotional, or sexual abuse, and neglect. I was affected by all four. Images shown in the videos reminded me of my misplaced childhood. Fortunately, I was better prepared to deal with these issues. I felt blessed to be a survivor

---

13. Brandon Gaille, "51 Useful Aging Out of Foster Care Statistics," May 24, 2017, Accessed February 4, 2022, https://brandongaille.com/50-useful-aging-out-of-foster-care-statistics/.

and ready to serve other children who experienced trauma.

Survivor.

It is a critical word. During my training, I whispered it silently.

Internally adopting the term survivor instead of victim aided me in healing my inner child. Becoming the voice for a child who desperately lacked an advocate was personal. Our training continued. Child abuse is not exclusive to one segment of the population. This topic was an ugly truth for all walks of society. Any child can be at risk.

Statistics about child abuse and neglect are unfortunate. One in seven children will experience child abuse or neglect in any given year. This might be an understatement, given how reluctant children can be to reach out to a trusted adult. Then there are the circumstances that are the most gut-wrenching to learn. In these worst-case scenarios, fatalities are a sad reality. Take 2019, for instance; it was a severe year. Reportedly 1,840 children died as a direct result of abuse and neglect in the United States.[14] In 2021, the number was consistent at 1,820. What needs to happen to bring these numbers down? Last year, while writing this book, nineteen children died from torture and abuse in my county, an increase over the thirteen deaths the year prior. The trend is going in the wrong direction for my community.

Understanding specific risk factors for abuse and neglect was also central to our training. We were informed about these factors and how they can lead to abuse and neglect. Poverty and drug or alcohol addiction were the most common root causes. Societal and family norms can have a negative impact on children's safety and well-being as well. Many parents were abused as children. They might have little knowledge about child development. Perhaps they were exposed to domestic violence as children. Many suffer from mental health problems or have no support systems.

---

14. Centers for Disease Control and Prevention, "What are child abuse and neglect?" Accessed February 4, 2022, CDC, https://www.cdc.gov/violenceprevention/childabuse and neglect/ fastfacts.html.

These factors fuel the cycle of abuse.

None of this was a surprise to me. I faced these issues in my family, but seeing these elements projected onto the whiteboard in the classroom made them real again. How can generation after generation keep perpetuating such heinous abuses on children? What could stop it? This segment made me wonder more about my parents' backstories. I knew so little about their families and their upbringing. Vivid images of my mother, maternal grandmother, and father flashed through my mind.

—

My grandmother was a horrible person. She whipped us with a torn electrical cord from a non-functioning iron while babysitting us during our primary school years. She kept it wrapped around her walker for safekeeping. The multicolored fabric binding frayed from age exposed us to the sharp bare wires. This was often a lunchtime ritual.

We walked home from elementary school for lunch recess. "Gram" would become enraged at me because I often cut through the fields on the corner streets and had dozens of "stickers" stuck to my knee-high uniform socks. She saw them immediately. The tan color stuck out on my navy-blue socks like stars in the dark sky.

"I'll crown you!" she screeched.

The ironing cord was swinging above her head like she was a cowgirl getting ready to round up cattle.

I grimaced as the frayed cord smacked from behind across my shoulders. My button-up sweater cushioned the blow.

There was no lunch for me, and I was forced to pick each of the stickers off my socks only to collect more on the way back to school. The cycle continued.

It was easy to accept what the researchers were saying. Generational abuse is an epidemic. Early prevention never occurred in my household either. My siblings and I were too scared. We recanted far too often. We also ran around and closed the windows daily to keep secrets within the walls of our house. We were brainwashed and terrified.

What were the risk factors in my household? I wondered. Were my parents abused? My grandmother whipped us, so I assumed my mom likely faced the same abuse. Did two major wars, WWII, and the Korean War, damage my father's emotional well-being? Had he been abused?

Was there a genetic component to my parent's alcoholism? My grandmother and mother both drank alcohol to excess, but I did not know anything about my father's parents. Where did he get it from? I cannot recall my paternal grandparents being talked about when I was younger. These and other questions churned in my mind. I found it helpful to be reflective on my past experiences to stay laser-focused on the problems in my community.

Remarkably, when shown some of the horrific truths about abuse in Bexar County, Texas, it did not initially alarm me. I could hear and see the physical reactions several trainees had in the classroom when listening to or watching the videos on abuse. They shifted uncomfortably in their seats and had normal shock responses to the vile stories and images.

Was I alone in my experiences in the classroom? It was not likely. The statistics proved that I could not be the only one. I trusted that the motivations each of us had in undergoing this training were pure and just. Similar personal stories had to motivate other volunteers. My past experiences initially immunized me to the shock or awe of the images. These were subjects and experiences with which I was deeply familiar. As the video played on, discussion in the classroom began.

"It is a travesty," stated one trainee.

"How awful," echoed another.

Gasps were distinct.

I remained quiet. Visions of my abuse played like a movie reel in my head long after the classroom video ended. No one knew what I was thinking. I was glad I had handled it well, or had I?

———

This particular year, 2018, there were 5,751 children in the care of CPS in Bexar County. These children represented 11 percent of the 52,397 children in foster care in all of Texas. Bexar County was leading the state with the highest number of children in the care of CPS. Harris County, which includes Houston, the fourth largest city in the nation, ranked second across Texas with 5,670 children in foster care.[15] It was heartbreaking to comprehend these numbers. Bexar County had a problem, and I was grateful to be part of the solution, along with the dozens of other trainees beside me.

Why were so many children in care? How could we improve the system? Did anybody have an answer to this crisis? These questions and others would eventually affect my desire to have a more considerable impact at the state level. For now, one case would be my initial focus.

———

Child Protective Services

I had a basic understanding of who Child Protective Service (CPS) caseworkers were before my training. Questions about how I navigated the system as a child emerged. Why could I not remember more about my caseworker? What trauma was locked away deep inside my core being?

We were provided an overview of the CPS department, and our instructors defined the foster care process. None of this instruction filled in the gaps in my memory. The training was exhaustive but could only partially explore the enormous roles and responsibilities of the CPS department and how the State of Texas runs the system. We were

---

15. Data.Texas.gov, "CPS 2.3 Children in DFPS Legal Responsibility by County by Fiscal Year," Accessed December 3, 2021, https://data.texas.gov/dataset/CPS-2-3-Children-In-DFPS-Legal-Responsibility-by-C/929f-jvud/data. CASA, "Chapter 1," 12.

encouraged to learn more independently including from the caseworkers
with whom we collaborated.

I discovered that it is CPS who investigates allegations and reports of
child abuse and neglect, not the police. CPS is responsible for gathering
information, interviewing all parties and witnesses, and determining
whether the children are either safe or unsafe. Only CPS investigators make
a ruling or disposition on an allegation.

Perhaps the major mistakes in my childhood were because, as children,
we mostly made outcries to the police. We did not know how to call social
services or CPS. We recanted regardless of who came knocking at the door.
Once Joey and I entered foster care, we had no contact with one another. I
never knew what he experienced in the boy's group home. I did not know
if we had the same caseworker either. Our foster care experiences never
addressed or erased the trauma we endured. Joey's trauma followed him
until his death. I was fortunate to survive with the grace of a loving God.
There had to be a better way, but as a child, I did not know how to utilize
my caseworker and communicate my needs.

As I absorbed the details in our training, it was easy to recognize
how committed the people in the child welfare system are to protecting
children. There are many variables, and so much can go wrong with kids
in foster care. Children primarily belong with their families, but when the
state must intervene—more attention is warranted to their situation.

I worried about the children in my community as I listened to the
instructors. It was obvious that all the trainees around me were worried for
the same children. We shared familiar sighs and glances. It was comforting.
This helped shield me from exposing my emotions and the grief of Joey's
passing. It was difficult not to think of losing Joey within the foster care
system and then losing him forever shortly after. *Keep them safe.* Such
thoughts looped silently in my head. I wanted to make a difference.

Proper handling of our outcries was utterly lacking in my youth.
Investigators rarely asked more than a few questions. My imperfect
memory has eroded the actual involvement of the police or CPS. After

countless "investigations" of our house over seven years, Joey and I were eventually removed. I do not know what made the difference that day. Someone intervened for us. Today, I hope the process is better in Texas and all cities and states.

In Texas, when CPS determines that children are unsafe and at risk, they can recommend services to the family, open a family-based safety services case, or initiate legal action to remove the child or children from the home.[16] When the children are removed from the home and placed in foster care, a legal caseworker is assigned to manage the case. We met several legal caseworkers. They attended our training to explain their role in a child and family's lives.

Initially, none of the caseworkers before me triggered lost memories about my caseworker. My memory was an abyss. I struggled to focus on the classroom discussion and continued to daydream intermittently.

What was my caseworker like?

My imagination conjured up images of someone who was likely kind and committed. I needed to believe that reality. Finally, an image did occur. It made me feel better for an instant. It was the back of a woman's head. The brunette with long curly hair was driving an old sedan that creaked and moaned with every rough spot on the country road. I was in the backseat of my caseworker's car on the way to the Barkleys, my first foster home.

"We're here," I heard as she turned to look back at me. "You're going to be fine. See, other children are playing outside."

The image was fuzzy and quickly faded away.

The panel's insight was valuable. We learned how the caseworker is principally responsible for the children. Their caseload can vary from a

---

16. TDFPS, "Child Protective Investigations (CPI)," Accessed January 31, 2022, https://www.dfps.state.tx.us/Investigations/default.asp.

dozen children to upwards of thirty or more. There is no magic formula. Abuse and neglect are grim problems in Bexar County. There are too many children and not enough caseworkers. The system is overburdened. Maybe that was the problem when I was younger. Were there not enough caseworkers to pay attention?

This training made it easy to understand how caseworkers have demanding jobs. They are professionals with extensive training to address the needs of the family and the children. They are ultimately responsible for each child on their caseload. They have a detailed policy manual to dictate their responsibilities and govern the rights of the children in their care.

Rights!

My eyes widened. I wondered if Joey or I had rights back in our youth. I scribbled notes in my training manual. The children I would represent and advocate for would know their rights. I would make sure of that. This was a promise I internalized.

The caseworkers continued to speak of their experiences with having a CASA advocate assigned to a case. The caseworkers in my class were straightforward and honest in their opinions. They had tremendous respect for the community volunteering to help address gaps in the child welfare system, specifically through the CASA program. They reported successful experiences with volunteer advocates' input and feedback about a child's best interests. Admittedly, they informed us that a CASA advocate and CPS caseworker may not always agree, but they appreciated the tenacity of the volunteers in most circumstances.

My training also triggered an interest in resolving other questions about my foster care experiences. Several years later, I would reach out to the New York State Office of Children and Family Services to submit a release of information request for all records related to my involvement with the department while in foster care. What were the details I had blocked out?

What was not disclosed to me as a child in foster care?

My initial request would fall flat. I would wait for a second reply and follow up again if needed. Eventually, I learned that the New York Central Register records are destroyed ten years after the youngest child on a case turns eighteen. I was twenty-three years too late in my search. I would never be able to unlock the past now. Accepting the unfortunate response as a conclusion to my history was complicated. As a new volunteer child advocate, I pledged again to educate children in foster care about their rights. They need to understand how to seek answers when ready.

The Legal Process

Each confirmed child abuse or neglect case undergoes a predetermined series of legal proceedings. There are strict timelines and procedural rules to follow. Every state is governed by different laws and procedures. Every child's case is unique. I paid careful attention.

In Texas, exigent circumstances defined by law allow a CPS investigator to remove a child from their parents at any hour of the day. These processes differ across jurisdictions around the country. When the judge rules that the state should have temporary managing conservatorship granted at the hearing, the children enter what we call the foster care system.

Texas directs an attorney ad litem to represent the children. The parents are assigned individual attorneys as well. If there are multiple parents, each has a separate attorney. As an agent of the state, CPS is represented by their department attorney, an assistant district attorney.

We learned about the types of court hearings that focus on the children and parents under the department's scrutiny. The first hearing after a child is removed from their home by CPS is held within 14 days. At the final trial, a child may be returned home or placed in lengthier state conservatorship.

The judge determines if the state is taking conservatorship of the children. They may expressly state that a volunteer advocate should be appointed to the case. Otherwise, a CASA staff member present for the removal hearings may flag the case for further review and request that an advocate be appointed later. There are far more cases than volunteer advocates. Historically, CASA advocates are assigned to the most severe or challenging cases as quickly as possible, while other children with pressing needs may remain unserved. The resolution: more volunteers!

When the children enter foster care, they may be placed with a relative or closely related friend (often referred to as "fictive kin"), a foster family, or a residential treatment facility. The needs of the children and placement availability affect their situation. Meanwhile, CPS caseworkers work with the parents on service plans to attempt to regain custody. A service plan is a detailed list of tasks or assessments the parent or parents must undergo. Some of the service plan requirements could include parenting classes, counseling, drug or alcohol treatment, or even drug testing, to name a few. These community resources are afforded at no cost to the parents in the hopes of a successful reunification after mitigating the risk factors.

The conclusion of a case at the trial could result in a child or children returning home. That is the primary goal of CPS. Family preservation is also a priority for lawmakers who craft new legislation or rewrite existing laws from legislative session to session. Sometimes, however, a trial does not officially close a child's case. Some children do not get returned to their parents after the trial.

When this happens, these children enter a new CPS stage called permanent managing conservatorship. In this situation, the child remains in foster care under the state's conservatorship. The child could be pending adoption, in a permanent kinship placement, or potentially stay in foster care until they reach age eighteen, the age of legal maturity. Some children can extend their care until the age of twenty-one in Texas. Children in a permanent managing conservatorship, or long-term foster care, also need someone to continue to advocate for them.

Hearings are routine for children in any stage of the state's conservatorship. Children who are veterans of the foster care system are equally as important as those first entering care. A CASA can benefit them by assisting the caseworker in researching permanent placement options through more in-depth relative searches, for example. Occasionally, a local or state organization can aid in family genealogy searches. Family reunification with a parent is also possible, even after the termination of their parental rights.

This information interested me. No one was assigned to assist my caseworker in finding suitable permanency options for me or Joey. The judge never got the complete picture. This was where we were failed the most. I was sent home and faced more abuse. My brother stayed in the state's conservatorship, but according to my mother, only because she "did not want him."

Such horrible past mistakes.

CASA advocates serve such a critical role in making recommendations about placement. I wished every child in foster care had a CASA or GAL advocate.

The staff reassured us that the first year on a legal case could be intense, but good results were absolutely possible. It may seem overwhelming to play such a critical role for a child in foster care, but the professionalism and confidence of the staff provided reassurance. They were encouraging and supportive, and every step of the way, we were reminded that they were here for us, and we were here for the children. It was comforting. The role was essential to improving children's outcomes.

I appreciated this process.

I had no recollection of having an attorney represent me. My visions of the judge were vague. I explored these earlier images of him, trying to fill in the blanks. My judge was a man. He had asked me to describe the sexual abuse. I wanted to comply. The abuse was scarred permanently in my brain. The details were vivid.

An image of a smaller me gazing at the older gentleman with white hair appeared in my mind. He wore the customary black judicial robe and sat behind an oversized wood desk with ornate carvings along the top edges. We were in his chambers. The walls were covered with dark wood veneer paneling, and his law degrees and other certifications hung in decorative frames on the wall.

I seemed uncomfortable in my memory. Shifting in the heavy wood armchair, I noticed my feet did not reach the floor. My mouth was open in this vision, but I did not hear myself speak. Did I disclose the painful memories? I had no idea. Questions again surfaced before me. My mind drew a blank. My recollections were muddied or non-existent.

I would leave training every day feeling disappointment about my past. Listening to music on my drive home helped me stay in the present and not sink into depression. My playlist included music I had heard as a child. Back then, I had found a way to fall asleep with the music blaring. It drowned out the fears and anxiety I faced before my father came home. I used it now to drown out the memories and lack of memories surfacing throughout this process. The voids hurt the most, but this tactic worked.

There were so many hearings and legal processes to understand. The children and families affected must have been overwhelmed. Briefly, peace passed over me. It was a peaceful feeling derived from not knowing all the details about my case. I reasoned that as a young teen, I would have felt more overwhelmed than I likely was at the time. Maybe I did not need to remember all the details. I grasped for an explanation to erase the past. Awareness of the facts in the present can be a good thing and a not-so-good thing. How do children and parents today avoid becoming overwhelmed in this process?

Specialty Cases

Specialty cases piqued my interest right away. Advocate Supervisor Ashley provided the training. I knew her name only as my husband Andy's supervisor, which meant she would most likely become mine when I passed all the requirements.

She began her presentation by defining crossover and permanency cases. The crossover, also called dual status cases, are cases in which the children in CPS custody, through no fault of their own, are also somehow involved in the juvenile justice system. Permanency cases are those I previously described as permanent managing conservatorship cases where the children have not found permanency yet and remain under CPS's legal guardianship or conservatorship.[17] There were also more hearings to learn about. The legal system was a complicated entity! Presentations and specifics were presented logically, and assurances were made again.

Ashley discussed the horrible truths about children in permanent managing conservatorship and how their placement stability, educational needs, medical needs, and long-term effects of running away, homelessness, or sexual exploitation could occur. Many of the consequences or outcomes for children in long-term foster care are bleak.

Children who age out of foster care only graduate high school at a 74 percent rate compared with 90 percent of the general population in the United States. Another 40 percent of these youth will experience homelessness at least once by age nineteen.[18] These were not favorable odds.

---

17. Child Advocates San Antonio, "Chapter 3: Specialty Cases," in *New Advocate Training*, (November 2018), 2-3.

18. Gabriella Franklin, "Words from a Mentor: Aging out of Foster Care," THRU Project, Accessed December 22, 2021, https://www.thruproject.org/words-from-a-mentor/?gclid=EAIaI-QobChMIgtu50eD39AIV_xXUAR3QDQSIEAAAYAyAAEgKVWfD_BwE.

Joey aged out of care in late 1984. He beat these odds—briefly. Graduating high school and joining the army appeared to be positive strides toward his future and success. Unfortunately, tragedy struck. He committed suicide. Why, Joey? We were not told of statistics for this type of alarming outcome. I felt a heavy burden as if my chest were being crushed. I was scared for these children.

Aging out of care at age eighteen is a legal passage for entry into adulthood for more than twenty-three thousand youth each year.[19] This is a difficult transition. Each detail we learned emphasized the crisis for hundreds of thousands of children experiencing foster care in the country. For perspective, in 2019, approximately 423,997 children were in foster care nationwide.[20] That equates to about 5 or 6 percent leaving foster care at the legal age of majority each year. Better outcomes would mean that these youth were reunited with family or even adopted.

The training on permanency continued with comprehensive information about working with young adults. This was my target population. I had longed to serve teenagers for thirty years. I was thrilled to know my soon-to-be advocate supervisor was as passionate about this population as I was. Helping teens survive foster care and prepare to enter adulthood at age eighteen would need to be balanced with all other required advocacy efforts.

I remembered several tremendous challenges I faced during and after foster care. There were lessons I learned that might help me help a teen today. Efforts to connect at Covenant House in Alaska long ago also flashed through my mind. I gave up without making an impact. Giving up today was not an option. Meaningful connections would be of the utmost priority as a CASA advocate. This was going to be a long-term commitment.

---

19. Gaille, "51 Statistics."

20. Child Welfare Information Gateway, *Foster Care Statistics 2019*, Accessed December 22, 2021, https://www.childwelfare.gov/pubs/factsheets/foster/.

The fact that I had no professional to help me navigate transitions into and out of foster care or even through college motivated me. I had to rely on others, primarily teachers or professors, who informally mentored me. My blind trust in their guidance kept me moving forward in my army career until I could develop an internal compass and resiliency. It was no different than what I did for AJ. At least now, I could play a more significant role for a child who needed extra attention.

Children's rights came up again in training. Familiarity with foster care rights would help us follow a timeline and communicate with the CPS caseworker about pending requirements. It would also ensure that the child was viewed as a person and not merely a number or statistic. I learned about rights in a Texas system that were probably afforded me in New York, but I was uninformed in the 1980s. Many children in foster care often need an advocate to speak up for them and voice their rights. I know I did. Sometimes, that advocacy can shape value and self-worth in the child, eventually resulting in learned resilience and advocacy for themselves.

My instincts and experiences warned me that children in foster care should not have to figure out the system alone. Navigating social services and CPS custody by myself was akin to swimming in peanut butter. There had to be a better way, and I concluded it was better with a supportive CASA.

Throughout this training, I learned of all the ways these teens would benefit from having a volunteer advocate provide constancy and be a helpful resource. There was so much to learn about the challenges these youth faced. Equally, their benefits could not be mastered in a day.

As a foster care alumni, I understood how overwhelming it is for other children in care. I committed to learning as much as possible about foster care benefits and services afforded them throughout my tenure as an advocate. I was grateful for this initial training because it solidified my earlier desire to work with these older youths.

The Courts

We were introduced to the children's court at the Bexar County courthouse on Dolorosa Avenue during our final training days. The historic courthouse is one of Texas's oldest and largest operating courthouses. The distinct granite and red sandstone is unique and sets this structure apart from the other historical buildings amid an eclectic mix of modern architecture in downtown San Antonio.

The children's hearings are held on the third floor in several courtrooms. The architectural details are opulent in both the hallways and courtrooms. The unique tiles and carvings that appear throughout the building reflect a Spanish influence. Inside the courtroom, a small gallery can only accommodate roughly two dozen observers or witnesses. The seats reminded me of the pews from Saint Ambrose, the Catholic Church I attended as a child.

I took my seat and slid to the end, allowing my fellow trainees to squeeze into the cramped space. Several people stood near the door as all the available seating was filled. A small commotion occurred every couple of minutes as people entered and exited the single entrance to the rear.

As I turned my attention to the front of the courtroom, I noticed the judge's bench, which was higher up than all the other seats. A court reporter and witness box were positioned to the bench's left and right. The bailiff was closest to the observers like me. Three large wood tables with a handful of chairs were set kitty-corner to each other in the center and to my right. I noticed CASA personnel at a smaller table to the left, directly in front of me. They were perpendicular to the judge. It appeared to be the best view of the courtroom, other than the judge's view.

We were required to observe the docket to become familiar with the formal proceedings. Our instructors showed us where we would sit, who the parties were, and how various hearings and motions would cycle in and out of the court. I scanned the room, noting people's faces in all the predesignated or assigned seats in front of the judge's bench. No one looked familiar outside of a few staff members I had recognized from my CASA program. I do not know what I was searching for. I shook my head to clear the cobwebs out. The people present that day were not present in the courtroom in 1981. I had lost myself momentarily.

"All, rise. Court is now in session," the bailiff commanded. His voice was loud, and the courtroom chatter stopped as the judge entered from his chambers behind the bench.

"Please be seated," announced the judge. "We are on the record. The court calls cause number—"

The pace was fever pitch, but the content was thorough. Parties were usually well-prepared, and the CASA role was recognized as powerful immediately. When the judge called a "cause" number, and all the parties were seated and sworn in, he always asked whether a CASA advocate was assigned to the case. After testimony from the assistant district attorney, CPS caseworker, and attorneys for all parties, he would usually ask, "CASA, what do you have to report?"

The volunteer advocate or advocate supervisor present provided input, and the judge weighed the testimony cautiously. He carefully reviewed the court report submitted by the advocate, paused the action in the courtroom, and occasionally redirected questions to the CPS caseworker. He sought an explanation or plan from the department for the concerns and recommendations he learned from the CASA report. Sometimes breaks were granted so the judge could go to his chambers and speak with the children in private.

I was impressed with the proceedings and the temperament of the judge. These were weighty proceedings, and even though the judge cared primarily about the children, he demonstrated his sensitivity to the parents' situation when needed.

No doubt, the people I observed in the court hearings, a turnstile of attorneys ad litem, CASAs, guardians ad litem, and CPS caseworkers, were a strong cross section of those involved in child welfare and child advocacy. The child was always the focus. I was ready for the challenge. What I witnessed in the courtroom was the best reference and insight assembled about the importance of a child having a CASA advocate.

Distant memories emerged of the judge in my case. I wish I had known more about what happened. As an adult with little insight into my childhood abuse case, I understood how foreign this process would be for a child today. Doing right by my CASA children was necessary so no child had to leave care with questions haunting them for decades. My duty as an advocate was personal.

The Role of a CASA

CASA advocates are volunteers, and while most CASA/GAL programs across the country are non-profit organizations, all are independent of CPS. The volunteers do not investigate whether abuse occurred or what has happened in the past. That is a CPS responsibility. We advocate for the "best interests" of children in foster care.

Ultimately, volunteer advocates seek to ensure that each child's needs are addressed, and that a safe and permanent home is found or reestablished with their parents. We check CPS's plans for the child and monitor the child's progress. Advocates often work to identify services the child or children may need since entering state custody and share our recommendations with the court, the child's attorney, and CPS.

CASA advocates work closely with the CPS caseworker, the child's attorney ad litem, or any guardian ad litem if appointed. We are a collaborative partner but remain completely independent of the department. An advocate supervisor always provides oversight, direction, coaching, or support. Advocates are never alone in this process; they have contact with other central figures such as the parents or their attorneys, case managers at residential treatment centers, foster parents or other caregivers, teachers, mental health professionals, and others.

Communication can occur with other parties, but it serves the purpose of fact-finding. For example, an advocate may ask a teacher about a child's attendance, behavior, academic progress, and any challenges the child has in the classroom to develop a game plan to address identified needs. The advocate cannot answer the teacher's questions about the child's time in foster care or with whom the child may ultimately live. The CPS caseworker has the ultimate authority over the child and information about the child.

Information is sacred. One of our most important roles is following the rules for gathering information and not sharing confidential information with anyone other than our supervisor, the CPS caseworker, the child's ad litem, and the child. Confidentiality is critical in all aspects of the child's case.

Established minimum case expectations dictate specific monthly and quarterly requirements for volunteer advocates. These serve as a guideline or checklist that facilitates proper volunteer involvement. In training, all expectations and responsibilities are made clear. Advocate training is precise. We are constantly reviewing relevant information about the child or children to make recommendations to the court.

CASA advocates are expected to report an assessment for each child on the case. We must get to know the children by visiting them monthly or more often. Participating in any meetings related to the child's well-being is also required. There are many considerations to make. Is the placement meeting their needs? How are they doing health-wise? Are there any concerns at school? Are their behaviors appropriate? What medications is the child on? Are additional services needed? This is not an exhaustive list. The insight provided by the volunteer advocate is essential to the judge.

Volunteers in this program can have a full or part-time job, career, or family and manage to dedicate the right amount of attention to their case. It is a balancing act but should not deter a career-minded person from exploring a volunteer opportunity with their local CASA/GAL program. You would be surprised how many advocates successfully balance their careers with this form of advocacy.

—

If you have become curious about child advocacy while reading this story, please explore the CASA or GAL programs in your community. I could not possibly provide every detail or "what-if" scenario a volunteer advocate faces. Your local program is your guide. You will find a link at the end of this book.

We can make a difference for the children. CASAs have a well-deserved reputation for being as thorough as possible because we often oversee a few children at a time. In contrast, a CPS caseworker has a much greater caseload with upwards of dozens of children to manage. As advocates, we provide written court reports to the judge before each hearing. Objective concerns and recommendations are summarized for the judge so they can make an informed decision about the child and family. The judge heavily weighs these recommendations and reports as well as any oral testimony we make in court.

"Happy endings" for the children are what everyone involved wants. CPS and the attorney ad litem representing the children form independent recommendations, and we do not always have to agree. The final decision will always be up to the judge. The Casey Foundation reports that nearly 250,200 kids left foster care in 2016. This trend repeats almost every year. While most of these children, about 66 percent, were reunited with family, nearly 25 percent were adopted.[21] What happened to the rest of the kids? Did they age out? Become homeless? End up in jail? Worse?

Finding permanency is paramount. This is why it is critical for the

21. Annie E. Casey Foundation, "Most Kids Existing Foster Care are Reunited with Family," Kids Count Data Center, September 13, 2018, https://datacenter.kidscount.org/updates/show/211-most-kids-exiting-foster-care-are-reunited-with-family.

CASA advocate to be as thorough and objective as possible when stating to the judge what is best for the child. Expressing the child's desires is equally important. Being able to voice concerns and recommendations starts with listening to the child. The volunteer is merely the link.

⚊

If I'd had an advocate assigned to me as a child, they could have notified the judge or CPS about the weekly shakedowns at the Barkleys. Barbara stole my life savings. I was treated as insignificant and threatened with a juvenile delinquency report and worse. A CASA advocate could have filled in my vacant memories about the second foster home. What was keeping me from remembering? They could have asked for a safe, permanent home instead of the judge sending me back to my parents to be abused again. Maybe someone could have advocated for Joey and me to be reunited. The prospect of having a volunteer advocate was not afforded to Joey or me. That disparity strengthens my commitment to spreading the message about CASA and GAL advocacy today.

Joey and I did not have a happy ending. I desperately did not want children to experience what we faced with no one in our corner. We were led down an unfortunate path paved with additional trauma and absent memories. Professionals involved in our foster care experience meant well, but we did not get the attention we needed. I survived my misplaced childhood and am grateful to have positive memories of my brother. Joey's legacy was alive within me and influenced my strong desire to succeed in this process.

⚊

Before finally obligating to this journey, I had to commit to serve at least one year on a case. This struck me emotionally as very sensitive and compassionate. I would not want to give a child hope only to quit the process and crush their spirit. It would be devastating for a child who had lost so much. This was where the term constancy was repeated several times.

Please understand how resolute this single requirement is for those considering becoming child advocates or currently serving as advocates. I made it personal and agreed to serve the year minimum commitment or longer if that is what it took. Do not ever quit on the child! It could cause irreparable harm.

***

Reflections

The training I underwent as a CASA was founded on a professional and organized curriculum that empowered my confidence in serving abused and neglected children. Early in my training, I recalled looking around the room and silently praying that everyone with me would be sworn in in a little over two weeks. We were.

Throughout this training, tips for what a volunteer advocate can or should do were provided in an organized and inspiring manner. The staff believed in the material presented. They believed we would be best prepared at the end of our thirty hours. I felt this too. Our advocate supervisors were supportive and informative professionals. They guided us through each case, offered tips and advice, and ensured we stay on track if doubts ever surfaced.

Joey and I needed an advocate back in our day, but alarming numbers of children today still need CASAs more than ever. Unfortunately, downward trends have appeared in volunteerism across the country. The pandemic is likely the cause, creating a renewed sense of urgency for new volunteers to fill the ranks in advocacy centers. Join us.

⸻

Swearing-In

Near the end of the training, I discovered that all my references, background investigations, and application items had passed the required scrutiny. I mastered all the mandatory training and passed my final tests. I was ready to be sworn in as a court appointed special advocate.

The next day came, and I was delighted to have my husband in the courtroom. Three months after he began his journey, I joined him as a volunteer child advocate for children in foster care.

A family court judge formally swore me in. It was as if I was granted a "license to care."[22] I first read this phrase in Gay Courter's book *I Speak For This Child*. It features her guardian ad litem experiences in Florida. "License to care" was a perfect analogy for those of us who become court appointed special advocates or guardians ad litem. We are volunteer representatives for the children and are provided court orders to be factfinders and advocate for their best interests. It was the judge's directive. Caring was necessary, but we carried the power of the judge's order with us. Objectivity would be critical. It reinforced the importance of this type of work.

I was about to embark on one of the most extraordinary journeys I could ever imagine—advocating for children formally in court. It was official. I was going to speak for the abused and neglected! Be their voice when needed. The role of a child advocate for children in foster care would be filled by someone who had once stood in their shoes.

This was the challenge I felt born for.

Thinking about the analogy I mentioned earlier—"flipping this life"—I consider many of today's vulnerable children symbolically as buildings

---

22. Gay Courter, *I Speak For This Child: True Stories of a Child Advocate*, (Lincoln: iUniverse. com, 2001), xvii.

too. Like I was, they are also in various stages of disrepair, abuse, and neglect. They need project managers and restoration. As a voice for their care and future, I am their project manager if they want me to be. I am ready to listen and speak as needed. Advocating for them is the first step to empowering them.

A week later, I officially met my new supervisor, Ashley. I was thrilled. This was a perfect match for me because Ashley was an expert on the staff regarding older youth. She taught the class about young adults early in training, and her class stuck with me. My capacity to learn more about the teen population in foster care would expand under Ashley's tutelage.

Chapter 15
The Asterisk

I will never forget the day I signed onto my first case. My advocate supervisor, Ashley, had three case files on her desk. She selected each from dozens for my consideration. Each story involved situations of children who were new to the foster care system. This was anticipated. They were temporary conservators of the state. Ashley had selected cases involving teenagers removed from their homes for abuse or neglect. These were some of the worst cases resulting in CPS removal. Teenagers were also the age group I wanted to represent.

"These are challenging cases. I want you to be aware of that," Ashley told me. "Teenagers can be difficult. They are smart. They may need more one-on-one attention."

My impression was that teens were often left to fend for themselves and that "the system" worried more about babies and toddlers. It may have been a false impression, but that was the understanding etched in my mind even though I now knew CASA had not existed in my community when I'd needed them.

Yes, Ashley was exactly right.

Teens can be difficult. I was a difficult teen, I said silently.

Mrs. Kane and Tina worked hard to gain my trust, yet I always struggled with relating to them. I was lucky to have them looking out for me at school or in therapy, but they could not impact my foster care experience. Civilians and random adults usually have no say in a foster child's treatment.

The "swimming in peanut butter" image appeared in my mind again. I imagined Joey felt the same way. Foster care was not something we were equipped to navigate alone. Since that period, the CASA/GAL difference in thousands of children's stories has been a game-changer nationwide. No child should be alone in the process.

An advocate would have been a blessing for me at age fifteen. So much needless grief, stress, and anxiety could have been minimized or prevented if I had had someone to help me then. A safe home was never identified. My best interests were not considered during that period of my life. The system failed Joey and me.

Even though I never had a CASA, past experiences prepared me to make a difference for a teen with similar experiences. System failures could be averted. My journey resulted in me developing resiliency beyond my trauma; this was the most significant asset I brought to Child Advocates San Antonio. The children in these case files deserved to discover a resiliency within themselves.

There are several possible outcomes for older youth including finding permanency through a successful reunification, fictive kin, or a smooth transition from high school into independent living. Whatever the future held for these youth, I wanted to ensure they had a voice in court, and they learned to find their own. The children needed to be heard and not processed as numbers, statistics, or forgotten stories within the system.

Right now, however, I had to select one case. I could only accept one child or one sibling group's story. Ashley picked three quite different cases for me to choose from. Three nondescript manila folders separated me from the children whose shattered lives hung in the balance.

⁕

Opening the folders in succession, I quickly scanned the first page of each. It was titled "case information sheet." There was a case or cause number and case name, followed by each child's name and date of birth. Other parties involved in the matters were listed—the assigned judge, the assigned CPS caseworker, parents and the foster parents' names, fictive kin, or the facilities where the children were temporarily housed. Each folder was arranged the same.

Closing my eyes briefly, I envisioned my name and Joey's name on a similar file in a Buffalo social services office. The judge, caseworkers, and placement names could never be revealed now; too many years had lapsed. I daydreamed briefly. Our file was destroyed. My mind produced fuzzy images of pages from our CPS records being shredded forever. I may have even heard the annoying crunch-crunch sound of the paper as it was shredded into tiny pieces in my head.

I let out a sigh.

Ashley looked at me as if to say, "It will be okay." As I turned my attention back to her and returned to the present, I blocked everything out temporarily. I was not sure if she did speak to me. I could only pick one case. What if the other two cases were shredded? Dread washed over me.

The next page in each file was an internal form CASA used to screen removal cases day after day in the children's court at the county courthouse on Dolorosa Avenue. These were the handwritten case details which an advocate supervisor had first scribbled during fast-paced court hearings. These notes required additional attention. I recognized the information on the neatly typed case information sheets. This indicated how these files had been carefully reviewed to ensure correct details.

An asterisk got my attention not once but twice in one file. At the top of the form, I noticed *strong advocate written in ink. The back of the page had additional notes about the unique concerns about these children. There it was again: *Judge requests a strong advocate! This manila file no longer seemed ordinary.

I flipped to the next section. An eight-page report contained more details about the children's situation. Moments ago, concerns about choosing the proper case flickered in my mind. What if the two other cases never got an assigned advocate? I had to make a tough choice.

Selecting the case needing the most attention was my priority. I was retired and could devote countless hours. Believing the CASA training and my life experiences had prepared me for this moment, I decided to pick what seemed like the worst-case scenario.

"Pick the case that suits you!" Ashley reminded me as I scanned the three cases she provided.

The asterisk kept drawing me back.

"There's something about this one, Ashley," I replied. "The judge emphasized assigning a 'strong CASA advocate.' He was serious about this case," I muttered while agonizing over being unable to pick all three cases.

This judge had a reason for requesting a strong advocate. The advocate supervisor who constructed the file also had heard enough details at the removal hearing to understand that these children could not wait any longer for an advocate.

"I am inexperienced. This is my first case. How can I be considered a 'strong' advocate?" I looked up, asking Ashley with a puzzled look.

"Do you think you are a strong advocate?" Ashley asked me.

"Yes, of course," I replied confidently. "My training prepared me. I am not afraid of a tough case."

"Well, there is your answer. It's your confidence. You will be a strong advocate for these kids!" Ashley replied.

My doubt was immediately erased.

———

As I carefully read the report, I grasped the magnitude of what these children faced. Several children were removed from their home after recommendations to mitigate removal failed. I knew how this could occur. Joey and I endured years of additional abuse prior to removal because the authorities needed a clear and convincing argument for removal.

These children, like Joey and I, were eventually removed from their home primarily due to substance abuse and abuse towards one of the children. The children were deemed not safe in the environment they were living in with their family members. Multiple fathers were not involved in the children's lives either. The children had not been enrolled in school. They lived in what can only be described as a temporary makeshift shack behind a small run-down home in a low socioeconomic neighborhood within the City of San Antonio limits. It was clear from reading the papers that these children had more complicated issues. I was shaken and awed by the details I read. Maybe I was not as immune to secondary trauma as I assumed during training.

This was real. Closing my eyes, I saw Joey and me in the back seat of the black social services sedan leaving Mariemont Avenue. We were leaving our childhood home for the first time. I was doing this for kids like Joey and me now. A sudden fear of the unknown washed over me. I could no longer visualize the red siding or brick steps from my house. The scene on Mariemont Avenue faded like a tunnel narrowing and collapsing into darkness.

What did these children feel? I redirected my reflections to these four teenagers. I wondered if these children felt the same emptiness I experienced when they were driven away from their home.

Did they embrace one another?

Were they scared?

Learning that the children were all separated by CPS concerned me. What if they never saw each other again like I had lost Joey? The enormity of their separation and the potential for long-term side effects bothered me.

Fixing my attention on the documents in my hands, I processed what I read. Every statement documented in the file before me was underscored by the date it was noted. There were so many red flags from the initial intake report years prior. My mind searched for answers as to why these children had not received closer attention before this removal. The children had continued to suffer in an unspeakable environment for too long. Exploring possible explanations, I wondered if these children denied abuse or neglect or recanted a previous outcry. Why did this go on for so long without action being taken?

The world can change and evolve over generations, but children are consistent. Fear of abandonment or separation from what is considered normal is a typical response. I felt those feelings as a young child despite my terrible suffering. Recanting outcries, often out of fear, worsened my situation. The trauma persisted and multiplied. Finding answers to my concerns about these children stoked a new anxiety. My mind was open to embracing these children's stories.

Flipping to another page, I found a possible answer. CPS tried to assist the family. This was protocol. CPS did its job as required. They tried to preserve the family unit, but it left these children in a crisis. Processes meant to preserve family integrity when an urgent danger is not present were the standard. Subsequent experience with other cases reinforced this model. CPS usually tried to prevent removal as the first course of intervention for children and families.

Unfortunately, events and situations continued to deteriorate for all the children in this environment. My heart sank. I sat down and read the documents while my mind sifted through my experiences. Flashbacks played like a scratchy 8mm film reel in my mind. Moments later, the tape broke, and the glow from the fluorescent light in the ceiling of Ashley's office brought me back to the present.

Over ten months, their parents were given many opportunities to resolve the abuse and neglect allegations by completing service or safety plans. The department documented all its contact with the parents and attempted to provide instruction for the children's needs. The parents were unwilling to cooperate with the plan, had an extensive history with CPS, and failed to make any lifestyle changes or show a willingness to protect their children. The case file revealed that this was what took time. These are the requirements established for each case before a child is removed.

I did not need to read the other case files as closely as this case now. There was no doubt in my mind that this case required immediate action. My supervisor filled in additional details as I read each page and responded aloud to confirm what I was discovering.

Ashley asked me again, "Are you sure you want to start with a tough case?"

My answer was unequivocal. "Yes. These kids need someone now. I am ready."

She smiled approvingly and stated, "Alright, the sixty-day status hearing is approaching fast. I will get your court order as soon as possible."

"Thank you. I will get right on this one," I replied.

Ashley had confidence in me and the advocate training program. She affirmed my choice. I knew I would need to lean on her and learn from her experience to ensure these kids got the strong advocate the judge had asked for.

Speaking for these children's best interests and meeting their needs for as long as it would take was my priority. Applying all my training, looking to my past experiences, researching to grow my knowledge, and leaning on my supervisor from time to time would ensure I stayed on top of these children's needs. There was no room for failure. I would draw on nearly every topic from my training manual to meet the needs of this case. I was preparing to face every possible situation imaginable.

I immediately signed a document stating that I accepted the case as well as the advocate minimum standards form I was expected to comply with each month as part of my court appointed obligations. There were limits set on these expectations, and I knew I would go beyond those minimums. This case would unexpectantly grow to the maximum! I was well prepared to face the challenges and felt confident that this was a good fit because of my training.

A sixty-day review hearing was already fast approaching and exactly three weeks away. There was a lot to do to become familiarized with the case, meet the CPS caseworker, and meet the children. Multi-tasking was necessary to meet all the demands and submit a complete and objective CASA court report for the judge ten days before the hearing.

I had no time to spare and hurried from the office. On the way out the door, I heard Ashley shout, "I believe in you!"

The fall air was crisp, and I felt energized by it. On the drive home, I was consumed with processing what I had committed myself to. I was on autopilot because it seemed like I blinked, and I was home already organizing my additional thoughts and making a to-do list. My action plan started immediately.

My husband, Andy, also a court appointed special advocate, would be co-signed on this case to allow us to share thoughts, experiences, and recommendations throughout the case. He would provide me with balance when I needed a steady partner to dump my feelings on after exhausting days or when it felt like things were not happening fast enough.

After all, "finding these children a safe, permanent home, as fast as possible,"[1] also known as serving their "best interests," was one of the founding principles I learned in my training. I did not have this at their age, but I would ensure they did. There was no turning away from these children. Those asterisks were meant to get my attention. This case did not dissuade me.

My enthusiasm for meeting the kids was growing!

---

1. CASA, "Chapter: 1," 16.

Chapter 16
The Kids

The children I would meet on my first case had suffered gross neglect and abuse. This was common for most cases that passed through the children's court in Bexar County. Could I get them to believe in and trust me when their lives were turned upside down? Could I help them each find success and see their way through the mess? Preparation was necessary. I took the case file my advocate supervisor had provided and reviewed it carefully several times.

In my home office, a college-ruled notebook sat before me. I carefully jotted down all the people affiliated with the case and their roles on one sheet while recording pertinent notes about the case on the next. Finally, I developed questions for each placement and the children on several more pages. Considering what I would have liked my CASA to know helped me carefully craft questions for the kids I was assigned.

Grrr. I wish I'd had a CASA back then. If only—.

The notebook with the green cover would accompany me on many excursions during my case involvement. It became tattered and torn after several years when my notes filled every page. I added a second notebook in the later stages of the case.

The four teenagers were placed at four distant locations within the foster care system. I immediately attempted to contact the placements to arrange visits. Responses were prompt, and I prepared to meet the kids.

———

Ben

I met Ben, the fourteen-year-old first, four days later. His placement was an hour outside of town. The large rural two-story home I pulled up to had been converted into an emergency shelter for youth recently removed from their families. My credentials cleared my entry, and I was taken upstairs.

Ben sat at the end of a folding table.

"Ben, this is your CASA," the staff member said.

There was no reply from Ben. He did not look my way and hid his face in his hoodie.

"Ben, I am a court appointed special advocate for children in foster care, like yourself. That is what CASA means." I sat down and slid my business card across to him.

He slid the hoodie from his head and stated, "I do not want to stay here. I want to go home."

His voice cracked a bit and showed signs of stress and anxiety. I pressed on, trying to develop a rapport with him.

"I understand, Ben. I am sorry that cannot happen right now. I have been assigned to advocate for your 'best interests.' I will help you and your siblings get through this process."

Gazing patiently at Ben, I gave him an encouraging smile as he made eye contact. We sat quietly while Ben's eyes darted back and forth. I imagined he was thinking rapidly.

"Ben, tell me about yourself."

"What's there to tell?" His tone was more matter of fact than question.

"Well, tell me about your life before CPS, your siblings, what you like—" I redirected while pausing to gauge his reaction.

I understood his fear but not altogether. Ben's story is his. It is unique. Yearning to help him, I needed to relate with him authentically. While I sat patiently, Ben suddenly looked at me. He had deep brown eyes. They were bloodshot as if he had recently been crying. Tears welled up, and he fought them.

"Ben, I know this is a difficult time. How can I help you?" The silence in the room was uncomfortable. "I can tell you I know a little bit about what you are going through." No response. Ben remained quiet. "I was in foster care around your age," I added, hopeful of breaking the ice.

The statement seemed to shrink his aloofness a bit. Ben's demeanor and body language started to change. He appeared open to talking with me, but I sensed his underlying anxiety and suspicion. Considering the trauma he had faced, this was normal.

Ben talked about an extended family that included aunts, uncles, a stepfather, siblings, and his mom. He had an intense sense of family, evidenced by his choice of words. Several people he referred to as family members were actually close family friends—fictive kin. These facts were revealed in some of our back-and-forth conversations.

"My mother raised us to trust one another. We do not need anyone else," he stated.

It was apparent that Ben had a distrust of authority. Now I understood why. His mother wanted secrets preserved, sort of like my mother. An uphill battle to gain his trust was ahead. But any trust would help in spades down the road. I was much older than Ben when I realized my parents had brainwashed us. I wondered if his mother's motives were similar. We were distrustful of adults at his age. My parents had us convinced there would be worse trouble if we spoke about what happened in our lives—behind closed doors. Threats of being taken to "Baker Hall" were also dangled over our heads.

Baker Hall has operated as an orphanage and boy's truancy center since 1864 in Erie County, New York. After the 1950s, it was expanded into a residential program for adolescents with emotional or behavioral issues. My siblings and I knew the location on the corner of South Park Avenue and Ridge Road in Lackawanna. It was barely a mile from Mariemont Avenue. We lived close, so my mother and father took turns torturing us with a drive to the institutional-style brick building on many occasions. It was located directly across the street from the hospital I was born in. We were reminded of how we could have been left there from birth, but my parents liked to exclaim how fortunate we were they did not leave us! I never felt fortunate.

⁂

Now, here sits Ben in his Baker Hall, and he did nothing wrong. He did not want to be there. Ben was scared. I wondered what he had endured.

I explained my advocacy role and asked him how he was holding up. He offered little in response to what he had been through. He was removed from a parent he loved only three weeks earlier, which was an additional trauma he struggled with. He never knew his father.

As we talked, I could hear the anger in his voice. He did not understand why he could not see his mother. He was close to her despite whatever he had endured. Shifting the topic of conversation to school was my attempt to decrease his anxiety. Ben was like any average teenager, so many "good" and "fine" responses were mixed in our talk.

"Do you feel safe here?" I asked.

"Yes, ma'am."

"Are the staff nice? Is the food good?"

"It's okay," he replied.

This was his second placement in three weeks. He was initially placed with his older brother Will at both locations, but Will was moved. He had had no contact with any of his siblings since.

"Tell Emma I'm worried about little Tony." Tears welled up in his bright eyes and began to fall. "I love Tony. I do not think Emma can take care of him alone." He sniffled quietly as he spoke.

"When I see Emma, I will ask if I can take a picture for you. In fact, can I take your picture?"

I got a respectful, "Yes, ma'am," in reply.

Ben sat back and raised his head to smile. He was a handsome young man. I snapped a photo as a staff member returned upstairs to check on our progress. Dinner was ready, and my visit was over. Before turning down the stairs, I focused directly on Ben again. His face held the smile. I thought I sensed hope.

"Ben, I will speak with your caseworker. You are right. You need to see all your siblings as soon as possible—it is your right! I will see you in a few more days."

"Thank you, ma'am."

I had started to make a connection.

"No, thank you for meeting with me," I echoed as I descended the stairs.

Downstairs, the staff member explained, "Ben is a sweet and polite young man, but he's not adjusting well since his brother was transferred."

"Please explain more about his behavior," I said.

"Ben has anger issues and is starting fights at school and here at the house. It started after Will was moved."

"What happened to Will?"

"Will told us about his 'juvie' (juvenile detention) record, and we had to move him because of that record," said the staff member.

I was concerned about how much longer Ben could keep his anger in check. Immediate action was necessary with my fact-finding probe. He also needed to see his siblings.

"Thank you for your time. I will come back to see Ben again this weekend. Please call me if I can do anything for him."

After a brief conversation about both teen brothers, I was fully informed about their time at the shelter. We exchanged contact information, and I departed.

Emma

The next day I met sixteen-year-old Emma at her placement far outside the other side of town. I waited in the residential treatment center's case management office. Emma came in and dramatically plopped herself into a chair across from me. Her arms flailed, and the chair banged against the wall behind her. It was theatrical, and I was secretly impressed because I liked the spark I observed in her!

I introduced myself and explained my role as a CASA advocate. She sat with her arms folded across her chest.

I looked at the case manager. "Ma'am, do you mind if I speak with Emma alone for a little while?"

"No, of course not. Call out if you need anything," she replied, leaving the door open as she departed the office.

Emma told me she was also on her second placement already. She was angry. Her language contained vulgarities and derogatory statements about why she was "here—in CPS care." I let her express herself with no corrections. After several minutes, she grew quiet and appeared calmer.

"Shit, I hate my roommate," she uttered after the brief silence. Suddenly, she caught herself and self-corrected. Her demeanor shifted from angry to slightly playful. "I am sorry, ma'am. I am sick of this bullshit." She cursed again, recognized it, and laughed. She covered her mouth but did not effectively withhold a smile.

Her case manager poked her head in the door. "Is everything okay?"

Emma and I gave the young woman a nod and a smile.

"We're getting comfortable," I explained. A wink from me sent the case manager down the hall again. "Okay, more PG language, please? I am too old for the R-rated stuff," I said and directed the comments back to Emma.

Smiling at her, I communicated that I was not there to scold her. Emma and I continued to talk alone. She told me about her nine-month-old child, Tony. I learned she had dropped out of school when she was pregnant. Now in CPS custody, she was enrolled in the ninth grade locally and performing well.

Emma called out for her case manager. "Can you bring Tony to meet my CASA?" she asked.

I was delighted I was going to meet her son. Emma seemed to be connecting well with me. Emma appeared very mature for her age. She carried herself confidently but was guarded. As she spoke, I learned of her frustrations in caring for her son and his teething. She disclosed a short temper with him and with her peers.

"Boundaries are a challenge," her caregiver confirmed when she returned with the little boy.

They shot each other sarcastic looks, and Emma jokingly rolled her eyes.

Emma held the fussy child, and I observed her impatience with him. The case manager remained in the office and relieved Emma of the problematic child. We continued our conversation.

"Do you have any contact with family?" I inquired.

"I talk to my sister and my mom. Have you seen Ben, Zoe, or Will?" she asked.

"I met Ben yesterday," I replied. "I was appointed to your case recently and will speak with everyone as quickly as possible—"

"When can I see them?" she interrupted.

"I will speak with your caseworker. That needs to be arranged as quickly as possible."

"And my dad? I am worried about him. He is ill," she informed me.

"When was the last time you saw your dad?"

"I saw him and my half-brother a few days before CPS removed us. My brother lives with him and my stepmom—I mean his girlfriend." There was another eye roll when she mentioned the word "girlfriend."

Okay, I thought. *There's tension with the girlfriend or stepmom.* But I need to learn more about Dad. There was little about him in the case file.

Emma was opening up more. I encouraged her to continue.

"My dad said he was sick and could die soon," she exclaimed, adding passionately that she needed to see him and ensure he was all right.

I contemplated what I read in the initial case file about her father. This medical information was not revealed in prior documentation.

"Do you know what is wrong with him, what his diagnosis is?"

Emma shook her head and pursed her lips as she searched deeply for an answer.

"I am not sure what he said. Maybe something about—?" Her expression indicated doubt as the words flowed. "I just don't know ... he says he is very sick," she continued.

I asked the case manager for answers, "Who is on Emma's contact list?"

The case manager pulled her file and replied, "Her brothers, Ben and Will, sister Zoe, her attorney, the caseworker, and I'll add you as her CASA."

I turned my attention to Emma, replying, "I'll speak with the caseworker."

That was my job. There is a delicate balance to advocating for children as a volunteer. They are clients, and I am supposed to act in their best interests. However, their best interests did not always mean doing everything they wanted. There was much more to learn on this case, and I made no promises other than to inquire on their behalf. I needed to learn more before I made solid recommendations on the children's behalf.

We switched topics back to school instead of family. She saw her charter school as a step towards public school and eventually college. I could tell Emma was driven and fiercely independent. Something struck me about Emma. She had goals for her future. Despite her inconsistent upbringing, she was making plans for her future—a positive sign!

We talked for a while, but I sensed that getting her to believe in me would be tough. Her maturity might have been her street smarts. I discerned that Emma had been the caregiver or support system for her siblings, her child, and maybe even her parents.

The case manager joined the conversation intermittently. "Emma is welcome to stay here as long as she needs to," she confirmed. "We are one of only a few specialized facilities equipped to care for teen moms and their children."

This was reassuring, but I worried her short temper could lead to internal problems. How she related to her peers and her lack of boundaries could cause conflict.

The case manager handed Tony back to his mother. He was peaceful and not fussing anymore. The case manager seemed good with children. Suddenly, serenity filled my mind as I recognized the positive influence this facility could have on Emma.

When it seemed like our conversation had yielded a good deal of information and created some warmth between us, I motioned that I was ready to depart.

Emma spoke first. "Can I give my CASA a tour before she leaves? I need to take Tony back to daycare anyway." She paused and looked back at the case manager.

I also looked at the case manager, hoping to get an insider's glimpse into what life was like at this facility.

She nodded.

I followed Emma through a maze of hallways and rooms. The facility was a sprawling one-story brick farmhouse with several additions. The layout confused me, but Emma navigated it with authority, pointing out a daycare center, laundry, the supply room, the pantry, an enormous kitchen, the living room, and her bedroom.

Emma was somewhat mischievously bossy with girls we encountered along the way. They responded to her with a similar attitude and profanity. She frequently turned and smiled at me. I liked this young woman. The teens seemed to have a familiar way of communicating, and no one was quickly offended. Teens, I laughed to myself.

I departed out the backside of the building and strolled back to my car. The facility was in a remote country setting. I knew Emma would be safe here. *The meeting was interesting*, I reflected, and it foreshadowed many challenges that would emerge throughout the case.

There were only three weeks left to produce a sixty-day hearing court report with recommendations and concerns for the children's court judge. It was an accelerated pace to meet all the children, talk with the CPS caseworker, and read the official CPS case file. Hundreds of additional documents and details about this complex case needed review in the coming weeks.

Zoe

I met with the youngest child, Zoe, the next day. Zoe was nearly an hour in the opposite direction again, like my previous two encounters. These children were spaced so far apart and outside our dense metropolitan area. Zoe was with a family friend; we call it fictive kin. The relationship was not easily explained and seemed to be a loose connection.

After speaking with the caregiver in the small apartment kitchen, she called for Zoe to come out of the bedroom.

Zoe did not reply.

The caregiver went to the door and opened it. "Come out," she said sternly.

Zoe reluctantly emerged from the darkened room. She dragged her tiny feet, and her black slides, too big for her, tripped her up. She abruptly sat at the table. Her entrance immediately reminded me of Emma.

Zoe was a meek and quiet child. Her body language was curiously withdrawn and slumped over. Guarded would not describe enough how shattered she appeared. She was so small. Barely four feet tall and probably only eighty pounds. She wore pajama bottoms and a purple princess-themed T-shirt, reinforcing and symbolizing how young she was—thirteen.

I flashed back to how fragile I was at her age. I wanted to proceed gently with her.

The caregiver introduced me and asked Zoe if I could speak with her.

Breaking the ice was difficult.

"Zoe, how long have you been staying here?" I spoke cautiously, trying to elicit any response from her.

"A while," she said, her reply barely audible.

This was going to be tricky. The case file did not specify how long she was with this family friend. The caregiver talked through the moments when Zoe would not speak.

I continued to lean forward and look at Zoe. I was smiling to show her warmth. She was broken. Her slight figure did not move. Her shoulders were hunched over, evidence of her unease. Pressing her further was not ideal. I explained my role as her CASA advocate and gave her my card.

"I could try another day," I told her.

Zoe looked up and startled me momentarily, "When can I see my dad and brother?"

I was about to get up but quickly regrouped. "Emma asked about them yesterday too. I will let the caseworker know you are asking as well."

Zoe began to talk a little more. Her voice was so soft that I had to concentrate and stay focused on her lips to hear her words.

"Emma calls me now and then," I heard.

"That's good," I said softly.

"How is Ben doing?" she asked, finally looking at me with a side glance.

"Ben is okay, considering everything that has happened." I smiled and raised my eyes so she could see I was also concerned about him. "Ben is going to school. He wants to play basketball. What do you think about school? Are you in any sports?"

"I don't like my school."

"What don't you like about school?"

"School is stupid. I hate my teachers."

"Do you like anything about school?"

"I do not know ... " she paused. "I like soccer. I guess—" her voice faded away.

"Oh, soccer is fun. I played in high school but was not particularly good," I told her.

"I just started. I think I am rather good," she complimented herself and did not even realize it.

I parroted the positive words to her, and she smiled slightly but did not look up from the floor. Zoe was reserved. Self-esteem was clearly a struggle for her. She engaged me more, and I assured her I would seek answers to her questions. She was trying to make a connection as carefully as I was trying—another positive sign.

The caregiver walked me back outside. She filled in some of the blanks. Zoe was with her before the CPS case was opened, and no one had come to move her. The caregiver disclosed how depressed and rebellious Zoe was but offered no verification that she could support her. The caregiver was noticeably young and inexperienced with children.

On the drive home, I left a voicemail for the CPS caseworker. She was responsive and returned my call a couple of hours later. We exchanged information I had learned from the children and the placements, and she updated me on information she was discovering. We were both new to the case. I asked for sibling visits to be arranged within the next three weeks. Holidays were approaching, and the children had already been separated for nearly a month. I questioned the stability of Zoe's placement with a caregiver who was in way over her head. The caseworker confirmed it was likely that this placement would fail. This was unfortunate and would probably be scary for Zoe. When the CPS legal case was opened, Zoe was already in this temporary arrangement, so CPS was a little behind in ensuring it was the safest and most permanent environment. I thought, *this is something to stay on top of*, and committed it to memory.

Will

The caseworker prepared me for the meeting with Will. I explained my difficulties when phoning the psychiatric facility where he was temporarily staying. Their privacy requirements were strict, and my court order was ineffective unless I had his unique patient code. "I'll text you his patient code and the unit's name," she informed me.

The caseworker told me her impressions of the older brother Will. According to the therapist, he was in a psychiatric facility for immediate "stabilization" but was now ready for discharge. "The challenge will be finding a suitable environment where he can receive the treatment or services he needs," she stressed.

⎯⎯

Eleven days after signing onto the case, I gained access to Will at the psychiatric facility. Will's small stature struck me. Physically, he did not even remotely appear the stated age of seventeen.

"Hello, Will," I began with a greeting and an introduction to my CASA advocacy role.

Will struggled not to slur his speech. He was heavily medicated. His eyes were heavy in his head. This worried me.

"Can you bring me some clothes?" he begged. "I'm so tired of these hospital gowns!" He was dramatic as he pulled at the two layers of hospital gowns he was wearing.

"I completely agree." I made a note to ask the mental health workers where his clothing was stored and what he was permitted to have.

Will walked around the room.

"I am ready to get out of here!" he stated, pretending to bang on the group room windows.

"How are you feeling?" I asked.

"I'm a ten out of ten!" He was excited and continued to offer unsolicited responses. His speech was rapid and random.

Will's mood and fluctuations in his speech did not indicate stability to me. His declarations did not mirror what I was observing in him. He stated he was diagnosed with many complicated mental illnesses. I am not sure he really knew what he was telling me. It seemed that his medications, whatever they were, were clouding his judgment. He openly talked about how he ended up in "juvie" and eventually a hospital. I needed to learn what he was on.

His version of events was distorted.

"What is the big deal?" he announced. He was questioning what had happened in the past. "I want to go home," he shouted.

I glanced out the transparent glass window and noticed staff hovering outside.

I tried to redirect Will. "How are you doing in here?"

"This place isn't so bad. They are nice to me. No one can call me! I want to talk to my mom, but I do not know her phone number."

I knew Will was restricted from communicating with familiar adults until it was "therapeutically recommended." This was commonplace for delicate situations where safety and stability were paramount in protecting the children until assessments could be completed.

Will was the first child to talk much about his mother. I sensed from Ben that he loved her, but the girls' avoidance of talking about her seemed more of an attempt to protect her. I wondered if I could identify enough with Will and get him the help he needed before he turned eighteen and became a legal adult.

He told me an abbreviated life story and candidly divulged his feelings about what happened with his current situation. Will's lack of discretion in his story and choice of words were remarkable and alarming, given that he had only met me today. This was his third placement. He was marking time here, not receiving any treatment for his unusual behaviors or trauma. The admission was to immediately stabilize his current mental health only.

I doubted he was "stable."

His mood and affect frequently deviated while he spoke.

"Will, slow down," I calmly pleaded. "I will see what I can learn about your discharge from the caseworker. I am sorry you do not want to be here. I will try to help you the best I can."

There was no reply from Will. His pacing stopped abruptly, and he stood silently in the middle of the small room.

"Who is your therapist?" I asked.

Will gave me the name, which I wrote down in my notes.

Speak with him ASAP, I wrote next to the gentleman's name. Answers and plans for Will would become clearer after a thorough consultation.

Will could not sit still again. We were in a group therapy room in the psychiatric ward. Glass windows allowed the mental health staff to observe every few minutes. They were concerned about his erratic movements and probably heard him speaking loudly through the door and windows again. A knock at the door interrupted our conversation.

"Medication time," the male worker dressed in hospital scrubs called out.

"I will bring you clothes and personal care items in a few days," I stated as I looked at Will again. I paused briefly, waiting for an affirmative response from him before standing up to leave.

It was hard to measure whether he understood our conversation and my role. He sprang up from his chair and hurried out the door to line up for medication. I barely got a chance to say goodbye as he ran by me.

I watched him interact with his peers in the facility as I was led out of the locked ward. There was brief horseplay, but the staff stopped it immediately. Will was playful and animated with his peers. I made a call to the caseworker following this visit. It was important to share my observations to ensure Will was treated appropriately.

<hr />

An intensive records review was the next course of action. I spent several hours at the CPS office reviewing all the records related to this case. The official case file was more extensive than what I had been initially provided. The caseworker dropped four enormous three-ring binders on the table. A child's story was behind each thick black plastic cover. There were references to multiple past CPS cases throughout the files. I jotted down dozens more names referenced from prior CPS investigations. The children's contact with CPS spanned years before removal. It would be essential to figure out how all the players were involved or linked to the children. Finding family connections for the children was important at this stage.

I also reviewed placement history, medical evaluations, family-based service plans, therapy notes, psychological evaluations, and internal CPS staffing notes—all required documents. They are part of every case. The caseworker gave me the contact information I had previously requested for the four schools and therapists. The caseworker was unable to arrange sibling visits immediately. She was working tirelessly like I was, but she was spread thin. I needed a bit of patience and urgency at the same time. Intervening and making the visits happen on my own, at least temporarily, could go a long way with the kids.

This case was beginning to show me a pattern where intense attention was required for trauma therapy, sibling contact, finding both suitable and safe family, and meeting the children's pressing education needs. These were priorities. We searched exhaustively for family or fictive kin to reintroduce into the children's lives during the first year. The caseworker was deeply committed to supporting the children and resolving family issues to mitigate further trauma. It would be an extremely challenging case, but we worked tirelessly, even 'round the clock some days, making contact with family and reuniting members of this large sibling group in the hope that we could establish a permanent relationship and placement.

Time moved slowly for the children.

We tried to work faster.

We needed to help these kids.

Chapter 17
Outcomes

N one of the children had a clear idea of where they stood academically. Ben spoke of staying home and playing video games because his mother did not enroll him in school. Emma had previously stated she dropped out due to pregnancy, and Zoe disclosed she did not go to school regularly but offered no insight as to why. Will also did not provide much discussion about his school history. None of the children was enrolled in their age-appropriate grades. CPS did the best job possible of assessing the children for where they were currently enrolled. They were all several grades behind.

Contacting their current schools yielded a small electronic record of those schools in the Texas centralized educational database. There were also codes for other schools and school districts in each report. I would dedicate over a month to tracking down every school the children attended and developing an educational portfolio of their academics to provide CPS and the judge with a clear picture of their deficits.

Each child had repeated two or three grades and had wide gaps where they were not enrolled in school during their life before CPS removal. I developed a spreadsheet documenting each school, enrollment dates, and each child's withdrawal or transfer from kindergarten clear to their present grade. That the children attended sixteen to eighteen schools in their short lifetimes, including their time in CPS care, was not uncommon in these cases. I was fortunate that I never changed schools while in foster care, but these children had endured so much. Their entire lives were uprooted several times. There had to be a better way.

The absences from non-enrollment or truancy added up to several hundred days on the low end for Zoe to even more days for Emma. Will and Ben's deficits were similar. Most academic school years are about 180 days, and my research and calculations revealed that these children had all missed the equivalent of three to four complete academic years. It was a dire situation needing an action plan.

As noted, the teens' academic portfolios were alarming. I collaborated with the schools to get special education evaluations, and participated in every individualized education plan or admission, review, and dismissal meeting, asked for grade placement hearings, tutoring, credit recovery, additional intervention classes, and maintained contact with all teachers and guidance counselors in person, and by phone or email.

I advocated for a specially trained educational advocate and guardian ad litem (GAL) to be appointed to the case. A lawyer served in this capacity, and the GAL became another voice of reason when addressing schools for the most appropriate and individualized services and accommodations. This was helpful when my concerns were not appreciated by some of the schools. Teaming up with a like-minded GAL was a favorable experience. Our local CASA program is not a GAL program yet, so having an official GAL appointed by the judge was a bonus.

My constant presence in all the children's schools made a difference; I noticed improvements in their performance as a result. The children needed to have a future after leaving care. They were damaged and entered care late in their young lives, much like I did. Their futures needed to stay within sight and reach. I spent countless hours listening to the children and communicating with them—goals, hopes, and dreams were a constant topic of discussion. I believed they could succeed with encouragement.

I wondered if I would make it back when I was their age. It took me decades of seeking help and, eventually, divine intervention to develop resiliency. These children deserved to have every opportunity available to them. Education is critical to success in life; these children deserved my undivided attention. And, yes, with extra attention to their needs—their resiliency started to show.

※

The children also changed placements across the state at least four or more times due to ever-evolving complex behavioral needs. I requested more intensive services and interventions when they were needed. I spoke with each teen's therapist and guidance counselor and documented my significant concerns. Conversations with therapists were routine to help me assess the children's progress. Conscientious of the children's privacy, I never asked the therapists to disclose personal issues that the children discussed. My need for information concerned whether they were making progress, had well-established therapeutic goals, felt safe, and participated in therapy. Additionally, the caseworker, guardian ad litem, and I worked closely throughout the case.

There were challenging times that tested my determination. At any step along the way, the case could, and did, "blow up." One child ran away, another was caught with drugs, and yet others were hospitalized or in fights. And that was just in one week. These children tested me with everything they had. They were crying out for help, control, and freedom—crying out for their rights and crying out to be heard.

The acting out was the manifestation of trauma in them and not a personal grievance towards any particular person. Tears would be shed after these trials, and I would listen again and learn more from them. We were a team. Advocates who establish a special connection with the kids they are serving tend to have the best results with the kids. For me, this came organically. Drawing on my personal experiences and my passion for wanting them to be heard ignited my energy to keep up with them.

※

Developing monthly plans to reunite the siblings on outings, sibling dates, spa days, and video calls challenged my creativity. The children needed this contact. Permission was granted to take the children to see one another, with few exceptions. The outings were some of the best days of their young lives and gave them respite from the congregate care arrangements they were residing in. We explored numerous sites, cultures, and venues across Texas—learning together and establishing trust.

They were patient every time we made sunrise-to-sunset drives across the state. Teenagers generally prefer to avoid waking before sunrise, but if it was for me to pick them up at one facility so we could travel to another, pick up a sibling, then travel three or four hours to see another sibling, they endured with no complaint, ever. I learned to respect them for their deep hearts, which deepened our relationship and fostered excellent communication for many years.

One of my fondest memories from working on this case was observing the siblings' love for one another. The hugs and tears were genuine. It was moving, and I experienced what sibling love looks like for the first time in my life. Affection and the expression of love were absent in my household, and I briefly envied these kids' bond. That envy was quickly replaced with pride within minutes of witnessing their heartfelt connections.

Visits with the children occurred weekly and more often as needed. I was developing a rapport and gaining their trust. My listening skills were improving. The children were articulate about their needs and wants.

—

The first year on the case was trying. It pushed me to my limits. My supervisor was concerned about how much work I put into the case. I worked hard to cultivate bonds with the children and for them to build strong bonds with each other. I had to become the fierce strong advocate the judge had first asked for. Subsequent years were more of the same.

The endless driving to and from visits or meetings was soothing as I drifted into the past with music on my "Mom" playlist—Queen, The Rolling Stones, Pink Floyd, Elton John, Bob Dylan, and others. I stepped back into the 1970s on each drive home. It was so much easier to flip back and forth through the pages of my life now. I could see the connections with the children on my case, and those resonated with me. The pain dissolved. I dreamed about their futures and promised to stay connected should they ever reach out after achieving permanency.

My interest in music and even using it for healing became an opportunity to share coping skills with the children. They all loved a variety of music. I was unfamiliar with most of the artists they listened to and was surprised when Ben expressed an interest in opera. Emma's taste could be loud, profane, and smattered with fast-paced lyrics. Zoe was amenable to all music. She was the most eclectic in her tastes. These drives were some of the most significant periods in our relationship—music, talking, and listening!

On another occasion, Emma caught me off guard. We were visiting at her placement in the country and playing with her son. Random songs played on her radio in the spacious bedroom. The room was sparsely furnished, so there was little buffer to dampen the sound and decibels. I could not recognize a single artist. She played her music with a heavy bass mix that drowned out the lyrics.

"You are so old!" she delightfully cried out to me.

She made a game out of asking me to guess the song or artist, but I lost every single time. Her laugh was the prettiest sound I had ever heard. It was unrestrained and wholesome. One could envision a colorful bird chirping delightfully in a tree lit by gorgeous sun rays. That was the effect she had on me. It was genuine. We often laughed together, and I always felt those belly laughs were therapeutic for her. It felt reassuring to relate to all the kids this way and discover their unique interests and tastes. Sharing these experiences helped them develop and refine their coping skills.

Eventually, I would cultivate a relationship with one of the fathers and gain his trust. The girls' father introduced me to his father and stepmother, finally leading to permanency for one child. At a challenging moment, the father faded away, avoiding additional contact. He was suspicious of CPS and feared they would take his other children from him. He even stopped communicating with the children, which crushed them.

Mom had her demons, but she was consistent at finding and maintaining work. Employment, unfortunately, was a higher priority than the children at first. I knew I needed to stay engaged with both parents to help them prioritize the children's needs. But like most families struggling to raise children and make a living—even just staying above the poverty line was a tremendous burden. Socio-economic deficits and generational norms were strong predictors of current lifestyles. Helping this family break their generational cycles was one of the most significant obstacles ahead of me.

My calendar stayed full while working on this case. Phone calls. Messages. Emails. Texts. Trips to see the kids and lengthy discussions with the caseworker and attorney ad litem consumed nearly all my time each week. The children needed the attention. This case would take several turns.

———

Regrettably, Will aged out of foster care after only six months into the CPS case. There was not enough time to affect change for him. He resisted most efforts to help him while in care. I do not judge him for this. He had unique needs that the state could not address in six months. We could not establish and implement a carefully crafted action plan fast enough despite anyone's efforts to intervene.

I imagined it was the most difficult for him to adjust, as the oldest child removed from the home, when adulthood was on the horizon. I lost contact with him for a long time. Periodically, I would learn how he was doing, and I was grateful to see him recently. It is unsettling to this day how Will did not thrive under the state's conservatorship. Collectively, we must do more for all children in foster care, no matter how short or long their care plan is.

Will had endured unspeakable trauma, and there was not enough time to fully help him rebound. I felt sorry for him. He had no appropriate outlet to work through his emotions and impulses after leaving care. My concern for him spanned years following his discharge. Society did not help this young man early enough. He needed CPS intervention a decade earlier; it was hard to understand how that did not happen. There is no single answer, and finger-pointing is not appropriate. I pray that Will finds peace and can integrate into society and become a productive member of our community one day.

———

Emma had been surrounded and wrapped in so many specialized services and supports, yet it seemed she rejected the education and aid provided over time. She resorted to the behaviors she was familiar with in her past. She developed what I call a "foster care fatigue." It was no surprise. It is an extremely stressful experience. The kids literally have no control over any aspect of their life. For teenagers, that is akin to adding more insult to injury. Emma and I had a mutual trust in one another during her time in care, but she grew tired of being in care and longed for freedom and everyday teenage life. Who can blame her?

Emma aged out of care a year after her brother Will. It was challenging to find ways to maintain even intermittent contact with her. Eventually, her social media accounts went dark, and her phone was disconnected. I lost track of her but heard she was pregnant again. Giving up was not an option for me.

A year later, I re-established contact with her. It delighted me to see her happy again and thriving. Nowadays, we engage in routine communication—texts, phone calls, and in-person get-togethers. She was about to move out of the state recently, which made me sad, though I knew it would be an excellent opportunity for her. This bird needs to spread her wings and soar high. Emma inspired hope within me about the thousands of teens in care in Texas. The maturity I recognized in her on day one is even more evident now. She is a strong, independent woman seeking God and faith in her life. She knows what she wants and will get it one day. I believe in her.

My most treasured thoughts about Emma are summoned up when I hear her laugh. Those contagious belly laughs are always accompanied by a smile that brightens any room she enters. Her children deserve to listen to her cackles and see her smile over them every day. She is now a mom of two young children and demonstrates compassion and resiliency in her pursuit of happiness. Emma was always goal driven. I believe she will accomplish the goals she shared with me. She has the mental toughness and drive to succeed.

Ben had a prolonged period of stability and rapidly advanced in school with plenty of professional help that I coordinated with the GAL and caseworker. He even skipped a grade through dedicated work in a charter school. He was significantly behind but seemed determined to make something of his life.

Reminding him that he was loved, supported, stronger than he felt, and not falling short were always priorities. Ben struggled to open up in therapy for years. Contact with his mom would occasionally send him into deep bouts of depression, aggression, acting out, and even a brief period of rebellion. It was two steps forward and three steps back over and over. The caseworker and I worked closely with Ben to stabilize him and reassure him that he would get through the low spots on several occasions. Ben sabotaged good placements numerous times hoping he would be returned home.

When he was close to age seventeen, Ben started to envision life after foster care. He was doing better, but it was a long road for him. I visited him weekly as often as possible and daily when he was in a psychiatric hospital. He matured rapidly and adjusted to his situation. He is now resetting his behaviors, goals, and treatment plans.

I reconnected with his biological mother with Zoe's assistance. Mom's case was closed with the termination of her parental rights at trial after the first year the kids were in foster care. Zoe was allowed contact with her by her guardian. This was pivotal in Zoe's healing, and now it was possible for Ben's healing. This unlikely connection, the result of listening to the child and waiting for the right timing, would become valuable for Ben.

Mom was doing better and had recently graduated from a drug treatment program when I reconnected with her. She did this of her own volition. It was an impressive and lasting change. She had a lengthy and stable period of sobriety. It showed on her face and was also apparent in her speech and thought process throughout our in-person conversation. She was ready to be reintroduced to Ben again. This was always Ben's number one wish. I encouraged the caseworker to arrange contact between the two.

Ben would need her to be part of his family therapy before he aged out of care at eighteen, which was imminent. There was no way we could reject his plan to return to her. I prepared his mom with my expectations that their contact should be about Ben's future, hopes, dreams, and goals and not about her or the CPS case. If we collaborated with her, and she worked with us, Ben's overall outlook would benefit. She agreed with the plan, and the caseworker initiated the connection between mother and son.

There was hope yet. Ben had his first official contact with his biological mother on his seventeenth birthday, three years after entering care. This graduated to video calls with her twice a week, followed by weekend visits and reunification. A happy ending!

Ben is now the happiest I have ever seen him. I am optimistic that his mom is the safe and permanent home he needs. Mom continues to impress me daily. She overcame great odds and faced her struggles with addiction directly. She sailed through recovery with surprising resiliency herself! She is the "glue" that has united all the kids again. It is nice to be part of that connection today. I am proud of her too! The reunification appears to be a success.

My greatest sentiments at present are with Zoe. She had the most challenging time in CPS custody over the past four years. Zoe is strong now and is not the meek, slight, and quiet child I first met years ago. She is a vibrant, attractive, funny, and friendly high school student. She has goals and ambitions. She has found her voice. She is resilient and knows it!

Zoe was the child I was most worried about from the start. Her situation required additional hours of my time every week. Time was not an issue for me. Whatever it took and wherever she was, I stayed in touch and told her she was loved, supported, appreciated, and worthy as often as possible. She has blossomed into a wonderful young lady.

When Zoe turned seventeen, she was finally adopted by her paternal grandparents. It was a laborious task to track down a family member with whom any of the children could be placed, but it was well worth the extra effort. Zoe is flourishing. I am so proud of her. She is a strong young woman. Long gone are her struggles in school and truancy problems. Tutoring has helped immensely. As a freshman, she received her first report card with five "A" grades. Her accomplishments increased year after year. She believes in herself too. The academic successes were as instrumental to her personal growth and triumph as her trauma recovery effort.

Today this case is long over. Maintaining contact with the kids is fulfilling for all involved. Ben and Emma have occasionally asked for assistance seeking employment and are self-sustaining now. Before Emma moved out of state, I helped her purchase her first car and taught her how to obtain insurance. Zoe and I even went on an outing to a family axe-throwing venue. It was a first for both of us, and we let out frustrations and joy while throwing an axe forcefully into a wood target. There will be plenty more reunions and adventures for all of us in the future. I have even seen Will recently. He has grown into a young man; his boyish features are gone. All the children are connected with their mother again. I am also happy for that connection and value any opportunity I have to be supportive.

<hr>

Child advocacy is not a "one size fits all" process. No case is the same, and no advocate, caseworker, or ad litem will approach the case in the same way. The caseworker, the attorney ad litem, and I often disagreed. Undeterred, we respected one another and worked closely to formalize plans with the children's best interests always at the forefront. What was best for each child individually was what mattered the most.

While none of the kids need my services anymore, I am happy they recognize their resiliency. They counted on me and fully believed in my support and advocacy for them each year. I was always careful to detail concerns and recommendations to the court at each hearing. Their best interests were always my priority.

I was pleased to have established an excellent relationship with the legal CPS worker and two additional CPS workers throughout this case. The attorney ad litem was always responsive, and I kept him equally informed of the children's needs at every road bump. Everyone cared so much for these children. We were all personally affected when one of the children had a setback, but their resiliency equally touched us all. Collaborating with these professionals while having little to no recollection of who represented me years ago never affected how I related to them. I respected their roles and the professional services they brought to the court case.

The judge always took the time to read my court report at the beginning of each hearing. I could see him agonizing over several concerns on numerous occasions. He knew this was a demanding case, and he challenged CPS constantly to step up and meet the recommendations from my report. These children had a unique misplaced childhood. They had to grow up faster than I'd had to. They deserved every opportunity I could articulate and advocate for in court.

<hr>

Not all cases are so demanding. I chose this case knowing it would require enormous time and effort. I did not have a predetermined specific skill set to meet the needs of the children on this case. My experiences and training gave me a firm foundation to stand on. I do not want to scare anyone away from CASA or GAL advocacy because of the difficulties I faced in this one example.

My supervisor knew about my past and the circumstances that led me to advocacy. As a social worker, she is never surprised that people who have been hurt seek service in a profession where they can help. She was always supportive and able to mentor me through the case when situations were beyond my volunteer experiences.

As an advocate, you must have stability in your life to project the same to children. God redeemed my life and gave me the internal peace needed to reach this. Every transitional step through my life was at His planning and according to His timing. I am grateful for the people that guided me toward Christ. I could not have found peace and comfort in this demanding work without faith in my higher power and all the available resources I learned through spiritual recovery.

This is valuable work. The greatest reward is knowing a child has a fighting chance at success because *you* made a difference!

In my first year of advocacy, 751 volunteer CASA advocates in San Antonio served 1,882[1] of the 5,751 children in care. More advocates are needed to serve the rest of this population. Year after year, the same trend in removals occurs in Texas and other states.

More advocates join the cause each year. But there is also attrition for whatever reason—illness, work, relocation, retirement, or other personal decisions. The pandemic has also contributed to multiplying those

---

1. Child Advocates San Antonio, Report, *FY2020 Annual Report*, (San Antonio: CASA, 2021).

attritions. Court appointed special advocates are volunteers. It is a constant effort by the organization to recruit and train dedicated advocates to represent some of the worst cases of abuse and neglect in our community year after year.

More can be done outside of taking the worst children's abuse and neglect cases. I wanted to expand my reach and remain vigilant to prevent burnout. Ironically, asking for additional cases did turn out to be the answer.

PART 5
OUTSIDE THE BOX

"I am only one,
but still I am one.
I cannot do everything,
but still I can do something;
and because I cannot do everything,
I will not refuse to do the something that I can do."
Edward Everett Hale, Poet

Chapter 18
Pilot Program

After my first year as a rookie CASA advocate, I was interested in taking on additional cases. My advocate supervisor reinforced my confidence, and my desire to impact other youths was robust. Ashley told me about a new program designed to improve college graduation success rates for children in foster care and foster care alumni; it was in its initial stages, a "pilot program" exclusive to Bexar County, Texas. Since it involved teenagers, I was more than willing to learn more. My husband and I immediately signed up for an information session at our CASA office.

At the information session, we were introduced to this community partnership called the Bexar County Fostering Educational Success pilot program. The unique program was conceived and established by community leaders from San Antonio and a prominent university in 2019 with support and funding from the Texas State Legislature.[1] Partners in the community included the Bexar County Children's Court, several local colleges, and Child Advocates San Antonio.[2] We were eager to become involved. Learning about the concept of the program and the intelligent

1. Courtney Cleavenger, "Youths with history of foster care discover pathway to college," *UTSA Today*, December 18, 2020, https://www.utsa.edu/today/2020/12/story/2021-fostering-educational-success.html.

2. Child Advocates San Antonio, "College-Bound Docket: Orientation," in *Bexar County Fostering Success Pilot Program*, (December 3, 2019), 4; Bexar County Fostering Educational Success, "Strategic Framework," Accessed December 3, 2021, https://www.bcfes.org/.

efforts put into its launch was exciting. Children who experienced foster care were often well behind their peers regarding higher education—a fact we learned on our first cases. If efforts were established to help these children, we wanted to be part of them.

***

From an early age, I knew I did not want what happened to me to define me. Liberation was possible, and academic success was the cornerstone of my plan. Life in or out of foster care is hard enough—but compound it with the complexities of higher education—and it becomes overwhelming. These kids need a break, a fair shot at success like their peers. This pilot program was an excellent opportunity to assist teens in developing their skills to break down barriers they faced.

I had broken through the intangible barriers. It was a demanding experience with many painful memories whereby I initially lacked the coping skills and self-esteem to be successful. College success eventually became far-reaching for me. Applying myself academically was a necessary vindication of my tough beginnings. Becoming a bookworm was a sensible approach to escape my dysfunctional home. Always having my eye set on an attainable goal gave me hope when life seemed hopeless. For me, that was graduating high school, college, and finally embarking on a career in the army. The army provided a ticket to graduate school, which was a bonus I never expected.

There were many difficulties with my educational aspirations. I performed okay in high school, but it required much effort. In college, I made the mistake of taking my hard-earned high school successes for granted. It was much more challenging. I skipped class, visited the library infrequently to research projects, and was somewhat lazy about the effort I put into assignments or studying. Initially, I did the bare minimum. Major Walker, Nancy Hale—my therapist, and several other unlikely figures steered me back in the right direction. I did achieve success, and much later, child advocacy eventually found a place in my life.

I understood how easy it would be for children in extended foster care or those who had recently left foster care to prioritize freedom over doing schoolwork. Adjusting to my new freedom and living on my own created a bit of an obstacle for me. My past was an excuse, even when I fell into a deep depression. I was immature. Often, I sought help from my therapist or professor too late. The professor was rarely willing to give me a second chance. Life can be hard and cruel at the same time. Lesson learned. Accordingly, success happened when I applied myself and persisted. Eventually, staying on course and becoming consistent in seeking guidance or mentoring, help in any form, made a difference in my academic pursuits.

The lessons I learned in college I was better able to apply in graduate school at the University of Pittsburgh. That is when I truly excelled. College life, friendships, family, maintaining financial stability or housing, and working can all take away from academics. Having a plan and using simple techniques I learned in high-school— note-taking, reading, re-reading, highlighting, researching, and using cue cards—made a difference. I was committed and breezed through my graduate studies with these tools. *What tools did these children know how to use*, I wondered.

Thoughts about my education permeated my mind while absorbing the details of this pilot program. What a terrific opportunity to demonstrate leadership, offer motivation, and provide mentoring. Child Advocates San Antonio and the Bexar County Fostering Educational Success program had a plan. I wanted in!

This pilot could make an impact within our community and was held up as a potential model for other counties in Texas. There were even higher hopes that it could be duplicated across Texas and perhaps even the nation with success. The principal goal of improving access, enrollment, success, and college graduation rates for children with a history of foster care interested both Andy and me.[3]

At the orientation, we were advised that only 2.3 percent of youth with a history of foster care earn a two or four-year degree by the age of twenty-four.[4] Additionally, we learned that more than six hundred foster care alumni currently enrolled in the partner institutions or colleges in 2019 were utilizing the Texas tuition and fee waiver benefit in our county.[5] Now, I understand how these benefits had been afforded to AJ for the first time. This data was genuinely relevant and captured in real-time during our training. There were a considerable number of youths who could benefit from the new program we were learning about.

Opportunities like this had not been available to me. The road to college was paved with complex decisions in my era. Joining the army was my primary plan to fund my college dreams. The training I received as an army medical laboratory technician transferred directly into college. I was awarded eighteen credits for the equivalent education, which advanced me to second-semester freshman status before I even set foot on campus. If I had to do it all over again, I imagine that I would still join the army and attend college.

Utilizing the GI Bill (a college fund available for military service members), drawing from federal financial aid, accessing a small grant, and serving in the army reserves, and finally working as a resident assistant in the dorm and at a local veterinarian's office, provided the additional resources I needed to afford college. How are kids today making ends meet to pay for college? Recent history tells us that far too many people are taking on enormous debts in the form of college loans. Programs are

---

3. BCFES, "Our Cause," Accessed December 3, 2021, https://www.bcfes.org/. CASA, "College-Bound Docket: Orientation," 4.

4. CASA, "College-Bound Docket: Orientation," 7.

5. CASA, "College-Bound Docket: Orientation;" 7; BCFES, *Year in Review*.

available in most states to assist children who were or are in foster care—but are these youths aware of how to access these resources? Was anybody helping them navigate the path? It was comforting to know that my county wanted to direct a new process.

I continued to wonder how teens leaving foster care navigated these obstacles today. So much has changed since I earned my undergraduate degree. Today, getting into a four-year college is more competitive than ever. The costs for higher education have also soared, making it unaffordable for many without a substantial family education fund. Some persevere through other means, often saddling themselves with enormous debt. The pilot program had many solutions to the problems teens with a history of foster care faced in Texas.

The pilot was established to focus on six major areas: college prep in high school, college campus-based support, racial equity and inclusion, youth voice and empowerment, data-sharing, and strategic action.[6] These six target areas were identified to collectively serve any children currently in foster care and those foster care alumni as early as possible. Engaging children in foster care several years before they reached college age was considered a critical step to increasing college enrollment. Ultimately, improving "systematic change and policy reform,"[7] was seen as the means to improving the overall outcomes for this at-risk youth population.

My excitement about this program grew as I listened to the briefing, and I was anxious to become part of it. The children's court previously identified the names of children in foster care who were already enrolled in college or getting close to college age and were potentially a good fit for the pilot program. They provided this information to my CASA program. This subset of teens was selected to become part of a college-bound docket

---

6. UTSA and BCFES Program Legislative Brief, *The Bexar County Fostering Educational Success Pilot Project for Students with a History of Foster Care: Year in Review*, (San Antonio: BCFES, Updated November 20, 2020), CASA, "College-Bound Docket: Orientation," 5.

7. BCFES, *Year in Review.*

under the "umbrella" of the pilot program. This was the part of the program that trained volunteer advocates like us were recruited for.

The college docket was named as such to initially track youth with open CPS cases while creating a court program where they would participate more frequently and directly with the assigned judge. The judge was the fulcrum of the program. He would become the "motivator in chief" for these teens alongside the outstanding CASA advocates. The college docket involved CASA, the children's court, the higher-education partner institutions, CPS, and the youth. We learned how to interface with these partners while working towards the youth's best interests and supporting their educational goals.

My husband and I immediately signed up for the program and were appointed to two more cases. This would bring my caseload up to four cases consisting of ten youths, nine of whom were teenagers. Again, we would intend to function autonomously on our assigned cases but provide support and additional structure for each other as needed. We always did. Being a married volunteer advocate couple generated plenty of internal support. I highly recommend this approach!

In the first year of this pilot, forty-seven youths participated in the college-bound docket program alongside thirty-two CASA advocates.[8] The CASA youths were under the legal jurisdiction of the children's court and CPS. There were 745 youths contacted by the pilot outreach and 142 youth[9] assessed for their services in the first year. The following year would double those contacts. The pilot program was well-intentioned to ensure children currently experiencing foster care and foster care alumni were not left behind. This program would continue to receive funding from the state

---

8. Child Advocates San Antonio, *BCFES Annual Report Template 2019-2020,* (San Antonio: CASA, 2020), 5-6.

9. BCFES Evaluation Team Report, *BCFES Retreat-Evaluation Report 2021*, (San Antonio: BCFES, December 3, 2021).

and achieve more noteworthy results.

Interventions with the teens at the college campuses involved campus coaches and foster care liaisons. They were the first line of contact with many of the youth. Staff informed us that approximately six to eight times more foster care alumni are likely to graduate from a four-year college if they have campus support.[10] Everybody in the partnership played a critical role with the participants.

Our roles in serving children through this pilot as CASA advocates would continue to evolve. Education advocacy would become one of my primary ambitions from this point on.

---

10. CASA, "College-Bound Docket: Orientation," 7.

Chapter 19
Education Advocacy

C hild Advocates San Antonio developed an additional training program for us, as volunteer advocates, to train and become "education advocates"[1] before being assigned a college-bound docket case. As volunteer advocates, we were already used to collaborating with many community partners. Now we would also join forces with the college representatives, which included foster care liaisons, college advocates, and other pilot staff. We would also work closely with the other CASA staff specifically focused on this program instead of only our individual advocate supervisor. Our support team from Child Advocates San Antonio would grow as we navigated this program with the assigned teens.

To become an education advocate, my husband and I received additional training to reinforce our initial advocacy training and enhance specific focus areas. Essentially, we re-learned every critical element that youth need to tackle when planning for college. Thinking back, the resources I had available to me were as outdated as black-and-white photographs and the Dewey Decimal System. What? Exactly, it was old-school. I was a dinosaur. The process evolved. Everything kids need to do today is online—but you better be adept at navigating the internet and tracking applications.

---

1. CASA, "College-Bound Docket: Orientation," 11-15; BCFES and CASA, *College Access for Students with a History of Foster Care Educational Advocates*, (San Antonio: BCFES, August 27, 2020).

Education advocacy would challenge my skillset for this generation and my ability to relate to the teens. There was much to learn, or rather, re-learn about the college process.

⸻

How did I find my way through college, let alone life? There was no help from within my family. My high school senior guidance counselor, Sister Marie Bernard, did not provide support or encouragement either. I recalled her criticism vividly when I had joined the army reserves and only applied for admission to one college within the same week.

Sister Marie Bernard told me both were "foolish mistakes."

"You need to apply to more colleges. What if you do not get admitted to Oswego?" she proposed.

"Sister, Oswego is the only college with Army ROTC and zoology programs in the state," I countered.

"You might be better suited to stay local and attend Buffalo State. Consider nursing or education as a career path."

"What!" I uttered, reasonably sure it had inadvertently slipped out from my mouth louder than I had intended.

"You could stay in South Buffalo, marry a nice young man from Bishop Timon and raise a family here. It is familiar to you."

These statements shocked me!

I rolled my eyes. That was her best "advice!" Sister Marie Bernard was always an intimidating presence. In those days, the Catholic Church had begun to move away from the strict dress code for nuns, but Sister Marie Bernard was old school. She wore the drab blue polyester two-piece habit. The color was lighter than the sky but darker than baby blue. She concealed herself in a crowd of students wearing navy blue and white uniforms— early camouflage. This probably helped her sneak up on her prey. She had caught me that day after receiving the senior student college applications submission list.

The senior class guidance counselor did not know my circumstances. I had plans. Why would she try to burst my bubble? I was determined to set her straight.

"Sister, I do not think so. Now that I am in the army, I do not intend to have a career as an enlisted soldier. I want to become an officer. The zoology program at Oswego is a pre-veterinary program. I want to be an army veterinarian." My answer was confident.

She frowned. Disapproval seemed to spread across her face. Discouragement from anyone at Mount Mercy had never happened before.

There was no access to the internet during my secondary education. I relied on the college manuals provided by the guidance counselor's office. There was no time for doubt to surface. I avoided Sister Marie Bernard for the rest of my senior year. Trusting in "hope and a prayer" for admission to Oswego, I went my separate way.

<hr />

Could persons be trying to disrupt the dreams of youth in foster care in my community? *Yes and no*, I reasoned. It would be easy to withhold support from them. Children experiencing foster care can change placements, and schools, multiple times even within the same school year. It would be easy for these children to slip through the cracks. Experiences with the teens from my first case revealed unintentional systemic discrimination as well. Oftentimes, they were not provided the attention they needed to excel.

I wondered how and why Joey joined the military. What kind of guidance had he received while in foster care? Did he have support in his high school? We had no contact during this period. It was not until he aged out of care after turning eighteen that I learned he had joined the army. He called my parents to tell them the news. I spoke with him briefly, and he was euphoric. He left for training the following week, and he and I only corresponded through letters afterward. College was not on Joey's radar. Maybe it was not the choice or future for all youth. I however had decided that both the military and college would meet my needs.

I wanted to ensure that the teens entering the college-bound docket program had plenty of support from all available resources. I also prayed there were no more Sister Marie Bernards out there! The experience I had in high school is funny to think about now. If she only knew my success. I secretly laughed. My decision to join the military and attend college were good choices for my future. My path was not exactly as planned, but it was a close second. Thank goodness no one talked me out of my choices!

<hr />

After our education advocacy training, we would be assigned to a teen or teens willing to participate in the college-bound docket program. We were expected to be one of the critical links in helping the youth access pre-college aides, get admitted to college, and provide support for success as long as they remained in foster care.

The "education advocate" role was born and realized from the Bexar County Fostering Educational Success pilot. This was meaningful to us, and we wanted to serve our youth in any way we could. Hesitancy or obstacles to attending college would be met with reinforcement from us as newly appointed education advocates.

We would also be involved in other activities with youth preparing for college and transitioning to adulthood. None was more paramount than respecting the teen's privacy rights after age eighteen. That would require a delicate balance between communicating with the young adult, their CPS caseworker, and their ad litem. Our principal role as education advocates would focus on education support to achieve graduation, placement stability, collaboration with partners, and community connections.[2]

After all, eighteen is the age of majority in Texas. A shift towards working with young adults to advocate for themselves and steer them in their personal decision-making would become critical for their successful transition from foster care. At age eighteen, it should be noted that some

---

2. BCFES and CASA, *College Access for Students.*

youth can extend their foster care relationship to age twenty-one. This was their right. Plus, their rights were deeply important to me.

Finally, as education advocates, we would be required to participate in at least eight hours of ongoing training each year on education topics.[3] This was out of the twelve required ongoing training hours we were already required to complete annually as CASA volunteer advocates. There were always opportunities available to meet these requirements in a group setting. Online webinars and books on special education laws and advocacy were other sources I used to meet my minimum requirements.

—

Michael and Kevin

I was immediately drawn to a case with two brothers at a residential treatment facility with more of a group home or cottage environment. The brothers had been in foster care for five years already. They had ambitious educational goals and needed an advocate for additional mentoring and steering.

Michael was a seventeen-year-old high school senior interested in the same major I had declared as an undergraduate. He was also working in his dream job within his chosen career field as I had done at his age. His younger brother Kevin, a sixteen-year-old junior, was dual-enrolled in a local community college and performing well. I already had so much in common with both teens and had not even met them.

I met the young men at their boys' cottage the following week. We sat at a large dining table near the kitchen. Kevin and Michael were cautious at the first meeting.

"Hello, I am a CASA and an education advocate."

---

3. CASA "College-Bound Docket Orientation," 14; BCFES and CASA, *College Access for Students.*

Kevin and Michael smiled, but Kevin did most of the talking.

"We had a CASA before."

"I have heard that," I replied. "Are you okay with me working with you in a different capacity?"

Both boys nodded in approval. "Yes," Kevin affirmed.

"Well, I was appointed primarily as an education advocate to assist you in navigating your educational goals. I want to help you both succeed in college."

"That sounds like a great idea!" Michael exclaimed as he moved his seat closer to the table.

"I do not remember our old CASA. It was a long time ago when we first came into foster care," Kevin shared. Neither spoke of familiarity with the advocate nor understood why no one was advocating for them until now.

"If you give me a chance, I'll be with you for the long haul," I began. "I was in foster care when I was your age."

"Did you have a CASA?" Kevin asked.

"No, volunteer advocates did not exist. I am sure having someone to keep me on track would have been helpful."

The boys nodded in agreement.

I discussed the pilot and college docket program with the boys.

"I struggled to adjust to college," I explained. "I took a couple of semesters off when I fell off track and became overwhelmed. I want you to know I will support you through this process. My experiences might also help give you both some perspective."

Both boys were respectful and listened intently.

"Let's talk about your plans," I suggested as I opened a notebook to jot down a few notes.

Michael and Kevin both indicated they were "A/B students."

"I took the standardized college tests this past November, but I don't know my score," Michael volunteered.

"How about you, Kevin? Have you taken a standardized test or prep course?"

"No, I need a prep course."

"I have a schedule for prep courses available at Café College," I said as I handed both teens a copy. "Café College is a local resource for educational support and career exploration. I can take you there if you wish." I looked at the boys for a reply, but they examined the material quietly. "If you are interested in any of those dates, I would be available to drive you," I offered.

"I cannot make any of these dates. I work every weekend from 9:00 a.m. most of these days until about 2:00 p.m.," Michael informed me.

"There might be another opportunity to make this happen," I replied. "First, we will need to access your test score at your high school. Next, we can target if you need any additional assistance. Maybe you do not need any."

The teens were polite and friendly during this encounter. I took notes as they answered my questions about their current educational needs, goals, career path, extracurricular activities, and some generic questions about their personal lives, interests, likes, and dislikes.

They had additional questions about some of my experiences with college and career planning. Michael was impressed with our similar college "major" aspirations and employment history. My transparency about my college struggles also answered some of their questions and lessened their concerns about moving on to college.

Complimenting them on their strengths came first and working on their college plans came second. This was especially true for Michael since he needed to start the process. He was entering his final senior semester in high school. Time was of the essence.

***

I got to know Michael and Kevin better over time. They were in a genuinely well-managed placement. I also learned that they were empowered in their choice to remain at this placement. They were used to support staff such as a case manager, house parents, rotating relief staff, and an education director at the facility. Having a CASA advocate was like adding a new member to the team for the teens.

When visiting the boys' high school, I provided a copy of my court order and credentials—my CASA badge. The counselors provided current transcripts for both boys. Michael and Kevin were consistent students. Kevin worked hard to maintain a top 10 percent ranking in his high school class. He was dual enrolled in a technical program at the local community college and was fascinated by the program there.

Kevin identified the community college program as a stepping-stone to a four-year university. He told me he was interested in the technology program he was studying. He proposed that he could earn a good living in that field while seeking a baccalaureate degree in a different discipline. Meanwhile, Michael steadily met his graduation requirements and was awarded two scholarships for his upcoming college journey.

Eventually, Michael turned eighteen, five months after our first meeting, and moved across campus to the supervised independent living program apartments. Entering extended care, he could stay until age twenty-one. He would continue to live on the same campus as his younger brother. I would transition from fully hands-on to a more reserved role, where he exercised more decision-making as a legal young adult. That was his right, and I respected it.

The CPS caseworker assigned to their case was familiar with the boys and spoke highly of them every chance she could. They were already equipped with their legal documents—an original birth certificate, state-issued identification, and social security cards. Both boys had jobs. They would also spend extracurricular time honing their leadership skills on the basketball court. They were both exceptionally talented amateur athletes, and I enjoyed attending several of their home games.

The teens asked extraordinarily little of me besides additional help navigating their future education and career exploration. I learned more about the teens' career aspirations, and it was becoming more evident that they both had similar plans. I researched their specific interests and provided them with a document summarizing their options.

"I want to get my driver's license," Kevin reminded me.

"Perfect, I can make a referral to the court manager to request funding."

"Thank you. I have been saving to purchase a car," he proudly informed me.

"Is anybody mentoring you on how to go about purchasing a car or budgeting for insurance and repairs?" I asked.

"Yes, I sometimes visit one of our former house parents. He helps me," Kevin added.

"It's great you have a lasting relationship with him."

"Yeah, I am a nerd. I like fishing and nature shows on TV. He likes that stuff too," Kevin exclaimed, more animated in his discussion.

We both laughed and agreed he was not a nerd after all.

"You have hobbies and interests," I reminded him. "They are essential in seeking a successful career and life. Some of my hobbies were chess and Latin club! How is that for nerdy?"

More laughter. My memory illustrates that I won the "nerd prize" that day. The boys were easy to relate to. They were stable and resilient. I enjoyed sharing stories and joking with them. Regarding their education, we were more deliberate and got down to business.

Both teens disclosed their educational and career expectations to me. I set out to conduct some research for them. I identified several four-year colleges in Texas with a curriculum meeting their needs. When we met again, we discussed the differences in programs and the strengths and weaknesses of each future campus. Together they decided to focus on a future transfer to Texas State in nearby San Marcos, outside Austin, after their local community college experiences.

Once the four-year path was identified, we focused on their immediate community college plans. Since Kevin was already in community college, he was familiar with the application and financial processes.

Michael was preparing to enter college in the fall. I immediately started an action plan for him. He had already chosen a college and declared a major. I helped him recheck his standardized test scores and encouraged retesting. I arranged for private tutoring funded by the college docket program before the next available test date. When Michael failed to meet the minimums again, I encouraged him and reinforced positives like goal planning, determination, grades, and work ethic.

I connected the teens with a specialist specifically contracted by CPS to assist these youth with the complicated college application and financial aid process. I ensured the teens had access to their official school transcripts and other documents needed for college. There was much preparation to do.

***

Aaron, Marco, and David

Meanwhile, my husband signed onto a case with three teenage brothers placed with their twenty-five-year-old brother, wife, and two toddlers. I went with him on the initial "meet and greet" at their apartment, as I was dually assigned to the case. We often signed onto each other's cases for continuity. The family of seven had been together for a little over a year and were remarkably emotionally stable. This was despite the youth of the guardians. It was a positive sign.

Our most significant concern was that their CPS-managed fictive kinship financial benefits had run out, and they were perched on the edge of homelessness. Initiating financial support from the state would need to happen at once. We immediately recognized they needed help becoming foster care licensed.

The teens were introduced to us as Aaron, an eighth grader close to turning fifteen; Marco, a sixteen-year-old freshman; and David, a seventeen-year-old senior. We noted immediately that the younger brothers were not on grade level. It is common to see children in foster care not in their age-appropriate grade level. Aaron and Marco were in this situation.

Efforts would be needed to address credit recovery in cases like this.

Marco expressed interest in credit recovery right away. Aaron was not as far behind and comfortable with where he was. The teens had never had a CASA advocate before, so we explained what a CASA was and introduced them to the pilot program.

We were pleased with how mature the teens seemed. They were polite, respectful, organized, quiet, well-adjusted, and ambitious. Although David was the only child identified for entry into the college docket program, we collected information about the younger brothers since they were eager and interested in the program. Each teen could articulate plans they wanted for their futures and college degrees. We collected information on their educational and personal interests and noted issues needing to be addressed immediately.

We planned to recommend the younger brothers for admission to the college docket program. The college docket court manager would later ensure this was accomplished, and all three teens entered the program together. This allowed us to provide pre-college aides to all the brothers instead of David alone.

During our first meeting, Javier (the oldest brother) and his wife spoke candidly about how their state-sponsored kinship support benefits had run out, and they were now struggling financially. They requested a wide range of services to help keep them afloat and support the teens' college goals. We knew we would need to assist this family right away and address the needs they spoke of. The teens' best interests had to be evaluated and advocated for while recognizing that they were already in their "safe and permanent" home.

The CPS caseworker wanted to close this case soon. The timing of the closure would affect a variety of benefits the teens could receive for education, medical care, and financial support. This situation rose to the top of our list of concerns. This case was unlike my case involving Michael and Kevin. Their CPS case was open and not in danger of closing. Permanency for them was granted to the state already. Michael and Kevin would remain in the care of CPS and could elect to stay in the voluntary extended foster care program until age twenty-one. For them, the decision was in their hands. This allowed them guaranteed access to the maximum state and federal benefits for children with a history of foster care. If my husband's case would close as soon as we were told, we needed to update Aaron, Marco, and David, their caregivers, and their attorney ad litem on the permanency options so they could work together to formulate the plan that met their needs best.

These potential disparities or inequities in case outcomes can happen often. This is why it is critical for a CASA or education advocate to be thoroughly knowledgeable about what benefits are unlocked at what age. Each case is different and must be judged by its unique circumstances and in the children's best interests.

The outcome of Aaron, Marco, and David's CPS case was hanging in the balance. My husband and I spoke with the CPS caseworker about our concerns and kept her apprised of the caregiver's financial concerns so she could also address them with the family.

Meanwhile, my husband and I acted swiftly to help the family obtain foster care licensing and reintroduce some needed financial support. There were many steps to undertake with the private foster care licensing agency, and the family was highly eager and compliant with the deadlines. The family became licensed within thirty days. This was an extraordinary feat that could not come soon enough. The additional state aid provided much-needed relief and support.

We also reached out to the court, specifically the college docket court manager, and obtained extra financial assistance to secure three separate beds for the teens to sleep in. Up to then, they had been sharing a crude undersized bunkbed. The teens identified themselves as San Antonio Spurs basketball fans, and I ordered basketball-themed bedding to give them a fresh start.

—

All five of these teens could be described as well-adjusted. Andy established relationships with his teens while I regularly visited my teens. We ensured all five boys had participated in college tours and connected them with the college coaches at their targeted college or university. The coaches were a vital link in advocating for the students at the campus and encouraging them to remain connected to their academic advisors. They were also crucial in trying to prevent an unintended dropout.

All the supports were present and organized. We had a firm handle on how to be education advocates. An unforeseen event emerged shortly after assuming these cases. It would challenge all of us. Unfortunately, the college docket partners, us, and our kids faced an unexpected trial.

It could derail their efforts.

Chapter 20
Falling Short

We continued to learn more about the pilot program during the first year. The college docket program included quarterly hearings with the judge. The first thing we noticed about how college docket hearings differ from legal hearings was that this judge conducted his courtroom in an informal setting, usually at a circular table. The judge sat at the table, not at his fixed elevated bench, where he usually presided "over" the court.

It was a welcoming environment for the teens involved. The judge often wore college apparel and recommended that the rest of us do so too. Seeing the different college alumni sweatshirts and polos represented in the courtroom was a pleasant change of pace. The presiding judge was the teens' biggest cheerleader. Well, after their CASA advocate in any case! Even outside the courtroom, the teens thrived and embraced his wisdom, fatherly advice, and praise.

The judge had a presence with the kids. His influence was strong. Michael and Kevin were always impressed that the judge would recognize them by name at outings sponsored by the pilot program or my local CASA program. This reinforced that the judge took their best interests intentionally and personally.

The court college docket manager was also actively involved in communicating with all the youth in the program. Her initiative and outreach with our teens remained constructive and opened doors for them to participate in activities with the other college-bound youths. This court manager demonstrated outstanding attention and service to the teens on the docket. She also got to know them personally and expressed compassion and encouragement directly to them. Relationships like these were priceless to the teens we served.

We would attend the college docket hearings in the courthouse or via video each quarter. The sessions were often quick. The judge would learn what the teens had been up to in their academics, be apprised of any concerns or obstacles, and the teens would participate directly with the judge and inform him of their goals.

The judge always had a plan that worked well to keep the hearings moving in an organized manner. No detail or need was overlooked. The children's court was incredibly supportive of all the teen participants. We maintained regular contact with the college docket court manager and were kept apprised of activities, funding, and other opportunities the teens could participate in.

The boys were all progressing with their goals early into the program. Despite their life experiences with abuse and neglect, the foster care experiences for the five boys demonstrated that they all had tremendous resiliency. They were well-rounded and ambitious goal-setters. They only needed the additional steady presence of a volunteer advocate to keep them focused during challenging times.

***

Michael and David experienced some difficult moments when the pandemic broke out. Both teens struggled with time management. The pandemic and remote learning were the most significant factors affecting their success. Their grades and college performance suffered. They had a strong work ethic and enjoyed earning money at their part-time jobs, so they prioritized work and remaining competitive in their jobs over their studies.

We advocated for frequent sessions between the campus coaches and the individual students to ensure success and put plans into motion. But we could not do the teens' work for them. Both rejected additional tutoring and became somewhat despondent about their academic futures. They did, however, continue to remain successfully employed.

Academic warnings ultimately led to self-defeating behaviors— oversleeping, class absences, incomplete assignments, and failure to communicate with their professors. This reminded me of the same mistakes I had made. The pattern was identical. After one year of college, both teens dropped out of school for a temporary absence. We feared that even a temporary break from school could lead to a permanent dropout. Yet what was most compelling was that we listened to the teens' concerns and supported them. Both teens remain in touch with us today and have promised they will continue their studies later.

In the end, we had to respect the teens' wishes. I also took time off from school when I was in their shoes. I shared my experiences, including both the highlights and the low points to encourage them to keep their options open. It was okay for them to choose work. They were both driven by responsibility and had found employment with which they were comfortable. They acknowledged they needed a break from college stress and adjusted their lives accordingly. Their state education benefits were locked in for life, so the state would always provide free public education in the future.

In the interim, we also focused on helping Marco advance as rapidly as possible in his high school academics. Marco was sixteen and only a freshman. He was assessed for additional credit recovery courses and participated in them during his freshman year and the following summer. Marco amazed us with his dedication. He rapidly advanced several grade levels through credit recovery classes and attending remote and in-person learning. Encouragement, court-funded tutoring, and sometimes a little redirection was needed, but in the end, he prevailed.

I worked closely with his special education team and high school guidance counselor. Marco overcame learning deficits that had warranted special education accommodations earlier in life. He was dismissed from several accommodations when he mastered key concepts and fundamentals in several core classes. Marco was impressed with his progress as were we.

Additionally, Marco and his brother Aaron were athletes like their older brother. They participated in extracurricular soccer, football, and softball while maintaining "A/B" averages in their coursework.

As for their permanency, their attorney ad litem had agreed with our assessment concerning their ability to lock in additional benefits if closing the CPS case was delayed a little longer. Eventually, the CPS caseworker would see this was in the teens' best interests and worked to support the goal. When Aaron turned sixteen, his caregiver, older brother Javier, would ask for permanency. All benefits were locked in. Javier indicated he was now fully competent and financially sound. He was ready to sever his younger brother's case from CPS and asked for the case to be dismissed. The teens also agreed they were prepared to leave the state's care. This was a big decision for all involved.

This was the best outcome for them at the time, and we were hopeful for them. If we had not been assigned to this case when we had, by the time Aaron got to college entry, he would have had far fewer resources than other teens who had experienced foster care. All three teens will receive full access to state and federal college resources when they are ready.

As a CASA, knowing what benefits are unlocked at what age, also referred to as "preparation for adult living" benefits, is critical in setting these youth up for maximum success. The case for Aaron, Marco, and David was officially closed, and as CASAs, we were no longer assigned the teens' case. The brothers may have left foster care, but Aaron and Marco decided to remain in the college docket program. Instead of a CPS caseworker and CASA support, they are provided direct support from a CPS aftercare program and the court college docket manager. Their needs are being met to this day.

Meanwhile, Kevin graduated from high school in the top 10 percent of his class as planned. He had been inducted into two honor societies, received two scholarships, and had thirty credit hours of college-level courses. He had sights on finishing his associate degree this year and planned to attend a four-year university after completing the initial degree program at a community college.

When things seemed perfect for Kevin, however, he abruptly announced that he would drop out. The pandemic was too much. Remote classes, he said, "were impersonal and not stimulating." He questioned the academic path he was on. I never saw this coming. It was a reminder of how fleeting life's goals can be for youth experiencing foster care. The pandemic knocked many teens off track. Both brothers often speak about returning to school in the future.

Concurrently, Kevin also moved into a supervised independent living apartment through the voluntary extended foster care program at his group home close to his brother. He maintains close contact with his former cottage staff and family. I helped coordinate a driver education program funded by the children's court after his eighteenth birthday. Driving was always a significant "normalcy" goal for him. Kevin was determined to get his license and buy a car with the funds he had saved for years. This year, I helped him accomplish that objective.

My husband and I felt we had fallen short of our end goal: helping all the teens successfully complete college. The pandemic was unexpected, derailing college dreams for three of the boys. The social distancing, campus shutdowns, remote learning, and even our ability to visit in person, disrupted their plans.

Even though three boys struggled and decided to take time off from college, the two younger teens remained with the college docket program. They all have potential and will eventually find their path and purpose in life.

The experiences both my husband and I had with these five young men were positive. I could share life experiences with the youth we represented every step of the way. Transparency about my college adjustment and academic struggles reassured the teens that taking a break and pursuing their studies after some time off was okay. I continue to mentor all the boys whenever they reach out to me.

They are all thriving.

We are no longer officially advocates for any of the boys. I am grateful for contact with them today and welcome their calls. We may feel like we fell short, but one thing is for sure—these boys all have a bright future!

They did not fail.

Chapter 21
Legislative Advocacy

Advocating for children in my community was extremely rewarding. I felt proud to impact a child's life directly and helping each navigate the painful experiences and the loneliness of being in care. The children I worked with longed for a permanent family, free from CPS. Many wanted to go home. I wanted to help them reach their goals.

My upbringing was in stark contrast. I longed to be safe and free from harm but needed a longer time in foster care. It was not as safe as I had wanted, but at least being away from home allowed my physical wounds to heal. My emotional wounds took much longer likely because I was returned home despite my parents not having changed their ways. I believed those experiences gave me perspective on the children I served that added value to how lawmakers shaped public policy in the child welfare arena.

My experience as a CASA made me question CPS policies and Texas family law governing how kids were cared for in general. Could I influence the writing of state laws to make lasting positive changes in the child welfare system for the community and my state? These questions and others pointed me in another direction.

The pandemic slowed down the in-person contact and activity with all the children. In my spare time, I turned my attention to completing several online training opportunities. A legislative advocacy training program was available through our state program office, Texas CASA. Without any delay, I signed up for the seminar series.

The timing was perfect. Learning about the Texas CASA legislative agenda was convenient as it was being developed for the next legislative biennial session. The Texas legislature meets in a regular session in odd-numbered years. It was a few months away.

Immersing myself in the training and the online resources available through Texas CASA's public policy staff satisfied my curiosity about the legislative process in Texas. I was anxious to advocate for children and families on a larger stage at the state level. It could be called "the big stage!" This became my new mission.

I wanted Child Advocates San Antonio to have a permanent seat at the table with our local politicians to share our mission and impact on the community. At the same time, I wanted to cultivate relationships with politicians to shape the future of child welfare across the state. Our children's stories must be shared to influence a permanent change.

The online seminar series introduced a broad range of topics on how our state legislature works. Budgeting concerns for our local programs, child welfare considerations in community-based care, and how federal laws impact child welfare in Texas were covered thoroughly.

While navigating the training resources, I discovered that Texas CASA had guided the development of standalone legislative advocacy teams or LATs at thirty-eight of the seventy-three CASA program offices across the state.[1] Could San Antonio become the thirty-ninth team to form and join the statewide legislative effort? For a moment, I was plagued with doubts. I would need my local CASA organization's approval. Thoughts about my dysfunctional childhood seemed like a distant memory. Had I come full circle to be instrumental in advocating to our lawmakers? Yes, my motives were pure, intentional, and grounded in righteousness for the marginalized

---

1. Texas CASA, "Impact Numbers," Accessed September 16, 2021, https://texascasa.org/.

children in Texas.

Approaching my supervisor for permission was the first step in spearheading a legislative advocacy team at our local office. The executive staff granted permission after a few follow-up questions. I was pleased and allowed to serve as chairperson for our team. Texas CASA established the model for developing a local LAT in my state. It was up to the local organization to have a grassroots campaign to start it up, recruit team members, and keep it running. Our grassroots team began shortly after approval.

After drafting a formal presentation for our local training, I coordinated with several advocate supervisors to recruit members. At this time, we advertised legislative advocacy as an opportunity for volunteer advocates to communicate with their state representatives and senators about pressing child welfare needs in their districts. I was excited to begin communicating with our legislators and to share our advocacy mission with them from an experienced volunteer and constituent's perspective.

Texas CASA recommended that constituents, rather than staff, would be most effective at influencing a legislator on a bill. The engagement of volunteer advocates across Texas means that bills Texas CASA feels are important are much more likely to be successful.[2] Similar opportunities exist in many states across the nation.

We were a fundamental piece of the puzzle. I had come a long way from the scrawny girl scarred from childhood trauma with no one to speak up for me. This platform was now a place to inform the people who shaped the law directly about the atrocities children in my community suffered. I hid my anxiety and apprehension from those around me. Creating a legislative team, and heading it up, would mean working closely with the executive staff at my CASA program. There would be greater scrutiny on

---

2. Texas CASA, *Legislative Advocacy Guide for the 87th Legislative Session,* Public Policy, Accessed October 16, 2020, 5, https://texascasa.org/wp-content/uploads/2020/11/TexasCA-SA_LATGuide_Ver3_Pages.pdf.

each word and story I communicated to the legislators. Preparation was paramount.

It was important for lawmakers to hear from the "boots on the ground." Who better than a volunteer advocate to share their experiences? Well, of course, a foster care alumni! I was both. I could also share Joey and AJ's stories and those of the children I worked with. Every example would serve as a valuable lesson for the lawmakers to learn from. This was an opportunity for CASA programs throughout Texas to be a powerful force by speaking with one voice and collectively representing the best interests of children across the entire state.

Our voices would be heard from local courtrooms all the way to the Capitol, the big stage we wanted to be heard from.[3]

I reached out to staffers for the fourteen state legislators in our South Central Texas districts. It was best to cold call each legislator's Austin-based offices (our state capitol location) and, if needed, contact the local district office as a backup. Fear and uncertainty about the pandemic affected all in-person gatherings. Texas was not completely immune to shutdowns. We had to meet via video conferencing. Meetings were scheduled as quickly as possible. The legislative session was underway.

"Good morning, Representative."

My government relations supervisor opened each meeting and introduced our CEO, the programs and mission advancement vice presidents, and me.

The meeting was semi-formal over a video call. The representative and her chief of staff or another staffer were present from their offices at the state capitol. We were comfortable in our home offices.

Angie, my CEO, followed the agenda I had prepared.

---

3. Texas CASA, *Legislative Advocacy Guide*, 5.

"Representative, thank you for your support of CASA, particularly for sponsoring the 'House Resolution for CASA Day at the Capitol' bill."

Angie and the executive staff relied on the legislator's biographical information sheets and the agenda I provided before the meeting. They were prepared to address the legislators on a personal and business level.

"It is my pleasure. CASA does wonderful work in the community. We need you!" replied the representative.

I remained quiet, pensive in my thoughts. Waiting for my turn to speak, I listened to the executive leadership engage our legislative guests. My worries about every detail I had prepared on the legislative agenda soon disappeared as I realized I was not a scared kid revealing secrets within my home for the first time. My voice would speak for a larger population of children now.

A vision appeared to me during the meeting. I saw a brunette lady by my side in the judge's chambers when I was twelve years old. It was not a real memory. My mind created it to soothe my doubts in the present. The lady was me. The CASA advocate badge hanging around my neck identified my mission and purpose to the judge before us. She held my small hand. My body was tiny. My frame was slender, maybe seventy pounds. No wonder I was overpowered so many times. There was a lost innocence on my face. Fragile. It is a miracle how I survived without an advocate.

Looking down at my round face, I spotted a few freckles and soft green eyes, highlighting the formation of a smile. Safe. I looked up at my protector. This gave me confidence. For the moment, adult me advocated before the judge. She told him everything! The difficulties that I faced at home in the hands of my abusers, and how Joey and I sought help dozens of times. She shared my concerns—concerns that earlier I could not speak of—articulately and accurately. She cared about me. The judge would have the most informed details and recommendations to protect me and look out for my welfare now. This is what a CASA does. It is a decisive role to play in the lives of the abused and neglected. I smiled wide at the computer screen in front of me.

In the background, I heard my program's vice president speaking to the representative about the budget and the need for resources. The video call was steady, but I felt like I had traveled back and forth in time. It was a wonderful feeling. This was the voice I needed. Many children in our communities need it too. Working with our legislators was the best way to have an impact from the top—from the lawmakers right down to the agencies tasked with serving and protecting children.

Angie and Allison, my executive team, continued to speak and provided a brief overview of our local program's involvement in the community. They addressed the impact of COVID and the challenges the organization, children, and volunteers faced. They also ensured the representative was knowledgeable about our local program and what children in the community faced with or without us.

The representative leaned into her computer screen and paid careful attention. She jotted down notes. Her attentiveness affirmed my belief in her as a "champion" for children.

The conversation started to shift, and I reckoned it was my time to speak. "I want to introduce our legislative advocacy team chairperson and advocate extraordinaire!" Angie proudly boasted.

That was my cue. Knowing how much respect the leadership had for me as an advocate was a great boost. Humbly, the real story is about the kids, not us. My experiences are similar, so it makes sense for me to help now. I am incredibly passionate about the CASA mission, and Angie recognized and acknowledged this often.

"Joan has been tracking the legislative agenda and would like to bring a couple of bills to your attention."

"Thank you, Angie, and good morning, Representative. As Angie said,

I am a volunteer CASA advocate. I want to start by acknowledging and thanking you for sponsoring four historic house bills this session. You are truly a champion for the children in Texas."

The representative was warm and welcoming. "Thank you for your commitment to the children. It is wonderful that advocates like you take the time to speak up for the children," she replied.

Nervously, I kept both hands on my desk out of the camera's view. My agenda and notes were positioned in front of my laptop for me to follow with ease. My finger carefully held my place on the double-spaced notes I read aloud: "I have sent over the full list of Texas CASA priorities, but I wanted to highlight two important pieces of legislation we consider priorities."

I spoke of the bills. Both were related to keeping children in foster care out of the juvenile justice system. I knew the material and had over-prepared, as usual. Soon, I recited the remainder of my notes from memory. Being considerate and confident, I engaged the participants in the video call with direct eye contact.

"Often, responses to trauma can look like misbehavior," I explained. "One study found nearly 90 percent of children in foster care who experience five or more placement moves will end up in the juvenile justice system. This is not appropriate for low-level offenses."

The representative and her staffer listened carefully as I spoke from the heart and related experience and facts to her. The guests' facial cues and head nods affirmed that I was on the right track.

"Both House bills have a companion bill in the Senate. Your attention to these bills means a lot to us. Finally, I want to be respectful of your time and will share a quick story with you."

"Go ahead, please," she encouraged me to continue. This was my chance to become personal and tug at her heart sincerely.

"I have been a volunteer CASA advocate for four years and have worked on cases advocating for sixteen children so far. I am currently assigned four cases involving ten children. This is not a normal workload for a volunteer advocate, but it is necessary to meet the needs of children in Bexar County. I take difficult cases, usually cases with teenagers. I try to relate to my teens on their level while advocating as the fiercest adult in their corner because I was also a product of the foster care system as a teen in Western New York."

———

A brief pause allowed me to keep my emotions in check and acknowledge questions and comments. Childhood images reappeared before me as I glanced back at my computer screen. Recognizable faces of "new" attendees were on the video call. It was my fantasy, but I saw in my mind that Joey and I were smiling. We looked fresh and blameless. Did we smile at that age? In the thick of decade-long abuse and horror, I had no recollection. Trauma had destroyed happy memories. But this was different. Trauma was overcome.

This immediately reassured me about what I was doing and why I was doing it. If only I could high-five these images! I had arrived. Confidence rose from within. Joey and the "child me" would no longer suffer. I could convey stories about what I experienced and what the children whose lives I served as a child advocate endured to lawmakers. This was a chance to change futures on a larger platform.

———

My voice interrupted the fantasy, "There was no one available to advocate for my best interests, and surviving on my own was wrought with challenges, including the suicide of my brother after he aged out of foster care. I broke the cycle of violence by joining the army and serving my country, first as a soldier and, ultimately, as a commissioned officer."

"Bless your heart. I am so sorry and thank you for your service to the country and your community," the representative added.

"My pleasure—" I choked up briefly. "My experiences allow me to understand some of the situations and stresses the children are experiencing in Bexar County. Child Advocates San Antonio has reinforced my instincts with professional training, resources, and support from the staff. Like hundreds of advocates before and after me, I feel confident that I can advocate competently for these children. Children we serve have their whole lives in front of them and often cannot see it without an advocate in their corner. The kids are the future of our community, and they are in crisis now. We can turn those stories into successes with your continued support. We are on the front lines with the kids while they fight the most urgent battle of their lives." To wrap up, I thanked the representative for being a local and state champion.

A subtle wink to Joey and child me on the computer screen was an affirmation that the cycle of abuse was over. As an established volunteer child advocate, I was poised to take child welfare issues to a higher level while continuing to advocate for children on my cases locally.

That first meeting and twelve more to follow were all successes. We met with the elected official or a senior staffer on each video call. I did not need to summon twelve-year-old me back to the meetings. My presence each day on the video calls was evidence of how far I had come. Joey could be proud. His sacrifice, our story, means more today than it did yesterday.

At each meeting, I changed the introduction and tried to address a particular child's story from within their respective district while maintaining the confidentiality of identities. These stories probably impacted the officials considerably during our meetings. Caring about the community and protecting vulnerable children were common goals.

Because legislative advocacy does not stop after a legislative session ends, meetings were always followed up with an email and a handwritten thank-you note. This was done to thank the officials for taking the time to hear our concerns about specific legislation before them and to cultivate or grow a lasting relationship with their offices.

At the end of the 140-day regular legislative session, the governor required several special sessions to advance other priorities that needed attention this year. In the end, hundreds of bills were filed that year. Not all became law. We got behind the ones Texas CASA identified as priorities and communicated why we wanted support for them to our local leaders.

Those elected officials came through for us. Several of them championed the cause of child advocacy and wrote, sponsored, or helped pass numerous good pieces of legislation during this 87th legislative session. That year, legislation that passed impacted the areas of juvenile justice, human trafficking, parent or family rights, and support, support for older youth, the Federal Family First Prevention Services Act, and general child welfare system improvement.[4]

Analysis of the successes or challenges of the 87th legislative session could be summed up in several ways. That particular year was challenging as we navigated meetings during the pandemic, and Texas faced a dramatic and tragic blackout from an unusual and rare winter freeze. The legislators dealt with positive and negative legislation introduced in this session. Several bills were ultimately passed to improve the child protection system, but there was much-needed work ahead.

It should be noted that a federal lawsuit filed on behalf of children with a history of foster care in Texas loomed over the state's head. The suit was in its tenth year and affected why much of the legislation was introduced and how the new laws were eventually written. The system still needs work. Every day, the children need more advocates and activists in their corner.

In the end, our team's advocacy and other state programs collectively led to that one voice we were looking for. CASA legislative advocacy team programs across the state spoke for all children and families in Texas. This form of advocacy did not replace what I did to serve my specific children on their cases, but it was rewarding to know those stories could leave an

---

4. Texas CASA, "Bill Tracker," Public Policy, Accessed November 6, 2021, https://texascasa. org/what-we-do/leadership-in-public-policy/bill-tracker/.

impression on an influential lawmaker.

Lawmakers are ordinary people like us. They are fulfilling their purpose. Having a seat at the table with them enabled me to help protect children's futures. Being on this team was also a terrific way to collaborate with other advocates. It was rewarding to hear about different advocates' experiences. I would continue pursuing a voice and a seat with the lawmakers to reshape child welfare in Texas. This was influential work. Celebrations for the work of volunteer advocate constituents speaking as one for all children were in order! Check these opportunities out in your state.

Unexpectantly, I felt triumph for Joey and me throughout this process. Our stories had meaning. His sacrifice was not a secret anymore. Casually thinking about Joey connected me to the memory of Private Douglas too. Their stories were intrinsically and emotionally woven within me.

Remnants of PTSD, I reckoned.

PART 6
THRIVING

"I am not afraid ... I was born to do this."
Saint Joan of Arc

Chapter 22
Regrets

Trauma affects everybody differently. Even with intermittent interventions—professional help, talk therapy, whatever you want to call it—I was not immune from additional trauma. "Fake it 'til you make it" was my motto after Joey's death. Sure, there were many hiccups, but ten years passed—me skipping through life's ups and downs—between his suicide and the suicide of Private Douglas. It was not pretty, and my memory of Joey was not clear. He was taken from me years earlier. Why did trauma cause me to filter everything I knew about Joey's final moment on earth through my interaction with Private Douglas twenty-four hours before his death? Why do regrets tie us to the past?

The sound of retreat beckoned me to pause and look up from my desk. The bugle call from the installation loudspeaker ceremoniously signaled the end of each day on the military base. Soon, the national anthem would be played. Service members would stop their vehicles, exit, and exhibit proper respect for the flag—a salute. Etiquette was essential in the army. The workday had ended. This was life on Fort Lewis near Tacoma, Washington all those years earlier.

Looking across my desk at my inbox, I recognized I had much more work to do before calling it a day. Mounds of paper overflowed from the metal tray marked "in" on the front left corner of my desk. The opposite corner was like a mirror image but marked "out." I never liked to end the day without at least getting all the paperwork reviewed, signed, approved, or denied and into the outbox. My thoughts shifted to recent conversations with my boss, the troop commander at Madigan Army Medical Center. I was one of three company commanders under his supervision. It was my first command and success in this role was vital to the hospital's mission and my career.

"If I see your car in the parking lot after hours, I will relieve you of your command. You need to take care of yourself. Go home," he demanded in a facetious and deliberate tone. This was not the first time he had issued such an order. The commander above me could see the symptoms of depression building within me. My successes were evident throughout the hospital command. But he sensed I was struggling. I never handled stress well. While searching for meaning in my life, I poured myself into my army career and tried to block out my past struggles with trauma. I excelled at my job, but that is typically all I did—work—pretty much all day, every day. How could I not recognize that this was not healthy? Burying myself in work was satisfying, despite his warnings. My boss, bless his heart, was my biggest fan and equally my most significant "checks and balances" partner.

The lieutenant colonel, my troop commander, was genuinely concerned for my well-being. I understood his compassion and warmth as he guided my career with fatherly advice. He recognized stress in my performance before I had. I brushed it off. Working long after the duty day ended and into the evening each day was not unusual for me. I maintained this pace for over two years while I served as company commander of Bravo Company. It was the highlight of my career so far. Glancing back towards my inbox, the overflowing papers could wait, I reasoned. My commander was right. A break was warranted.

"Heidi, are you calling it a day?" I shouted to the clerk in the adjoining office space.

"Yes, ma'am, I'm outta here!"

Moments later, First Sergeant Sterling poked his head into my office. "Ma'am, go home. We got it."

"Thank you, First Sergeant. You're right. I need to go," I replied.

It was Thursday, and I rarely left the barracks, where my office was, before the sun went down. Thanksgiving was seven days earlier, and I had worked the entire week. Andy and I continued to date long-distance. He was on an extended assignment in Alaska, over twenty-three hundred miles away at Elmendorf Air Force Base, but we were making it work. Submerging myself in my job was a regular liability for me. I had no other life outside of it, which gave me little chance to explore the Pacific Northwest, sleep in, or be carefree with friends on the weekends. Work did not jeopardize my relationship since we were in separate states, so I continued to pound away at my job.

"All right, I'm outta here."

Dakota stirred from a deep sleep, raised her massive head a couple of inches, and set it back down, quickly closing her eyes again, signaling she was not anxious to go home. She was a welcome presence in my office, and at over one hundred pounds, she secured critical square footage near the door of my small office. She slept the days away on my office's dark blue and grey industrial-grade carpet. She did not expect an early departure. We had a fifteen-minute ride home to nearby Tacoma, Washington, ahead of us.

"Go for a car ride?" I uttered.

Dakota sprang up quickly now. She was a striking Akita. All white with a black head and mask. Her appearance resembled a bear. The soldiers in my unit loved when I brought her and Montana to the office. Dakota had been my companion since my college years. She was the surrogate I needed after my mother killed my dog, Captain.

At this point in my career, I found irony in Captain's death at my mother's hand, and now I wore the army captain's bars on my shoulders. A private's rank had adorned my uniform when I lost him. I never dreamed my life would take such an ominous twist. I shook off the disgust from my past and jumped from my seat.

"Where is Montana?" I asked, already knowing the answer. Montana was my second Akita. He was Dakota's companion. He was a rescue Akita acquired in Alaska on my first assignment.

"C'mon, girl," I rallied Dakota again, and we left the office. "Montana," I called through the halls.

"He's upstairs with Wright, ma'am," said Private Douglas.

"Thank you," I called out as I bounded up the stairs two at a time.

Private Wright's room was on the second floor, almost directly above my office. Wright was ironing his hospital uniform with the door ajar. Peeking inside, I surprised him.

"There you are, boy, ready to go for a car ride?" Montana leaped to his feet, slipping briefly on the linoleum floor. He shook his body awake as if shedding his fur of excess water from a bath.

"I'm sorry, ma'am, he was keeping me company," Private Wright said with understandable anxiety in his tone.

The soldiers in my unit were usually polite and respectful. It was a strange picture. The two of them "hanging out" in the barracks watching TV and ironing made me smile. Companionship for the soldiers, by way of my dogs, was my objective. It made me happy to know my dogs were positively affecting the troops. Wright and Montana had a special bond.

"Carry on, Private. Thank you for keeping him company. Let's go, boy." We descended the stairs to catch up with Dakota and head home.

"Wright, he's coming back tomorrow too!" I shouted back up the stairs.

"Have a good day, ma'am," I heard from the desk near the door.

Slowing to a stop, I turned to see Private Douglas behind the desk. He had one more night of extra duty after tonight. Seven weeks earlier, Private First Class Douglas was simply another military student assigned to my unit. He came and went without flare. He always kept his head low but was respectful to all he encountered, including me, on the occasions I observed him.

Private Douglas got caught up in the drug sweep. Why did he experiment with drugs? He had tested positive for marijuana use during a random company drug screen. The military required 10 percent of the unit to be tested monthly and 100 percent of the soldiers and officers yearly. As a company commander, I had a zero-tolerance policy for drug, alcohol, or domestic violence offenses. My soldiers knew this. Several prominent soldiers, noncommissioned officers, and even an officer were discharged from the army because they refused my offer to undergo addiction treatment instead of being discharged.

I did not know him very well, but for the previous six weeks, Private Douglas was present at the desk every day before his evening duty began. He issued me a polite "good evening" without fail. He held no grudge over his reduction in rank, extra duty, or the confinement order that kept him in the barracks except for school, chow, and church services.

Smiling at the private, I noticed he was grasping a book tightly. "What are you reading, Private?"

"Matthew 6: 14-15." He clutched the Bible, bound in a dark mahogany leather, and proudly waved it at me. His voice was filled with delight. Despite what was in store for him Monday morning, motivation and faith were evident.

Since his initial punishment, Private Douglas shared pieces of his story with First Sergeant Sterling and then with me. Over many weeks, we got to know a genuinely decent and pleasant young man who made one bad mistake.

He was an LPN, a licensed practical nurse student at Madigan Army Medical Center. We called them 91-Charlies. I learned he had been on a Division I college football scholarship before active duty. Injuring his shoulder while playing football cost him his full-ride scholarship. Not wanting to burden his family, he joined the army to make his parents proud. They were not aware of his current situation.

I enjoyed the daily interactions with Private Douglas. He did not strike me as a troubled youth or a disciplinary problem. If he was going to change his situation, he needed to speak up. First Sergeant Sterling and I encouraged him almost daily.

It was disappointing whenever one of the young soldiers made a horrible decision and wound up in my office for discipline. Private Douglas worried me. He had a bright future ahead of him, but he tested positive for marijuana. This was a couple of decades ago, and he was a military soldier—so no, it was not okay to use recreational drugs at that time.

Private Douglas fought the claim. "Barracks lawyers," who were fellow soldiers akin to jailhouse lawyers, may have influenced him and kept him from being honest and forthright at his initial hearing. They did not have his best interests at heart. The army's testing was ironclad. Lying only complicated the process. But I always offered a way out. Redemption was, without exception, possible.

Every day I pleaded with him to make a deal with me to erase his positive urine drug test and the subsequent administrative punishments from the army command above me. First-time minor drug offenses could be expunged through a short stint in "rehab." Because we had a recent rash of violations—nearly rising to epidemic levels—I referred all current offenses to my troop commander for steeper penalties to send a message. Stiffer punishments could deter additional young soldiers from making the same poor career decisions.

Make no mistake, I asked for the higher level "field grade punishment." I could have exercised a company-level punishment, but I was a stickler about drug and alcohol offenses. Company grade officers, like me, only wielded power to inflict fourteen days of extra duty instead of the lengthier forty-five days that a field grade or lieutenant colonel could impose. The strict approach usually dissuaded other young soldiers from risking their careers. My family members were addicted, and I knew recreational drug use could escalate for many and become detrimental to themselves or those around them. It was somewhat personal. Why did Private Douglas fight this process?

We were also a military medical unit. Standards needed to be high. So I referred the charge to the next higher command. Private Douglas would be chaptered from the army, like others before him, with a "general discharge under honorable conditions." This was not the same as an "honorable discharge." It would likely limit his Veteran's Administration benefits unless he came to his senses and asked for leniency. This is what I wanted for all my soldiers. But admitting the mistake and volunteering for rehab was paramount.

"Come see me tomorrow. You know my requirements. I will stop the chapter proceedings if you make a deal with me."

"I know, ma'am, I know."

"Rehab is only a small setback. You'll recover." As I stepped out the open double doors, I took another look behind me at the private. "Private Douglas, I mean it. You seem like a good kid. Let me give you a second chance."

Private Douglas closed his Bible and looked up as if he was going to speak, but he said nothing. His uniform was crisp and accentuated his muscular physique. His football frame and chiseled jaw represented the All-American soldier image like those used on billboards for recruitment. He stood tall and confidently. Delaying my departure momentarily, somewhat hopeful of an answer, I waited. There was no response.

"Douglas!" First Sergeant called for him, and he darted from the desk down the narrow corridor to his office.

"Company, attention!" The unit clerk called in a thunderous voice to let the soldiers know I was departing.

"As you were," was my customary response. "Have a good night," I called back into the building.

Private Douglas was serving his forty-fourth day of a forty-five-day sentence to extra duty. The punishment started at the end of each duty day and lasted through each weekend. Whatever tasks the first sergeant assigned him, Private Douglas did not complain and dutifully finished the assignments with little shame. He would likely be up many hours mopping and buffing the three floors of the barracks building and conducting other housekeeping duties like taking the trash out and organizing the common areas while others slept.

On the drive home, I reflected on the encounter. We exchanged the same pleasantries nearly every day for forty-four days straight. Was I finally getting through to him? A marijuana infraction was minor compared to a DUI, possession of large amounts of stronger narcotics, or even dealing drugs within the barracks. There had been a rash of illegal drug offenses recently. *Certainly, he would be the one to ask for help.* An allocution and request for help were all I hoped for. *He has another day. He will be the one*, I reasoned out loud to Dakota and Montana and continued my drive home.

※

The next day was a flurry of activity at my military unit. While the first sergeant prepared for a building inspection, I was occupied by meetings at the troop command and the hospital for most of the day. Private Douglas had left the building in remarkable shape the night before. The wax on the floors shimmered from the indirect sun flowing through the eastern doors and windows. A wide smile spread across First Sergeant Sterling's face. He was grinning like a proud papa. The kind and gentle soldier had a way with the young soldiers, and he was impressed with how the barracks looked this morning.

"He's a fine young man; Douglas is, ma'am."

"I know, Top," I said, using the traditional military nickname for the first sergeant.

Frank Sterling was the "top" enlisted soldier in the chain of command for our company. The chain of command is everything in the military. I respected him, and he was a great leader to have by my side. That day, the hospital command sergeant major, the senior ranking enlisted soldier at Madigan Army Medical Center on Fort Lewis, was visiting my unit. The increasing number of drug offenses had caught his attention too. This visit was an enlisted matter, but I supported First Sergeant Sterling's preparation.

My omnipresent and overflowing inbox greeted me as I stepped into my office, but it would have to wait until later. I had meetings to prep for. The unit clerk left an itinerary on my desk blotter. Hurriedly, I left the building. "Top" had everything under control. It was the sixth of December. The holiday season was fully upon us. First Sergeant Sterling and I had recently donned our dress blue uniforms and served "chow" to the soldiers at Madigan's cafeteria for Thanksgiving. Plans were underway for a repeat dinner and events for Christmas, and I had hundreds of "leave" requests to approve for soldier's vacations to see family and friends away from Fort Lewis.

By late afternoon I was back in my office. The wood chair at my desk was padded with leather on the seat and back. It swiveled from side to side and reclined just enough. A few seconds of rhythmic movement in my chair, pushing the wheels back and forth, gliding from side to side, and rocking, was all I needed to energize me to tackle my inbox. The massive amount of paperwork had tripled. It was spellbinding. Leaning back towards the desk, I grabbed my pen and returned to work. Before I knew it, the day was over. The sound of the installation bugle signaled retreat across the military base again.

"Good evening, ma'am," said Private Douglas leaning across the Dutch door into my office. His demeanor was chipper. Something was different today.

"Well, hello, Private."

"I was thinking about what you said. Can I talk to you before you leave tonight?"

"Yes, of course," I excitedly replied. "How about now?"

"Top wants me to touch up the entry since the command sergeant major is on his way."

"All right, that makes sense. Carry on. We'll talk later."

Yes. He is ready! Joy warmed me.

Regrettably, I fell into old habits and worked several more hours late into the evening. Glancing at my watch, I realized it was after eight o'clock.

The command sergeant major visit was a success, and he whisked the first sergeant away with him. The barracks were quiet for a Friday evening. Private Douglas never returned.

Readying myself to depart, I whistled softly for Dakota and Montana. The telltale jingle from their dog tags gave away their location when they scrambled to their feet. I envisioned them once again slipping on the finely waxed linoleum floors near the desk at the main entrance. The connection between the shimmering floors, evidence of Private Douglas's work ethic, and his request to speak with me eluded me at the time. Grabbing my briefcase, I made a beeline for the door, grateful I did not have to scour the barracks looking for the dogs. They were ready to go.

My Akitas were frequent visitors to the building occupied by Bravo Company on the Fort Lewis military installation. I never asked for any permission from the higher command. Dogs were an essential source of companionship for me, and the soldiers under my command could also use some additional attention or companionship from them. After all, our company motto was *Bad to the Bone.*

We were a medical company supporting Madigan Army Medical Center. A sergeant in my unit even designed the logo featuring a dog—a scruffy mutt sporting a syringe (suggestive of the laboratory he worked in at the hospital) as a military weapon. As a former army medical laboratory technician, I was additionally proud of the image. Everyone entering or exiting the unit would pass the remarkable mural on the wall near the front desk and understand our pride and esprit de corps.

It was dark outside, and my mind was fixated on my overflowing inbox. The work was exhausting, I grumbled to myself. My departure was without any fanfare tonight. The front desk was momentarily vacant, and an encounter with Private Douglas was also absent from my thoughts.

"Let's go for a ride." Dakota and Montana hopped into the backseat of my silver Dodge Intrepid.

Minutes later, I was home and feeding them dinner. I no sooner plopped down onto my sofa when I realized I had forgotten to speak with

Private Douglas.

Holy shit! No, no, no.

I had broken a promise.

Today was his final day of extra duty and confinement to the barracks. On Monday, he would be chaptered out of the army by the field grade Article 15, the punishment I requested from my higher commander, the troop commander.

Private Douglas had asked to speak to me. Was he going to ask for forgiveness and a second chance? I searched my mind for the Bible passage he had told me of the day before. Not immediately recalling it, I decided to intervene on Monday. We could undo his untimely dismissal from the army if he was ready for rehab.

Exhausted after unlacing my boots and kicking them to the floor, sleep overcame me, and I sank deeper into the grey leather sofa in my living room. My dogs lightly snored as I dozed off.

It seemed like I had only closed my eyes for a minute when I heard the phone ring.

Dazed, I reached for my glasses and turned on the light at the adjacent end table. Glancing at the clock above the dining room table, I was slow to register that the hands indicated 1:15 a.m. The phone continued to ring. I grabbed the receiver off the kitchen counter. "Hello."

"Ma'am, it's First Sergeant. I have terrible news."

My battle fatigues—the standard issue camouflage uniform issued in the army, were wrinkled and clung to me like a blanket. Less than half an hour later, I was at the Bravo Company barracks on Fort Lewis processing the account of Private Douglas's last moments alive. First Sergeant Sterling held Douglas's Bible. It was tabbed to Matthew, Chapter 6. It was about—forgiveness.

———

Twenty-five years separate today from this memory. Private Douglas's suicide opened a chasm in my past. I had been treading water for ten years when he died. My misplaced childhood was front and center once again. It would remain there riding shotgun and depriving me of the ability to thrive for many more years.

I made a grave mistake. I missed the opportunity to listen to my soldier. This regret and many others about my final years with Joey sucked the life out of me.

Had Joey reached out to his command before his suicide? Had they failed him like I failed Private Douglas? Was it a cry for help? I beat myself up endlessly for missing the signs. This was unwarranted. The truth is I did not know what the truth was. I blamed myself for years. Pain and regret sucked me deep into that peanut butter image, again.

It hurts recalling these events and writing these words. Yet it is vital to my story. When trauma occurs, a short stint of "talk therapy" may not cure it. Additional trauma can occur and complicate life. The belief that you have already dealt with certain life events can be broken like a two by four being smacked across your head when a new trauma occurs. It can disrupt your life, your stability, and your outlook. This was definitely my experience.

When I work with children in foster care today, the court may order or direct therapy—but I have yet to see any real success come from therapy. Fortunately, I hear that there are current efforts to address the frequent changes in individual therapists. How traumatizing to start fresh with a different therapist every couple weeks or after every change in placement. Children deserve a better opportunity to heal and not form regrets of their own.

This was an important discussion for me to share. One trauma can unravel a previous trauma. Today, my Akita dogs, Utah and Georgia, lie at my feet as I write this story. They are like a subtle link to the past. Dakota and Montana, the Akitas that wandered the halls to the delight of my soldiers and Private Douglas passed over the rainbow bridge long ago, but Utah and Georgia provide the continuity and comfort that I have found through animals my entire life.

During my career in the army, soldiers were fashioned like carbon copy cut-outs with green and brown camouflage patterns. You could not immediately identify their pasts by looking at them as they uniformly stood in a military formation. This was intentional. The army wanted uniformity, not individuality. We did not know their stories. It was not until late in my life that I realized that, as a society, we often look at children in foster care the same way. Society sometimes fails to invest the time to become informed. We look past the children, not seeing them. We cannot create meaningful change if we do not see the children and listen to them.

It took intentionality to discover who served alongside me in the military. Joey and Private Douglas did not initially stick out as exceptional among the ranks of other privates. Like other commanders, I focused on the unit mission. "Mission first, people always," we used to say. But I had missed an opportunity to put Private Douglas in the "always" category. I do not make that mistake anymore. Children in foster care need to be in everybody's "always" category.

Private Douglas's loss is a massive regret for me, but it is important to reflect upon and learn from where I went wrong. This was a pivotal moment in my life. It directly impacts how I treat people today. I interact more intentionally with people, especially children and teens. Recognizing how to impact youth means you must engage them. Everybody has an individual story. I want to know those stories.

Children, teens, and young adults are not carbon copy cut-outs in the present day. All children, especially those experiencing foster care, are unique, special individuals who need to be heard. Please take note of their stories. Engage them, and—listen. For those who cannot speak for themselves—be their voice.

I know better now. Thriving—living for pure and positive purposes in the moment, occupies my beliefs and actions today.

I listen.

I reflect.

I embrace the individual story.

I help others thrive.
"People first. People always."

Chapter 23
Rescue Plan

Two Saturdays had passed after I learned of my brother's death in 1986 when I stepped out of the limousine at Holy Cross Cemetery. This was the first reunion between Joey and me since being taken from our home and placed in foster care. I waited until Joey's remains were removed from the black hearse. The soldiers positioned his casket in the grassy field in the Garden of Joyful Mystery. It was chilly, but the sun peeked out from behind the fluffy clouds after a mostly cloudy month. It was a sobering moment.

Standing apart from my family and friends, I hung my head low, staring only at my brother's final resting place. A U.S. flag was draped over my brother's coffin. The placement of the blue union field on the coffin designated how my brother lay within. The field of stars was closest to me and meant I was standing near my brother's heart. My mother was seated near the foot of the coffin.

Father Stanton spoke. His lips moved, but I did not hear a word. My ears were ringing prematurely. Seven soldiers fired three rifle volleys in the distance, what is commonly called a twenty-one-gun salute. A lone bugler raised the brass instrument to his lips, and the iconic sound of twenty-four somber notes pierced the air. Family and friends stood silent with their hands over their hearts.

I saluted my brother. Unable to contain my tears, they flowed like water from a faucet. I sobbed loudly and uncontrollably. To this day, I still cry at military funerals. Whether the scene is from a recent news story or a movie on TV, hypervigilance is evident. It is a reminder of how much my heart ached when I lost Joey.

The six-man army honor guard carefully lifted the flag, revealing a standard military-issue pine coffin. I counted thirteen rotations as the soldiers ceremoniously folded the flag into a triangle symbolizing the thirteen original colonies. Their hand movements were crisp and exact. The precision was reverent and respectful. One of the sergeants had gathered spent "blank" brass rounds fired from the M-1 rifles. He placed three rounds within the folds. The senior noncommissioned officer made purposeful steps in slow motion toward my mother.

As the sergeant leaned in closer to my mother's level, he spoke the following words: "On behalf of the President of the United States, the United States Army, and a grateful nation, please accept this flag as a symbol of our appreciation for your loved one's honorable and faithful service."

My mother's emotions were not evident when she was presented with Joey's flag. The flag had blanketed him from Germany to Buffalo and was now removed at his final resting place in Holy Cross Cemetery. My mother, the person who rejected him and lost him to the foster care system, was now being honored with the flag presentation. It did not seem fair. I watched the clouds in the sky to dissociate again. *Why, Joey?*

⸺

These were the last memories of my brother. I never want to forget them. My dysfunctional past led to the discovery of a purpose-filled life, and by living out my purpose—my story is nearing completion. There was additional healing in documenting the journey. That was unexpected. Dedicating this story to Joey's memory was my way of telling him to rest in peace now. Old wounds have healed. Joey would be proud of what I am doing as a volunteer child advocate.

If only we had an advocate speak up for us when we were broken and incapable of following through with our outcries. Our trauma could have been addressed and we could have been made safe. The journey for both of us could have been different. Every child needs an advocate in some form.

The U.S. flag that once adorned Joey's coffin now flies high above Fort Sam Houston National Cemetery on Veterans and Memorial Days. It is an honor for Joey and the other soldiers who went before and after him, such as Private Douglas. His remains may lie six feet beneath the daylight in the pine casket in New York, but a piece of him is close to me again. He flies high in the sky over San Antonio. I was grateful my mother kept the flag through the years and carefully preserved it in a drawer. I retrieved it from her estate after she passed nearly fourteen years to the day we lost Joey.

———

My complicated past paved the way for me to become a child advocate. A complex and traumatic childhood is not a curse. It took over thirty years to realize that what I went through was not what defined me. This is the reality I remind the children I serve. It is the same for them. We all have had a misplaced childhood of some shape or size to overcome. What I have made from my negative life experiences is what matters. It is equally the same for them. My misplaced childhood was replaced with a new understanding of helping guide children through their shattered lives in and out of foster care. That journey is my forever path now.

What *did not* happen to me is in the past, along with the horrific tales of what *did* happen. The precious present is where I live life now. Focus on what is ahead. Use the past for good. What we do with our misplaced childhood is where purpose lies. Nothing is gained anymore by reminiscing about the lack of advocacy for Joey and me. It was so long ago. The story was now written, and it was time to close all those chapters in my life.

I survived. This is what thriving looks like.

There was a rescue plan for me long before I knew what was written about my life, and I was living it. What I experienced was not for nothing. This story can be used for change.

We need a rescue plan for all children trapped in poverty, neglect, or abusive homes. Lives can be altered for good. Broken pieces of their lives are not easily swept away. They should not be. They can be put back together. It may take some time, and you or the children you work with may need help.

You may even need a higher power—like I did. Realizing positive change can take less than a lifetime. Resiliency and resilience look different in everyone. I recovered from the difficulties in my life. It took a long time. My siblings did not fare so well. The difference may be that I recognized that living in my mess was not a solution before it was too late. Plus, I had help. I looked for kind and decent role models. These people believed in me. I now return the favor to the kids I represent by believing in them. Children in foster care need you to believe in them.

My decision-making record is not without flaws or errors. I could not fix my siblings when they became adults. Regrets about turning away from my family bothered me often. I escaped and left them to figure it out on their own—it was the way I always survived, but it does not feel right. Not being able to love my mother or forgive her before she died will always be a regret. Then there were regrets about how I recanted after making outcries—could I have ended the abuse sooner? Probably not likely. And finally, Private Douglas, not speaking with him hours before he committed suicide—I must reckon with these personal responsibilities.

Modeling responsibility and clean living would hopefully be enough, but it was not enough in my family. Today my sense of responsibility is toward the vulnerable children in foster care in our community. It is my way of giving back. Children need a strong adult, a voice to speak for them, and someone to steer them through life. More importantly, before you speak—listen to these children. Volunteer advocates can do that. You can do that too.

AJ came home recently with his wife and two children. They stayed overnight for my birthday. Looking at the young man before me, I no longer see a teen searching for purpose. AJ has that. He is a gift. He models responsibility for the soldiers under his leadership and his family. I am grateful for our relationship. Our age difference spans decades, but our friendship is permanent. Sometimes, when I look at him and his success in the military, I see visions of Joey—as if AJ is living the life my older brother could not finish. Moreover, I recognize what I wish my brother could have become. I am proud of AJ for modeling that success.

———

Surviving and thriving did not seem absolute when I was young. I almost left this world too early. My self-destructive period has passed. The only connection to my past now is my younger brother John. I do not communicate with him. As I mentioned before, forgiveness is a process. Sometimes we must re-enter the cycle when it is right for us. I am not there yet.

My extended family has grown and given rise to new connections. My cousin Jennifer, nephew Matthew, and many of my paternal Aunt Donna's relations now call me family. Whether I found them, or they found me, I am grateful to nurture these healthy relationships. This is thriving at its fullest.

I have no answer for my brother Joey's untimely passing. 1986 will always be remembered as the year I lost my dear brother. We had no one by our side. But it was also the year that started me on this journey. Losing Joey set me on a quest for purpose. You followed me on that quest by reading this story.

What purpose is ahead of you?

What is your story telling you?

There is no excuse for a child to face the foster care system alone in this era. If you know of a child swimming in peanut butter—be their jelly!

EPILOGUE

The story is complete (for now). However, the most challenging task I face as a volunteer child advocate is before me. How do I recruit others to join the call of CASA or GAL in their community? Did this story inspire you? Will you consider child advocacy or support for children in foster care in another form? If you are already a CASA or GAL, will you continue serving on another case? These were the questions I had when I decided to start this project. Advocates are needed locally—in forty-nine states and the District of Columbia, not only in Texas.

I hope this story helped you think about your purpose and path in life. We decide what motivates us, fuels our purpose, and drives our desires. You do not have to have experiences like mine, or any experience, for that matter, to become a court appointed special advocate or guardian ad litem. You only need to care. The license to care is a bonus!

No two cases are the same. Volunteer advocates are the glue that binds the facts together, not always in a neat package either. We bring consistency or constancy to the child. Children lose contact with family, move placements often, change schools, and even have multiple CPS caseworkers transition through during their case. The volunteer advocate, however, must remain with the child for as long as possible to find them a safe, permanent home. The CASA or GAL is the constancy the child needs in foster care.

Many advocates I have spoken with speak fondly of staying connected with many children years after their cases close. I love the connections I have with the kids from my closed cases. Getting a call, voice mail, or text message from one of the teens is always exciting. Even an emoji text lights up my day. I return the gesture hoping it reminds them how much I care. I want them to live their best life.

The training and case requirements may sound daunting but advocating for abused and neglected children is equally rewarding. My life has been remodeled forever. My childhood and life experiences may have paved my way on that journey for me. I found a purpose within a purpose. I knew I wanted to help children and teens my entire adult life, but it was all according to God's timing. I hope my story has touched you or ignited a purpose inside you.

Although I owe much of my strength to my spiritual renewal in Christ, I could not have found my path without the people who believed in me, prayed for me, or guided my life. Grief about what my brother missed out on no longer takes refuge in my heart. I remind myself occasionally—that I am resilient!

We can all model resilience by taking personal responsibility to do what is right despite the wrongs done to us. I never wanted to repeat the abuse my parents inflicted on my siblings or me as children. Determination to break the cycle of abuse was always at the forefront of my thoughts. It does not happen overnight. First, you must believe you are worthy, strong, and enough. After all, you are enough! We are all capable of more than we know. Finding your purpose and following it is where the work starts.

Now we must be there for the vulnerable children in our communities.

———

We need an army of volunteer advocates to meet the needs of all the children in the foster care system. Nearly every community needs more volunteer advocates to speak for these children. Last fiscal year, 818 active volunteers in San Antonio served 1,665 children.[1] This was incredibly different from the original thirteen volunteers in 1984. Additionally, National CASA/GAL reports that 97,900 volunteer advocates across the nation served 242,000 children in foster care in fiscal year 2021.[2] Volunteer advocates represented about half of the children in foster care.

Pause and reflect on that for a moment. Does this cause provoke you to do something? There is deep satisfaction in knowing you can make a real difference in the lives of children who need an objective voice in court.

---

1. CASA, Report, *FY2020-2021 July-June Champions of Hope Society*, (San Antonio: CASA, 2021).
2. National CASA/GAL, *Annual Report*.

The need for advocates is strong. The National CASA/GAL Association actively invites new prospective volunteers across the country to inquire about the program. If you do not feel called to volunteer in your community or continue serving as an advocate, consider finding another child welfare organization where you can be the difference. Consider foster care parenting as well. At the very least, spread this message. Please become part of the solution, whether with a local CASA/GAL program or another child welfare organization.

You *can* do this! You *should* do this!

Local and state CASA/GAL organizations are unique, with varying statutes, rules, and policies. The information contained in this book may not necessarily conform to each individual program across the country.

To find out more about the types of
Court Appointed Special Advocates (CASA)
or Guardians ad Litem (GAL)
programs in your state and opportunities to volunteer,
please contact:

The National CASA/GAL Association
100 West Harrison Street
North Tower, Suite 500
Seattle, Washington 98119

www.nationalcasagal.org

APPENDICES

APPENDICES

Angels Around Us

The following is an account of how ordinary people can contribute to children in foster care in other ways outside of the CASA/GAL model. These are examples of additional advocacy that I do beyond my immediate cases and the stories of how other advocates or former advocates contribute in unique yet very meaningful ways. I hope those who do not feel called to become CASA/GAL advocates feel inspired to seek another way to help children.

After settling into my role as a court appointed special advocate, I recognized a dire need for the children to be provided furniture either when placed with kin, returned to their parents, adopted, or when they embarked on independent living after aging out of care. Their story would continue when they received a permanent placement. Forever families were a new beginning for most of them. This was an opportunity.

It was not uncommon for children to move placements many times within a year. They often traveled from placement to placement with their belongings in a black trash bag. It was a humiliating journey. I was that kid too. As a volunteer advocate, I found community resources for backpacks, duffle bags, or small suitcases to make the transition less stigmatizing for the youth. They often lacked basic furniture when placed in their permanent and safe home. I began to use the talents God developed in me for "flipping" furniture for these youths. I wanted to provide a unique gift to the children or teens since they often had nothing personal to call theirs.

I started collecting dilapidated dressers from online market boards. Remembering how I once was like these broken pieces inspired me. My life was rehabbed long ago, and now I was driven to breathe new life into the furnishings and reached back into my DIY skill set. Moved by my father's fix-it skills when he was sober and fine-tuned by God through faith in Him as my creator, I set out to impact children in foster care in a unique way. Renovating dressers and donating them back to children who experienced foster care but were now entering their forever home in Bexar County, Texas, would become a new hobby or philanthropy effort!

Word spread throughout my organization about my goal. Fellow CASA advocates and supervisors conveyed their requests and children's wishes directly to me. I fulfilled twenty children's dreams (and needs) in the first year. The responses and requests for resources for youth were overwhelming. I was undeterred. Since the start, I have created over thirty-six custom dressers, one after the other, trying to keep pace with the waitlist.

The children voiced requests for various themes for their dressers: superheroes, favorite toys, television shows, toolboxes, cartoon characters, sports teams, princesses, chalk art, gaming, and others. After making much-needed repairs, I hand-painted each dresser specifically for the child I was told needed one. Moreover, I wanted the child to request a specific theme. I wanted to hear what treasured dream or wish the child had, different from what the advocate or guardian wanted for them. Having them participate in their gift-making was foremost to me. Their voices could be heard this way.

A bed, more dressers, and several small desks with chairs would follow. This is one of my other passions, and it provides children who otherwise have nothing something they can finally treasure as they enter their permanent forever home and leave care. Each piece validates how special they are. It supports thriving.

⁂

There was no inclination earlier in my life that watching my father hone his DIY skills in my childhood home would influence my life in such a way. The talent was buried deep within my past to show me the way out of pain. I used to see my father as a monster. He influenced me to work with my hands on construction projects and crafts. Monsters cannot do that. Those images were changed when I exercised forgiveness. I never saw this coming.

This was a new calling. Creating custom handcrafted goods for children was a purpose within a purpose. There was more healing for me through these projects. Because child advocacy efforts can stress advocates, I found peace and relaxation in painting the dressers. It was also self-care. I told my supervisor it was "art therapy!" Whatever it was, it filled a need in me and the kids who received the prized furniture.

DIY skills were an instrumental part of my life. It took me years to recognize that my dad, as evil as I believed he was, modeled a skill I eventually grew addicted to. I no longer have any sense of hatred or disgust toward my dad. I am grateful for the journey of forgiveness with him. My childhood is forever in my past. I survived with determination and new skills to put to use. The forgotten memories, my misplaced childhood, no longer seemed as pressing.

⸻

This passion is not unique to my story either. I found similar acts of service widespread across our organization. This story tells why I entered the child advocacy movement and shared my experience as a volunteer advocate, but there is more to this movement.

I met many other advocates who shared their talents beyond their casework. Sometimes I learned of their contributions through chance meetings. Other times I read about these advocates in social media posts published by Child Advocates San Antonio or even from stories on the local news. It was inspiring to learn about other advocates contributing in exceptional ways.

The love advocates display through their extraordinary efforts to help a child, even children from other cases, was heartwarming. There were so many individual stories like mine that demonstrated compassion and purpose. I felt compelled to meet some of these fantastic advocates and share their incredible stories.

⸻

Simeon and Laura

One couple I met briefly four years ago, Simeon and Laura, had received the Recruiters of the Year award for their efforts in advancing the local

CASA mission. I listened intently to the details behind their award and knew they were special. I ran into them at a couple of functions a few years later.

It was no surprise that they were behind renovating seventeen child-parent visitation rooms at our local CPS administrative building. I had seen the transformation from stark white government walls to colorful and playful child-friendly spaces and wondered who was behind it. The makeover was fabulous. How gratifying to learn that fellow volunteer CASA advocates were behind the project.

A visit with Laura and Simeon was necessary to learn more about the project's inspiration and accomplishment. Simeon spoke of becoming advocates around roughly the same time I did. They were now seasoned advocates like me. Their contributions came early in their tenure as volunteer CASA advocates.

Simeon and Laura, a husband-wife advocate team, saw a need when observing a child-parent visit at the CPS offices. Observing child-parent visits is a common activity we do to gather facts before making recommendations about the child or children to the judge. This is also one of the minimum case expectations we agree to. It helps our fact-finding and reporting. During their first case, Simeon and Laura noted how sad and unfriendly the government spaces felt.

Simeon recalls. "We were brand new advocates—fish out of water."

"The CPS building felt like a juvenile detention center each time we made our monthly visit to observe the kids on our case have court-ordered visitation with their parents," Laura added. "We were not sure we could make a difference."

Over several months, they knew they wanted to make a change. A breaking point emerged. The children were not thriving in this environment.

"Our CASA child had to celebrate his sixth birthday with family in a dingy government white-walled room," Laura lamented.

On the ride home from that visit, Simeon and Laura told me how saddened they felt about their child's experience.

"It was not a fun place," Laura recalled. "It was so unfair for these kids. Our biological children have a beautiful dentist's office—personalized and child-themed. We must do better than this for these traumatized children."

Simeon added, "We spoke with the CPS caseworker on the children's case."

They asked the caseworker, "What can we do to make these rooms a happy place?" The caseworker agreed the rooms "were dreadful," but their request did not immediately gain any traction. She was committed to helping them make a change, but it was difficult for her to connect with the right person at the CPS office building to approve their request.

"We asked if there were someone else we could speak to," Simeon said.

They hit a dead end but were not deterred; they contacted their advocate supervisor. Their supervisor suggested they contact the CPS director of community outreach. He provided them with her contact information.

Simeon's eyes grew big as he recalled the immediate response to his email from the director of community outreach at CPS.

"The answer from her was an enthusiastic 'Yes. We welcome your help!'" They had found someone with the power and connections to allow them to proceed.

They were eventually introduced to the new local CPS director, and she was also on board. The CPS office building is a rented space, so the community outreach director asked their landlord for permission to paint and redecorate the rooms into friendlier areas for the children to feel safe and comfortable.

Laura's single social media post resulted in "lots of love" from the community, and an online wish list was developed and funded by generous friends, co-workers, neighbors, and strangers. Soon paint, supplies, colorful rugs, furniture, and other items were donated to advance their cause. Simeon and Laura raised roughly twenty-thousand dollars and had nearly one hundred volunteers from San Antonio to help convert the spaces.

With the help of a friend for design advice, Laura spearheaded the themes and colors. Simeon managed the budget. CPS helped coordinate the renovation by blocking the rooms for a couple of weekends. Their CPS caseworker remained connected and engaged in the project as well. Over one hundred volunteers worked in shifts for three days over the two weekends.

Children with court-ordered visitation at the CPS building now have safe, friendly child-themed spaces for their visits. The colorful walls and images help break the ice when they reunite with their parents intermittently. These children have endured trauma that resulted in their removals. At the very least, the CPS visitation rooms no longer seem threatening or detention-like. Simeon and Laura went beyond their volunteer advocate roles. They are indeed angels to the children in our community!

<hr />

John and Nancy

John and Nancy are another extraordinary advocate couple and "angels" I heard about year after year. John volunteered as a CASA advocate for seven years. Nancy was also an advocate for five years.

John told me he was friends with Nancy several decades ago. They lost touch through the years but were elated to be reunited through a chance encounter at a local CASA seminar about ten years ago. John immediately noticed his old friend's name on the sign-in sheet above his. He was surprised and delighted to learn that Nancy was also an advocate. John and Nancy reignited their friendship and were even assigned a case involving four children at one time. They remained in touch and now collaborate and combine their skills on a toy-making project for children in foster care year after year.

I met with John recently at his home and workshop. His workshop was well-organized with an array of paint cans, tools, and various scraps of lumber. It was a dedicated space for John to create his masterpieces.

"How did you first hear of CASA?" I asked John.

"I was dimly aware of CASA near the end of my engineering career. I needed something to 'pay it forward' while caring for my gravely ill wife," John explained. "I had always loved children and working with children."

John did not have a straightforward career path. As we talked, I learned about this well-educated professional who served in the U.S. Air Force during the Vietnam era, held a master's degree in special education with an emphasis on learning disabilities, and received additional career training as a mechanical engineer. John put his education and career skills to work first as a teacher at an alternative high school. Next, he worked at a mental health facility serving children in San Antonio. Eventually, he worked as an engineer in the heating, ventilation, and air conditioning field.

John says, "I also worked as a carpenter when I went to school. So I developed some skills early in life. I bailed out of teaching after four years but knew I had an affinity for working with kids. That is where my wife and I first became friends with Nancy and her husband. We taught school together."

John's experience as a mental health worker profoundly influenced him. He recalled an incident at a psychiatric facility where a child was referred for evaluation.

"He's not a bad kid ... we can fix this," he began.

John was sitting at his kitchen table, propped up on the two rear legs of his chair. He became more introspective, lowered his chair to the floor, and leaned in, speaking of a particular child that "blew him away." As he described the small, underweight, misshapen child with physical ailments, he left me with the impression of a very vulnerable child, a "scared kitten." I understood the enormity of what he had experienced, and his face confirmed the gravity of the situation he had encountered so many years prior.

John continued to explain how he felt heartbroken about a system he believed "was corrupt, fraught with scandal, and broken." The year was 1975. John was navigating his life, family, and career choices but eventually found his way to child advocacy. "More people need to take ownership and make our community survivable," he emphasized. "The vulnerable children in our communities need us."

John tells me he served about six children as a volunteer advocate. He maintains contact with a couple of the children. He had lunch with one of his former CASA clients that week. He spoke fondly of the young man he first met at age thirteen and stayed by his side until he aged out of foster care at age eighteen.

Since retiring from work and volunteering, John and Nancy have spent countless hours building hundreds of wooden toys for Child Advocate San Antonio's annual Christmas toy drive. Their reach and impact on children have been enormous.

"Nancy is crafty. She's a real artisan," says John.

I concurred. I had seen the custom wooden toys—cars, animals, dollhouses, trains, and games. John's craftsmanship is well-evident, and Nancy's hand-sewn accessories and enhancements complete many designs.

A child from one of my cases also received one of John and Nancy's hand-crafted wooden ducks. John's smile was ear to ear as I spoke of the duck and told him of the toddler who pushed it across the floor of the bedroom he shared with his teen mother.

"The feet flapped and made a 'quacking' sound with every rotation," I told John. "The little boy loved it."

John has been making toys for children in foster care for eight straight years now. He "dreams up ideas" or fine-tunes examples he may have gleaned from a magazine. His colorful and custom creations are welcome gifts estimated to have lifted the spirit of hundreds of children over the years.

I met Nancy at her home too. Nancy tells me she tries to inspire John with innovative toy ideas. She sews the fabric and makes the toys "happy," she says, "but it's John's mission."

Nancy has collaborated with John for the past four years on the toy drives. Nancy says she "wants to make the world a better place for the next generation. Children are victims."

John and Nancy collectively make toys each February to December. John's workshop may lack the "elf assembly lines" from Santa Claus's workshop, but he surpasses all others in his heart.

John smiled through much of our interview. He is a genuine and humble man. The same goes for Nancy. She is a sweet and resolute woman. A statement she made stuck with me:

"We try to honor and validate children when we ask them what they like."

These two are true angels.

I was honored to speak with both and learn what fuels their passion. John and Nancy epitomize selflessness. The children gifted one of their custom toys may never know who made the toy, but they will see the "love" in the attention to detail.

Cathy

It does not take long for child advocates working with teenagers in Bexar County to learn about former advocate Cathy Hamilton's contributions to youth in need. Cathy is one of the most inspirational people I have met during my tenure as a child advocate. She served as a CASA advocate for five years and created a non-profit providing a "retail-like environment where our community's often-forgotten teens in foster care can shop for new clothes, shoes, and personal items for free."[1] As a volunteer advocate, Cathy recognized that the children in foster care she worked with needed

---

1. San Antonio Threads, "Leadership," Accessed December 18, 2021, https://sanantonio-threads.org/about-us/leadership/.

brand new clothes that fit them properly, not hand-me-downs.

Cathy realized she needed to "stop waiting for someone to do something." Her non-profit, San Antonio Threads, was born in her garage after she set out to canvas the community and draw in support to obtain new clothing for children. Her motivation was directed at helping disadvantaged teens in foster care or experiencing homelessness or poverty.

When I spoke with Cathy, she described an experience as a CASA advocate alongside a CPS caseworker when a particular child was moving placements. The child left Cathy with a precious memory from that day. It was stored deep in her heart and fueled her passion for helping children receive new clothes.

"The little girl kept the price tags and labels from gifts I had given her during my tenure as her advocate," Cathy recalled. "She kept them in her pillowcase. She slept on them every night."

Cathy realized the children she worked with "had memories worn in their clothes when moving from place to place."

"New clothes mean new memories," Cathy would recall another teen telling her.

"Please throw away my old clothes," the teens often told her or her staff.

Children who come through her shop "let go of their past."

There were naysayers along the way.

"Why don't you give the kids used clothing from an existing organization?" people would ask Cathy.

But no. Cathy was not deterred. She was on a mission.

Cathy will never forget the little girl who kept those tags—symbols of her gifts, maintained as a treasure in her pillowcase. Cathy affected that little girl, and the little girl significantly affected Cathy. Child advocacy is a rewarding experience that way. You never know how a child can touch you so deeply until the day it happens.

Cathy says to some of her clients, "I was like you. I wanted a fresh start too." The "shopping experience" for the teens at SA Threads is exceptional. The staff serve as personal shoppers and help each child handpick their

style and color of clothing. They assist with determining sizes and set the wardrobe in the dressing rooms for the youth to try on and feel whole again.

The handwritten thank-you notes from the children Cathy and her staff serve are among the first things that grab your attention when you step inside SA Threads' business space. Hundreds of messages and note cards expressing gratitude and praise for "new threads" proudly endorse Cathy's actions to improve children's lives.

Yet Cathy is humble. She found her purpose within her volunteerism at our local CASA program. She expanded her reach to vulnerable youth and filled a need for them with her non-profit.

She says, "Leaving Child Advocates San Antonio was not an easy decision. They did not want me to go."

Cathy had a vision that needed to be fulfilled. Since opening her shop five years ago, her organization has served over twenty-two thousand youth in the San Antonio area. The total was nearly ten thousand this past year![2] Remarkably, she has continued to grow her organization and now serves disadvantaged teens in other Texas cities by introducing Austin Threads in 2019 and Houston Threads in 2020. Austin Threads has unfortunately since closed, but Threads is thriving in San Antonio and Houston.

Before leaving Cathy's office, I noted a sign on the wall:

"Be the change you want to be in the world."

Cathy is that change. While working as a volunteer advocate, she saw a need and "did something about it." The children in San Antonio are benefiting from her mission and vision. Her service as a volunteer court appointed special advocate was part of her journey, but the five years she served as a CASA were only the beginning of her overall impact on child advocacy.

---

2. San Antonio Threads, Accessed December 18, 2021, https://sanantoniothreads.org/.

———

We are all capable of changing a child's story. Whether through direct advocacy, creating a non-profit that serves marginalized children, donating goods or services to support children and families at risk, or even fostering—the opportunities are endless.

Be an angel.

CASA ... Angel by Their Side

This original song was reprinted with permission from the songwriter, businessman, and philanthropist Rick Cavender.

Somewhere in the shadow stands a frightened little boy
Who holds a hand that guides him to the light.
He's never had a home or a love to call his own
But he finds a friend who saves him in the night.

Let's be there for the children.
Let's give them wings to fly.
Keep them moving forward with Angels by their side.

Chorus
In a sea of love your protector's here to guide you home.
Finding all the blessings you can know.
We never turn away.
We're stronger every day
Child Advocates San Antonio.

There's a child who lives unsettled.
One family to the next.
She hopes to find a home for good.
There's an arm around her shoulder.
There's a smile of tenderness.
To take her where she's loved and understood.

When their voices can't be heard
We find the spoken word.
To love and hold a child with trembling hands
To take them to a place with hope that they embrace
Where caring love is theirs to understand.

Let's be there for the children.
We hear the battle cry.
To keep them moving forward with Angels by their side.

Chorus
In a sea of love your protector's here to guide you home.
Finding all the blessings you can know.
We never turn away.
We're stronger every day
Child Advocates San Antonio

—Rick Cavender

Recommended Reading

These are books I have read and found helpful as an advocate. Some have touched me profoundly and solidified my desire to add my own to the growing list of stories. Nothing is more urgent to me than serving children and spreading the word to recruit others to the CASA cause.

*Please refer to my website: **www.joanulsher.com**, for a growing list of recommendations and to add some of your own.*

Experiences with CASA/GAL Advocacy:

Bryant, Yolanda. *One Child at a Time: The Mission of a Court Appointed Special Advocate* (CASA). (Freeze Time Media, 2014).

Courter, Gay. *I Speak For This Child: True Stories of a Child Advocate.* 2001 ed. (Nebraska: iUniverse.com, 2001).

Gharbo, Tracy, and Linda Palmer. *Reshuffled: Real Stories of Hope and Resilience from Foster Care.* (New York: Morgan Ben Publishing, 2021).

National Court Appointed Special Advocate Association. *Lighting the Way: Volunteer Child Advocates Speak Out.* (Washington, DC: CWLA Press, 2002).

National Court Appointed Special Advocate Association. *Someone There for Me: Everyday Heroes Through the Eyes of Tears in Foster Care.* (Washington, DC: CWLA Press, 2004).

Child Advocacy:

Wright, Amy Conley, and Kenneth J. Jaffe. *Six Successful Steps to Successful Child Advocacy: Changing the World for Children.* (California: SAGE Publications, 2014).

Education Advocacy:

Rief, Sandra. *The ADD/ADHD Checklist: An Easy Reference for Parents & Teachers.* (California: Jossey-Bass, 1998).

Siegel, Lawrence M. *The Complete IEP Guide: How to Advocate for Your Special Ed Child.* 10th ed. 2020. (California: NOLO, 1998).

Wright, Pam, and Pete Wright. *From Emotions to Advocacy: The Special Education Survival Kit.* 2nd ed. 28th printing 2020. (Virginia: Harbor House Law Press, 2006).

Childhood Trauma or Foster Care:

Ambroz, David. *A Place Called Home: A Memoir.* (New York: Legacy Lit, 2022).

Bruno, Holly Elissa. *Happiness is Running Through the Streets to Find You: Translating Trauma's Harsh Legacy into Healing.* (Nebraska: Exchange Press, 2020).

Elliott, Andrea. *Invisible Child: Poverty, Survival, and Hope in an American City.* (New York: Random House, 2021).

Hope Peterson, Tori. *Fostered.* (B&H Books, 2022).

Rhodes-Courter, Ashley. *Three Little Words.* (New York: Atheneum Books for Young Readers, 2008).

Rhodes-Courter, Ashley. *Three More Words.* (New York: Atheneum Books for Young Readers, 2016).

Toth, Jennifer. *Orphans of the Living: Stories of America's Children in Foster Care.* 1st ed. (New York: Touchstone, 1998).

Van der Kolk, Bessel. *The Body Keeps the Score: Brain, Mind, and Body in the Healing of Trauma.* (New York: Penguin Books, 2015).

Resources for Youth in Foster Care:

Jamison, Melynda Milburn. *Oscar's Family.* (Bookbaby, 2022).

Lindsey, Crystal. *Grit & Gratitude: The Former Foster Youth's Playbook for Adulting.* First ed. (Texas: 333 Publishing, 2020).

Mooney, Robert P.K. *A Foster Kid's Road to Success.* (Utah: RPKM Publishing, 2020).

Nash, Patrick. *Surviving the Teenage Heart Attack.* 2021 ed. (Nevada: 2019).

Russell, Nicole. *Everything a Band-Aid Can't Fix: A Teen's Guide to Healing and Dealing with Life.* (Minnesota: Wise Ink Creative Publishing, 2018).

Legal Advocacy:

Cobb, Sue Bell, and Bobby Cenegy. *There Must Be a Witness: Stories of Abuse, Advocacy, and the Fight to Put Children First.* (Alabama: New South Books, 2018).

Ventrell, Marvin, and Patrick Furman. *Trial Advocacy for the Child Welfare Lawyer.* Second ed. (Colorado: NITA, 2017).

Personal Growth or Inspiration:

Bradshaw, John. *Healing the Shame that Binds You.* Revised ed. (Florida: Health Communications Inc, 2005).

Callahan, Miriam. *The H₂O Workbook: A Biblical Path to Hope, Heal & Overcome for the Thirsty Soul.* Second ed. (Illinois: Tyndale House, 2018).

Duckworth, Angela. *Grit: The Power of Passion and Perseverance.* Paperback ed. 2018. (New York: Scribner, 2016).

Goggins, David. *Can't Hurt Me: Master Your Mind and Defy the Odds.* (Texas: Lioncrest, 2018).

Johnson, Spencer. *The Precious Present.* 1984 ed. (New York: Doubleday & Company, Inc, 1981).

Mackesy, Charlie. *The Boy, the Mole, the Fox and the Horse.* First hardcover ed. (Canada: Harper Collins Books, 2019).

McGraw, Robin. *Inside My Heart: Choosing to Live with Passion and Purpose.* (Nashville: Nelson Books, 2006).

Oher, Michael. *I Beat the Odds: From Homelessness to the Blindside and Beyond.* (New York: Avery Books, 2012).

Sources

American Society for the Prevention of Cruelty to Animals. "History of the ASPCA." Accessed December 2, 2021. https://www.aspca.org/about-us/history-of-the-Aspca.

Annie E. Casey Foundation. "Most Kids Exiting Foster Care are Reunited with Family." Kids Count Data Center. September 13, 2018. https://datacenter.kidscount.org/updates/show/211-most-kids-exiting-foster-care-are-reunited-with-family.

Bexar County Fostering Educational Success. "Our Cause." Accessed December 3, 2021. https://www.bcfes.org/.

_____Evaluation Team Report. *BCFES Retreat-Evaluation Report 2021*. (San Antonio, Texas: BCFES, December 3, 2021).

_____"Strategic Framework." Accessed December 3, 2021. https://www.bcfes.org/.

_____ UTSA and BCFES Program Legislative Brief. *The Bexar County Fostering Educational Success Pilot Project for Students with a History of Foster Care: Year in Review. (*San Antonio: BCFES, Updated November 20, 2020).

Bexar County Fostering Educational Success and Child Advocates San Antonio. Pamphlet. *College Access for Students with a History of Foster Care Educational Advocates.* (San Antonio: BCFES, August 27, 2020).

Callahan, Miriam E. *The H_2O Workbook: A Biblical Path to Hope, Heal & Overcome for the Thirsty Soul.* (Self-published: 2018). 63.

Centers for Disease Control and Prevention. "What are child abuse and neglect?" Accessed February 4, 2022. CDC. https://www.cdc.gov/violenceprevention/childabuseandneglect/fastfact.html.

Child Advocates San Antonio. "Chapter: 1." *New Advocate Training.* (November 2018). 6,12,16.

_____"Chapter 2: Child Protective Services, the Courts, and the Parties Involved." *New Advocate Training.* (November 2018). 2,6,11.

_____"Chapter 3: Specialty Cases." *New Advocate Training.* (November 2018). 2-3.

_____"College-Bound Docket: Orientation." *Bexar County Fostering Educational Success Pilot Program.* (December 3, 2019). 4,5,7,9.

_____"Mission Statement." *Course Overview.* (November 2018). 1.

_____Report. *BCFES Annual Report Template 2019-2020.* (San Antonio: CASA, 2020). 5-6.

_____Report. *FY2020 Annual Report.* (San Antonio: CASA, 2021). 1.

_____Report. FY2020-2021 July-June Champions of Hope Society. (San Antonio: CASA, 2021).

Child Welfare Information Gateway. *Foster Care Statistics 2019.* Accessed December 22, 2021. https://www.childwelfare.gov/pubs/factsheets/foster/.

Cleavenger, Courtney. "Youths with history of foster care discover pathway to college." UTSA Today. December 18, 2020. https://www.utsa.edu/today/2020/12/ story/2021-fostering-educational-success.html.

Courter, Gay. *I Speak For This Child: True Stories of a Child Advocate.* (Lincoln: iUniverse. com, 2001). xvii.

Data.Texas.gov. "CPS 2.3 Children in DFPS Legal Responsibility by County by Fiscal Year." Accessed December 3, 2021. https://data.texas.gov/dataset/CPS-2-3-Children-In-DFPS-Legal-Responsibility-by-C/929f-jvud/data.

The Edna McConnell Clark Foundation. "About Us." Accessed December 24, 2021. https://www.emcf.org/about-us/.

Forland, Ellinor. Letter to National Council of Jewish Women. "Brief History of CASA in San Antonio." (San Antonio: CASA, 2006).

Franklin, Gabriella. "Words from a Mentor: Aging out of Foster Care." THRU Project. Accessed December 22, 2021. https://www.thruproject.org/ words-from-a-mentor/?gclid=EAIaIQobChMIgtu50eD39AIV_ xXUAR3QDQSIEAAYAyAAEgKVWfD_BwE.

Gaille, Brandon. "51 Useful Aging Out of Foster Care Statistics." May 24, 2017. Accessed February 4, 2022. https://brandongaille.com/50-useful-aging-out-of-foster-care-statistics/.

Gaines, Chip, and Joanna. *The Magnolia Story.* (Tennessee: W Printing Thomas Nelson, 2016).

Mental Health Advocates of Western New York. "Court Appointed Special Advocates." Accessed June 3, 2021. https://mhawny.org/program/court-appointed-special-advocate/.

National CASA/GAL Association. "History." Accessed December 2, 2021. https:// nationalcasagal.org/about-us/history/.

_____ "It Was a Judge's Idea." Accessed December 2, 2021. https://nationalcasagal.org/about-us/history/.

_____ *National CASA/GAL Association for Children 2021 Annual Report.* Accessed March 21, 2023. https://nationalcasagal.org/about-us/reports/national-casa-gal-association-for-children-2021-annual-report/.

_____ "Our Reach." Accessed December 2, 2021. https://nationalcasagal.org/about-us/national-organization/.

New York Society for the Prevention of Cruelty to Children. "History." Accessed December 2, 2021. https://nyspcc.org/about-nyspcc/history/.

San Antonio Threads. Accessed December 18, 2021. https://sanantoniothreads.org/.

_____ "Leadership." Accessed December 18, 2021. https://sanantoniothreads.org/about-us/leadership/.

Texas CASA. "Bill Tracker." Public Policy. Accessed November 6, 2021. https://texascasa.org/what-we-do/leadership-in-public-policy/bill-tracker/.

_____ "Impact Numbers." Accessed September 16, 2021. https://texascasa.org/.

_____ *Legislative Advocacy Guide for the 87th Legislative Session.* Public Policy. Accessed October 16, 2020. 5. https://texascasa.org/wp-content/uploads/2020/11/TexasCASA_LATGuide_Ver3_Pages.pdf.

_____ "Who We Are." Accessed December 2, 2021. https://texascasa.org/who-we-are/.

Texas Department of Family and Protective Services. TDFPS. "Child Protective Investigations (CPI)." Accessed January 31, 2022. https://www.dfps.state.tx.us/Investigations/default.asp.

ACKNOWLEDGMENTS

I want to express my profound appreciation for my local CASA program, Child Advocates San Antonio. The support I received from my CEO, Angie White, helped me spirit this project through to the end. Angie believed this story was possible from the start. That belief opened a chasm to my past, unleashed the words in written form, and ultimately sealed the hole in my heart. This writing journey was cathartic and had a healing effect on my soul because of her support. Vicki Spriggs, CEO of Texas CASA, was equally supportive and encouraging. I am humbled by her endorsement. A special thank you to my advocate supervisor, Ashley Stutes, for believing in me as an advocate and reminding me of my strengths when challenges emerged. Your mentorship and leadership inspire me to be a better advocate daily!

My greatest sentiments lie with the people featured in this story, specifically the children I served as a CASA. I have advocated for twenty-four children in the past five years. Maintaining communication and sharing this journey with them has been important and adds value to all children both those currently in foster care and those who have left the system. May each of you find peace of heart and beauty in the path you are establishing for yourself. Your journey is only in the beginning stages, and I will never forget any of you.

Additionally, Jarmon Page supported this project very early. I am forever in awe of his accomplishments. Volunteer advocates Simeon and Laura Sutton and former volunteer advocates John Faultersack, Nancy Sedarat, and Cathy Hamilton welcomed my inquiry about their contributions to our community. Without their stories, I do not believe the complete narrative I envisioned would have been fulfilled.

This story could not have been told without the support of people I worked closely with on one of my cases. Jamal Rhadbane and Deitre Marquez taught me much about child welfare and shaped my evolving advocacy knowledge. I always respected how they approached the children's situation, even when we disagreed. Jamal routinely asked me, "How did you survive foster care?" This reminded me to think about my lived experiences and apply them to working with the kids on my cases. I sincerely thank both for how they continue to serve children in our community and strive to make the "system" a better place. They are the light in an otherwise dark child welfare system.

When I talked to family members about drafting this story, they rallied around me. Many from my husband's side of the family did not know what I had endured as a child. For that matter, my husband was in the dark as well. Kristi Barth, cousin and founder of the non-profit *Teens Finding Hope* and author of *Jared's Journal, The Making of Brave, Finding Rainbows, and Parent Diary,* gave me focused feedback throughout this process. Kristi helped me convert my initial story into one that could familiarize people with the CASA model. My extended family also offered encouragement and prayers for me to stay on course through this challenging journey. I am grateful for having you in my life.

Additionally, I owe a debt of gratitude to my CityChurch family. My spiritual revolution and discovery of my God-driven purpose was formed at CityChurch. Former Pastor John Witte was instrumental in helping me tell my story to the congregation many years before these words were arranged on paper. John also baptized me into my new life with Christ. Former Pastor Miriam Callahan, the author of *The H$_2$O Workbook*, provided insightful advice about the writing process. It was through Pastor Miriam and Pastor Yolanda Lopez's spiritual recovery programs at CityChurch where I found my path. Pastor Yolanda saw my purpose before I did. She knew I was a "hands" person. She recognized my talent for DIY long before I recognized God's plan for those talents. She always lifted my spirits and helped me realize the true plan for my life.

My dearest friend Wanda Longoria provided brilliant support and feedback from the start. Her patience and compassion in listening to my story helped me explore my deepest memories and experiences and craft this final written book. Finally, Kim Fairchild helped me weather the storms of life during my transformation and acceptance of Christ. Thank you for your friendship and prayers. My CityChurch family will always be an extension of my family. God bless you all!

I would be amiss not to mention my high school friends from Buffalo—yes, all of you! I treasure you all. Thank you for your support. When I first revealed my hardships many years ago, none of you turned your back on me. Heidi, Michele, Eva, Kathleen, Amy, Cari, Carol, Sheila, Kyle, and several others—I am not intentionally leaving anyone out. Your support and love through the years have helped me accept my past and repurpose my misplaced childhood into a life of service.

I would also like to thank the people who always stood by me, believed in me, prayed for me, looked out for me, or otherwise guided my life—whether they knew it or not. They changed the trajectory of my life: the late Madge Cleary, Myra Booker, the late Marty Felmet, Nancy Kane, Tina Duggan, Doak Walker, Nancy Hale, Kay & Pete Sears, Ken Privratsky, Art Ayala, David Aiken, Cordy Dickerson, Patty Emberley, Darrell Parsons, Mary Long, and the late Nancy Krasczyk. A special shout-out is reserved for Ted Williams; he deserves this separate mention. Dr. Ted opened my eyes to Christ—and he knows me better than anyone! I am deeply indebted to his commitment to healing me emotionally and spiritually. God works miracles in our lives, and he helped me realize His power. Thank you!

Thanks to the team at One Lit Place, owner and founder, Jenna Kalinsky, and my most awesome, inspirational writing coach and editor, Krista Foss. I never believed I could become a legit writer, but your encouragement was exactly what I needed. Additionally, thank you to Astrid Sucipto, my talented web designer, and Joe Perry at Joseph Perry Law, an exceptional attorney who offered brilliant literary legal guidance.

Finally, I want to acknowledge my husband, Andy. He attributes himself to "supervising me" as a self-described peer supervisor! Of course, he is not my peer supervisor; he is my forever partner! He has captured my heart for over half my life, taught me how to love, improved my cooking skills, and makes me laugh when laughing seems impossible. Thank you, Andy. I love you.

Above: My dad holding me as a 6-month-old baby with Diane and Joey.

Above: Easter Sunday: From left rear, Diane—age 7, Joey—age 6, me—age 4 1/2, and front left, John—age 3.

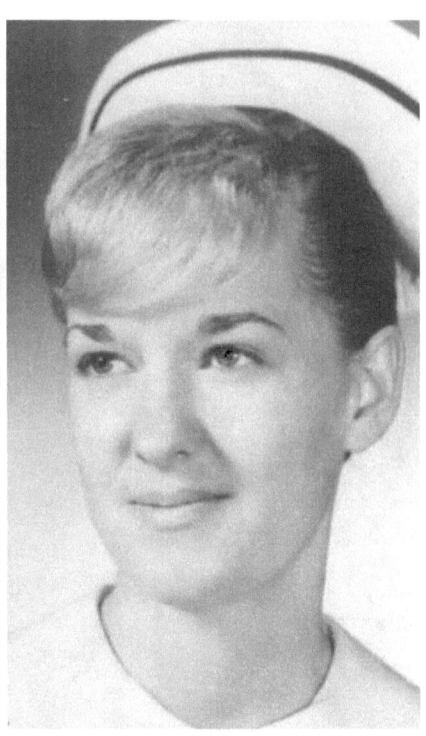

Above: My mom when she graduated nursing school.

Above: Diane's First Communion: From left, John, me, Diane, and Joey.

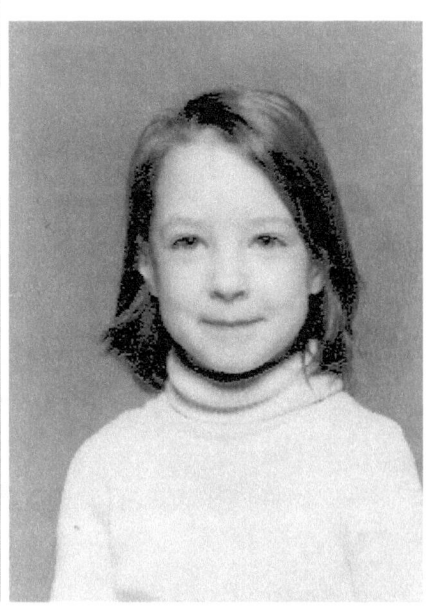

Above: Me in kindergarten.

Above: Joey in elementary school.

Above: My father and mother captured in a rare moment of cooperation.

Right: My dad with my dog, Captain.

Above: Me with the Great Horned Owl named Bruce, taken at the Buffalo Zoo. It was my birthday, and I was hired as a paid employee after a year of volunteering.

Right: Joey during U.S. Army basic training.

Above: When I found my brother's grave site and decided to write this story.

Above: Me during U.S. Army basic training.

Above: Me at advanced individual training as a medical laboratory technician.

Above: My promotion to captain in the U.S. Army with LTC(R) Art Ayala.

Above: Serving as a patient administration officer in Japan.

Above and Left: With AJ at the Dallas Cowboys training camp in San Antonio.

Above: With my friend Kim Fairchild when I volunteered at CityChurch.

Above: With AJ, his wife Lori, and their children.

Above: Visiting with children at the Pies Hermosos Asociación Civil, formerly the Casa Hogar Orphanage in Chihuahua, Mexico, as part of a CityChurch visit. Photo permissions: Pies Hermosos.

Above: Volunteering at one of several FeedSA initiatives at the San Antonio Food Bank with members of CityChurch.

Right and Below: Visiting with my Mount Mercy High School friends. They were understanding and supportive when they learned about my childhood experiences.

Above: My husband Andy with me and Judge Antonia "Toni" Arteaga on the day I was sworn in as a Court Appointed Special Advocate.

Above: My husband Andy the day he was sworn in as a volunteer advocate at the Bexar County courthouse. Photo permissions: Child Advocates San Antonio.

Above: College-Bound Docket Supervisor Samantha Barton from my local program and me after receiving awards from the BCFES pilot program.

Above: I made a play table for mini-brick toys and donated it to my local CASA for their children's playroom. Pictured from left to right: me, Allison Martinez—VP of Programs, and Ashley Stutes, my supervisor.

Above: Andy and me at an official event.

Above: Andy and me promoting the local CASA program.

Above: Receiving a volunteer award from the San Antonio Business Journal.

Above: Three of the many children I have worked with. I took them to the Empty Cross in the Texas hill country for a sibling visit.

Above: Several of the teens I worked with in Halloween costumes. Photo credit and permissions: the boys' guardian.

Above: Andy and me dressed in cowboy attire to deliver a cowboy-themed bed that I made for one of the youngest children on a former case. Permissions: granted from the guardian.

Above: College-Bound Docket teens with Judge Montemayor, Children's Court Judge.

Above and Right: Painting a gaming-themed dresser.

Left: Three children formerly served by a volunteer advocate with their princess-style dresser. Photo credit: Carey Schroeder Compton. Permissions granted from their guardian.

Above Left and Right: Local volunteer advocates Simeon & Laura Sutton at CPS. Their efforts spearheaded the renovation of seventeen child-family visitation rooms at the central office. Photo credit: Simeon Sutton.

Above: John Faultersack with program staff and dozens of his hand-crafted toys in December 2020. Photo permissions: Child Advocates San Antonio.

Above: Former advocates John Faultersack and Nancy Sedarat with their hand-made toys for children in foster care. Photo permissions: Child Advocates San Antonio.

Right: John and Nancy's toy creations assembled in his kitchen and ready to deliver to our local program. Photo credit: John Faultersack.

Above Left and Right: Two children formerly served by local volunteer advocates dressed in their favorite superhero attire to go with their custom dressers. Photo credit and permissions: from their guardians.

Above: Program staff and volunteers at the Bexar County Courthouse. Photo permissions: Child Advocates San Antonio.

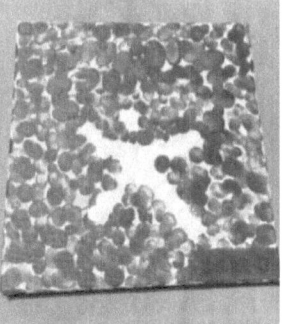

Above: Our local CASA logo as a finger painting made by children during an "Art and Soul."

Above: Cathy Hamilton, CEO and founder of SA Threads. Photo permissions: SA Threads.

Above: Cathy Hamilton and the staff of SA Threads at their storefront in San Antonio. Photo permissions: SA Threads.

Above: A child shopping for free clothes and shoes at SA Threads. Photo credit: SA Threads.

Above: One of the thousands of thank-you notes left by grateful youth. Photo permissions: SA Threads.

Right: A letter I received from one of the children I served as a CASA. Letters like this touch me profoundly and serve as a reminder that I am making a difference.

"Dear Joan,
I hope your doing fine and I made you a Minecraft Dungeons arcade card just for you. I also colored Armored Ironman for you could remember who I was to you. So I love you so much to the Milky Way galaxy and back. So I hope I can still call you, or FaceTime you. I'll always be your (name withheld) no matter what, and I'll still be that kid who made you laugh so much. So like I said I love you to the Milky Way galaxy and back.
Love, (name withheld)."

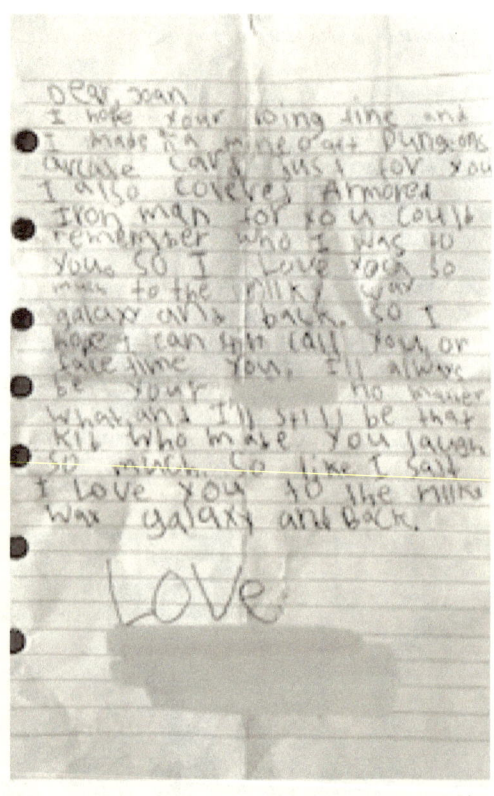

ABOUT THE AUTHOR

Joan Ulsher is a San Antonio-based writer, award-winning child advocate, and retired U.S. Army Major. A former foster youth and abuse survivor, her military career led her to become the chief contributor and editor of the *U.S. Army Medical Department Activity-Japan Patient and Staff Handbook 2000*, published in Japan in 1999. She was a Registered Health Information Administrator and Patient Administration officer before dedicating her post-army career to community service and philanthropy in 2005. She holds a master's degree in the combined program in Health Information Management and Health Information Systems Management from the University of Pittsburgh. Joan began her CASA advocacy in 2018; she spearheaded the development of a Legislative Advocacy Team in 2020 and serves as the Chairperson of that team at Child Advocates San Antonio. She has been awarded The Spirit of Mercy Award by the Mount Mercy Academy Alumni Association and was named Child Advocates San Antonio's Rookie of the Year, the *San Antonio Business Journal*'s Nonprofit & Corporate Philanthropy Volunteer of the Year, the Bexar County Fostering Education Success Program's MVP Champion, and Child Advocates San Antonio's Advancing the Mission awardee for her volunteer work in her community, most notably with CASA.